Ancient Britain

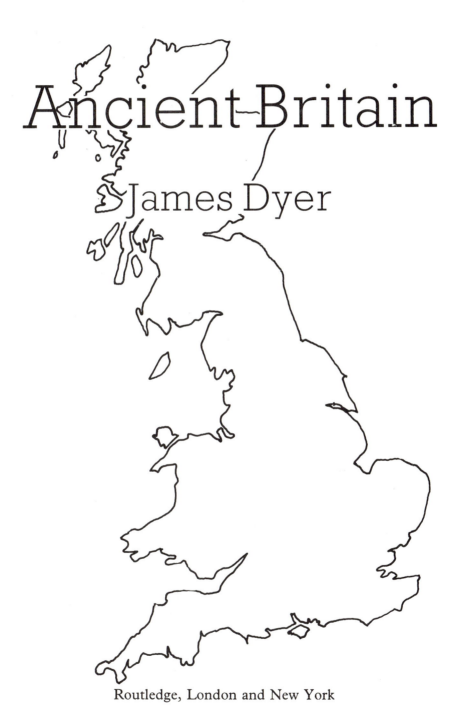

Ancient Britain

James Dyer

Routledge, London and New York

With gratitude to R.J.C. Atkinson
for introducing me to archaeology

First published 1990 by B. T. Batsford Ltd
Reprinted 1995

Reprinted 1997
by Routledge
11 New Fetter Lane, London EC4P 4EE
29 West 35th Street, New York, NY 10001

© James Dyer 1990

Typeset by Keyspools Ltd, Golborne
Printed and bound in Great Britain by
The Bath Press, Bath

British Library Cataloguing in Publication Data
A catalogue record for this book is available from the British Library.

Library of Congress Cataloguing in Publication Data
A catalogue record for this book is available from the Library of Congress.

ISBN 0–415–15151–1

Contents

List of Illustrations

Figures

1 The extent of ice sheets during the Anglian, Wolstonian and Devensian glaciations
2 The contorted soils covering the palaeolithic floor at Caddington (Beds)
3 Palaeolithic flint implements
4 Overhanging cliffs providing rock shelters
5 Upper palaeolithic art on pieces of antler and bone
6 Examples of later mesolithic flintwork
7 Star Carr
8 The spread of farming from the Near East to Britain
9 The effects of forest clearance
10 Plans of rectangular neolithic houses from southern Britain
11 Ground plans of typical causewayed enclosures
12 The distribution of stone axes
13 The principal axe factories and flint mines in Britain
14 A flint mine at Grimes Graves
15 Plan of the galleries at Pit No. 2, Grimes Graves
16 Typical neolithic flint implements
17 A reconstruction of the Sweet Track
18 Examples of early neolithic pottery
19 Three earthen long barrows
20 The portal dolmen of Dyffryn Ardudwy
21 Tombs in the Severn-Costwold tradition
22 The passage grave of Bryn Celli Ddu
23 Maes Howe type tombs of Orkney
24 Chambered tombs in northern Britain
25 Examples of late neolithic pottery
26 A single entrance henge and a double entrance henge
27 The probable development of Stonehenge
28 A plan of Stonehenge as it survives today
29 The lintel stones at Stonehenge
30 A plan of Avebury henge and stone circles

31 Major monuments in the locality of Avebury
32 Two stone circles: Long Meg and her Daughters, and the Rollright Stones
33 The recumbent stone circle of Loanhead of Daviot
34 The neolithic village of Skara Brae
35 Reconstruction of the great hall at Balbridie
36 Examples of beakers
37 Reconstruction of the section through the Rudston G62 barrow
38 Bronze Age costumes based on preserved examples
39 Using a saddle quern to grind corn
40 The position of primary, secondary and satellite burials in a round barrow
41 Reconstruction of a mace or sceptre from
42 Bush Barrow
   Objects excavated from the Bush Barrow
43 Typical round barrows of Wessex
44 Examples of Bronze Age metalwork
45 Examples of Bronze Age pottery
46 Late Bronze Age pottery
47 The formation of lynchets
48 The site of Itford Hill, Sussex
49 Moulds for casting metalwork
50 Late Bronze Age swords
51 The late Bronze Age settlement at Springfield Lyons
52 Reconstruction of an Iron Age farmstead
53 Reconstruction of Staple Howe
54 Reconstruction of the early phases of Dan y Coed and Llanwhaden
55 Reconstruction of possible gate structures in British hillforts
56 Plans of typical southern hillforts
57 Plan of huts excavated at Little Waltham
58 Reconstruction of Glastonbury lake village
59 Examples of coarse and fine decorated pottery

Sources of Illustrations

Annable, F.K. and Simpson, D.D.A., *Guide Catalogue of the Neolithic and Bronze Age Collections in Devizes Museum* (1964).

Armstrong, A.L., *Proceedings of the Prehistoric Society of East Anglia*, Vol. 5 (1926).

Ashbee, Paul., *Archaeologia*, Vol. 100 (1966).

Bartlett, R., *Current Archaeology*, Vol. 10 (1988).

Bradford, J.S.P. and Goodchild, R.G., *Oxoniensia*, Vol. 4 (1939).

Burgess, C.B., *Archaeological Journal*, Vol. 125 (1968).

Burl, H.A.W., *The Stone Circles of the British Isles* (1976).

Clough, T.H.McK. and Cummins, W.A., *Stone Axe Studies*, Vol. 2 (1988).

Cunliffe, B.W., *Iron Age Communities in Britain* (1978).

Dix, Brian, *Current Archaeology*, Vol. 6 (1979).

Drewett, P.L. (Ed.), *Archaeology in Sussex to AD 1500* (1978).

Drury, P. J., *Excavations at Little Waltham 1970–71* (1978).

Evans, J.G., *The Environment of Early Man in the British Isles* (1975).

Forde-Johnston, J.L., *Hillforts of the Iron Age in England and Wales* (1976).

Grimes, W.F., in Frere, S.S. (Ed.), *Problems of the Iron Age in Southern Britain* (1961).

Harding, A.F., *Proceedings of the Prehistoric Society*, Vol. 47 (1981).

Henshall, A.S., *The Chambered Tombs of Scotland*, Vol. 1 (1963).

Henshall, A.S., *The Chambered Tombs of Scotland*, Vol. 2 (1972).

Hodder, I. and Shand, P., *Antiquity*, Vol. 62 (1988).

Holgate, Robin, *Neolithic Settlement of the Thames Basin* (1988).

Kilbride-Jones, H.E., *Proceedings of the Society of Antiquaries of Scotland*, Vol. 69 (1935).

Lynch, F., in Powell, T.G.E. (Ed.), *Megalithic Enquiries in the West of Britain* (1969).

Mustoe, R.S., *Bedfordshire Archaeology*, Vol. 18 (1988).

Piggot, S., *Proceedings of the Prehistoric Society*, Vol. 16 (1950).

Piggott, S. and Powell, T.G.E., *Proceedings of the Society of Antiquaries of Scotland*, Vol. 88 (1948).

Pryor, F., *Excavations at Fengate, Peterborough*, Vol. 1 (1974).

Renfrew, C., *Investigations in Orkney* (1979).

Saville, Alan., *Antiquaries Journal*, Vol. 64 (1984).

Smith, I.F. and Evans, J.G., *Antiquity*, Vol. 42 (1968).

Smith, Worthington, *Man the Primeval Savage* (1894).

Stead, I.M., *Antiquity*, Vol. 43 (1969).

Wainwright, G.J., *Current Archaeology*, Vol. 12 (1969).

Willock, E.H., *Proceedings Devon Archaeological Exploration Soc.*, Vol. 2 (1936).

Acknowledgements

Many people have helped me in the production of this book. In particular I would like to thank John Collis, Robin Holgate and John Wymer for reading parts of the manuscript and making many most helpful suggestions. Others who have provided information, answered queries and supplied illustrations include R.J.C. Atkinson, Evelyn Baker, Richard Bradley, Aubrey Burl, Brian Dix, Philip Dixon, Claire Halpin, John Hadman, J.E. Hancock, Ian Longworth, William Manning, Francis Pryor, Ian Ralston, Colin Ramsay, Graham Ritchie, Alan Saville, Ian Stead, Neil Stephenson, Graham Webster and Alastair Whittle. Site reconstructions were specially drawn for me by Tracey Croft and Joshua Pollard. Edna Pollard transferred a difficult manuscript on to word-processor. My father, F.J. Dyer, once again read the proofs. To everyone I offer my sincere thanks.

James Dyer
Luton, June 1989

A Note on Dating

The majority of dates in this book are quoted in years before Christ (BC). Many of these are based on information derived from radiocarbon dating. It was originally believed that radiocarbon dates were the same as solar or calendar years. It is now known that this is not the case, and that many radiocarbon dates are too recent, and they have to be calibrated against dates obtained from tree-ring analysis. This is a far from simple process and there are many pitfalls. In the time chart on page 14 an approximate correlation is shown between actual years BC and uncalibrated radiocarbon years: bc. It must be made clear that this is only an approximate guide. For greater precision the calibration curve produced by Pearson *et al.* (*Radiocarbon* Vol. 28, 1986, 911–34) should be consulted.

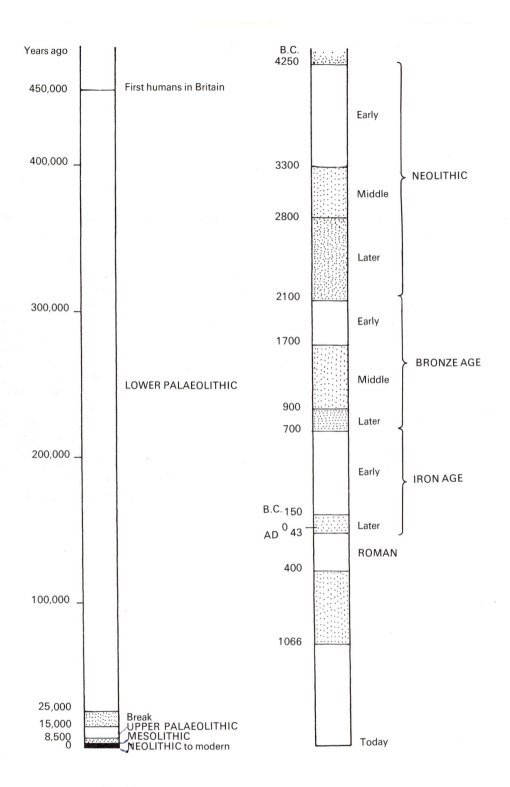

Years ago

450,000 — First humans in Britain

400,000

300,000

LOWER PALAEOLITHIC

200,000

100,000

25,000
15,000 — Break
8,500 — UPPER PALAEOLITHIC
0 — MESOLITHIC
NEOLITHIC to modern

B.C.
4250

Early

3300

Middle   NEOLITHIC

2800

Later

2100

Early

1700

Middle   BRONZE AGE

900

Later

700

Early   IRON AGE

B.C. 150

AD 0 43   Later

ROMAN

400

1066

Today

Time chart – whole of prehistory

Introduction

This book is for the layman, seeking a first introduction to the story of Britain before the Roman conquest. When I first began to take an interest in prehistory in my early teens the choice of books available to me was limited. There were a number of detailed studies by professional prehistorians like Gordon Childe and Christopher Hawkes but few introductory volumes for those taking their first steps into the subject. *Prehistoric Britain* by Jacquetta and Christopher Hawkes was a fine introduction, supplemented on methodology by Graham Clarke's *Archaeology and Society*. The book that had the greatest influence in my formative years was Stuart Piggott's *British Prehistory*, and it has seldom been far from my mind in producing this new volume. Piggott had the knack of telling his story in a way that appealed to schoolboy, student, layman and university don alike. He reminded us continually that prehistory is about people, and that whilst our vocabulary is dominated by monuments and artefacts, behind those words were people with emotions and feelings as real as ours. By the very nature of its evidence prehistory is stifled by thousands of unknown factors that we can never hope to retrieve. We may describe flint mines or burial mounds but we are rarely able to see what really took place there. For example, archaeology allows us few glimpses of prehistoric childhood with its toys and games, entertainment with music and singing, leisure spent in sporting activities or with loved ones and pets, or sickness with its medical care and herbal remedies. In this book I have presented an outline of the story of our island's first inhabitants. It is for the reader to fill in the flesh and blood; I have tried to give the clues where they exist. It is not the story of great lives and deeds: that is the realm of history. It is a simple account of our state of knowledge of life in Britain before the arrival of the Romans in AD 43.

Chronological Years BC	Radiocarbon Years bc	Period	Monuments	Events
4500				
4400				
4300	3500	Mesolithic-early neolithic overlap		
4200			Lambourn long barrow	Earliest long barrows Earliest round bottomed pottery
4100				
4000	3250		Fussell's Lodge long barrow Sweet Track way	
3900				
3800				
3700	3000		Balbridie, Hazleton North	Causewayed enclosures begin
3600				
3500	2750		Carn Brea, Hambledon Hill causewayed enclosure, Nutbane long barrow	
3400				Earliest stone circles
3300	2500	Middle Neolithic		End of causewayed enclosures Henge monuments begin
3200			Gwernvale, Arminghall, Fengate House, Isbister	
3100			Skara Brae	End of long barrows
3000				
2900	2250		Stenness circle	
2800		Later Neolithic	Stonehenge period I	
2700				First beakers, first copper objects, larger stone circles
2600			Avebury stone circles	
2500	2000			
2400			Arbor Low	
2300				
2200				
2100		Early Bronze Age		Wessex Elite
2000	1700		Stonehenge period II Stonehenge period IIIA	Climatic deterioration commences, beakers end
1900				
1800	1500			
1700		Middle Bronze Age		
1600				Arreton metalwork
1500	1250		Stonehenge period III B, Mam Tor	Cremation burial normal practice Acton Park metalwork
1400	1200			
1300			Cob Lane burnt mound	
1200	1000		Dinorben	Penard metalwork, Mount Heckla eruption Earliest hilltop settlements
1100				
1000			Springfield Lyons	
900		Late Bronze Age		Ewart Park metalwork
800				Hilltop enclosures, timber-laced northern forts
700		Early Iron Age	Staple Howe	Southern hillforts
600				
500				Duns and earliest brochs
400			Milton Loch, Cat's Water	
300			Glastonbury lake village begins	Developed hillforts Arras burials begin
			Little Waltham	
200			Walesland Rath	
BC 100		Late Iron Age		
0			Camulodunum	Aylesford graves, Caesar, souterrains Gallo-Belgic pottery imported
AD 100				Claudian conquest AD 43, Lindow Man

Radiocarbon dates based on Pearson et al (1986)

Time chart – mesolithic to Roman period

Chapter One

In the Beginning

The span of time

The first human beings moved into Britain about 450,000 years ago, a length of time so remote that it is impossible for the average person to comprehend. Throughout the greater part of it, human progress was so slow that the same stone tool types were used with little change for hundreds of centuries, and social economy changed only as climatic and environmental conditions dictated. It might help the reader to suggest that if Christ had been born yesterday, the appearance of the first people in Britain would have begun some seven and a half months before. On the same time scale all ensuing history from the arrival of the first farmers to the present day would have to be squeezed into the last three and a quarter days.

This vast span of time is best understood in geological terms. The Pleistocene period can be divided into a number of stages marked by changes of climate. These correspond to cold and warm phases referred to as glacials or interglacials but, in actuality, it would seem that the extremes of each (for example the presence of ice sheets or relatively warm parts of an interglacial such as the climate of the present day) only occupied a minor part of that time. For much of the middle and late Pleistocene period the climate would have been cooler than today in Britain. The cold stages are known as the Anglian, Wolstonian and Devensian, with the Hoxnian and Ipswichian warm stages in between them. Following the Devensian stage is the Flandrian warm period in which we live today. The Wolstonian stage was much longer than the others and spread over 250,000 years, but it was broken up by less cold periods called interstadials. In much the same way cold phases in the interglacials are known as stadials.

During the extremes of glacial periods great sheets of ice spread from the Arctic south to the British Isles causing a world-wide drop in sea level of up to 100 m. (109 yd), due to the water stored in the ice, and creating a land bridge between Britain and Europe (fig. 1). In the intervening interglacials when temperatures rose the ice melted and Britain became an island for a time. Throughout these changes people and animals wandered backwards and forwards between the continent and Britain, and adapted themselves to the climate.

During the coldest times mammoths, woolly rhinoceroses, reindeer and horses roamed over a treeless tundra-steppe countryside. In the warmer interglacials represented at such diverse sites as Barrington (Cambs), Victoria Cave, Settle (N. Yorks) and Trafalgar Square (London) warmth-loving animals such as the hippopotamus, straight-tusked elephant, lion, spotted hyena, bison and various species of deer flourished amongst extensive forests of birch and pine. None of the ice sheets ever covered the whole of Britain; there was always an area of southern England left exposed, where animals and humans could eke out their precarious lives, each preying on the other for food. We have a little evidence to show that they also travelled in northern Britain, at Pontnewydd (Clwyd) for example, although the glaciers would have wiped away most traces.

The palaeolithic period

The period of human activity which began 450,000 years ago is known as the palaeolithic or Old Stone Age; it is divided into two parts. First the lower palaeolithic period, from the appearance of the earliest people in Britain up to about 25,000 BC, when there seems to have been a break in settlement during the advance of ice in the Devensian glaciation. From around 15,000 BC occupation was resumed and the upper palaeolithic period got under way,

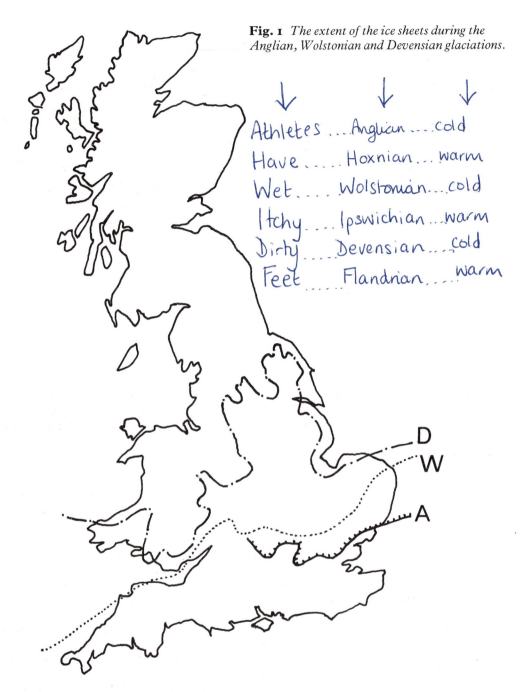

Fig. 1 *The extent of the ice sheets during the Anglian, Wolstonian and Devensian glaciations.*

↓   ↓   ↓

Athletes ... Anglian .... cold
Have ..... Hoxnian ... warm
Wet .... Wolstonian .... cold
Itchy ... Ipswichian ... warm
Dirty .... Devensian ... cold
Feet .... Flandrian ... warm

D
W
A

eventually merging into the mesolithic period around 8,500 BC.

The people of lower palaeolithic Britain lived in the open air, camping beside rivers and lakes, wherever they had access to big game. Cave sites and rock shelters are relatively rare in southern England, and Kent's Cavern and Westbury-sub-Mendip were both utilized. We can imagine small, nomadic family groups following herds of animals from place to place, and supplementing their meat diet by gathering wild plants and berries. Animal skins and

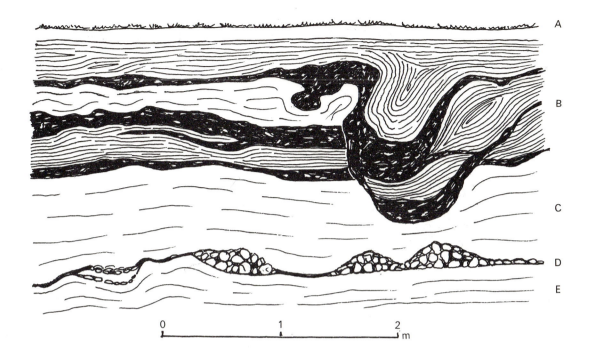

Fig. 2 *The contorted soils covering the palaeolithic floor at Caddington (Beds). A Surface soil; B Contorted glacial drift; C, E Undisturbed brick earth; D Palaeolithic land surface with piles of artefacts and flakes. At the bottom of the section are the piles of flint which men brought to the site as raw material for knapping into implements.* (After Worthington Smith, 1894)

branches would have been used to make temporary shelters, since permanent sites are unlikely. Occasionally traces of camp sites have survived, such as one beside a shallow, reed-fringed lake at Caddington in Bedfordshire, where a century ago Worthington Smith found the working place of stone-tool makers, whose piles of raw material for implement making still remained as they had gathered them (fig. 2). A detailed study of tools from the site by Garth Sampson was able to show that at least three knappers (flint-tool makers) had operated at Caddington. One was an experienced craftsman who recognized the best flint and worked it with few mistakes. Of the two others, one was reasonably skilful whilst the other was clearly only an apprentice who made numerous mistakes.

Four series of stone tools were made in Britain during the lower palaeolithic period.

The simplest are those known as Clactonian, named after a rich site beside an ancient buried river course at Clacton-on-Sea (Essex). Nodules of flint were taken and struck to detach flakes. It is these rather crude flakes that form the bulk of the Clactonian tools which were used for various cutting purposes. Sometimes the remaining cores of flint were used as chopping implements. Other Clactonian sites, all in waterside locations, have been found at Swanscombe (Kent), Barnham (Suffolk) and Little Thurrock (Essex). They seem to date from the Anglian glaciation.

Overlapping with the Clactonian tools, but surviving for a much longer period through the Hoxnian interglacial and almost to the end of the Wolstonian stage, were tools of the Acheulian industries, dominated by handaxes (fig. 3). This name is given to a variety of tools whose exact function is unknown; they did not

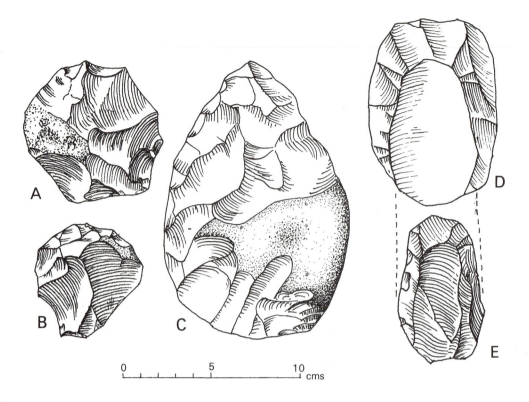

0   5   10 cms

Fig. 3 *Palaeolithic flint implements.*
A *Clactonian core;* B *Clactonian flake tool;*
C *Acheulian handaxe;* D *Levallois tortoise-*
shaped core; E *Levallois flake tool from core.*

have wooden handles and are unlikely to have been axes in the conventional modern sense. It seems more likely that they were multi-purpose tools with widely differing uses, ranging from throwing at animals to bring them down, to cutting meat and scraping skins. Handaxes were often rather crude but might also be finely chipped into elegant pear- and oval-shaped implements. They were made by detaching a series of flakes from a flint nodule until the core remained as the finished tool. The flakes were not wasted but made into a variety of knives, points and scrapers.

Acheulian tools have been found at many open sites including Swanscombe (Kent), Hoxne and High Lodge (both Suffolk). The Barnfield Pit at Swanscombe has also produced three fragments of a human skull. The face is missing but experts believe that it belonged to an early form of *Homo sapiens*, perhaps a quarter

of a million years old and ancestral to Neanderthal man. Modern man, *Homo sapiens sapiens,* did not appear in Europe until about 40,000 years ago. In Kent's Cavern at Torquay (Devon), early Acheulian tools were apparently found with the bones of bear and sabre-toothed cat.

The Levalloisian method of flint working was used in the later Acheulian. It used flake tools struck from carefully prepared cores; these cores resembled the shell of a tortoise until the desired flake tool was detached. Levallois tools are known in large numbers from a 'factory' site at Baker's Hole (Northfleet, Kent), where they were found accompanied by handaxes. Both types also occurred together at Caddington (Beds) and Crayford (Kent).

In a cave in north Wales at Pontnewydd (Clwyd) late Acheulian and Levallois style tools made from volcanic pebbles have been found with a few fragments of human bone from an adult and at least three children. Dated to around 225,000 BC, these people probably belonged to the extinct human species *Homo sapiens neanderthalensis* or Neanderthal man.

There is good reason to believe that they were members of a small group of hunters who used the cave as a shelter for very brief periods, perhaps seasonally, as they ranged freely across southern Britain and into Europe in search of game.

Probably dating to the earlier upper palaeolithic period is material from the Goat's Cave at Paviland (Glamorgan) where the bones of mammoth, cave bear, woolly rhinoceros and elk were excavated by William Buckland in 1823. He also found the burial of a young man whose corpse had been covered with red ochre, perhaps in an effort to restore to it some appearance of life. It lay together with a mammoth's skull, ivory rods, shells and an ivory bracelet, which were all part of an elaborate funerary ritual.

The last handaxes to be made in Britain are

Plate 1 *At least three caves in the Cheddar Gorge (Somerset) were occupied by upper palaeolithic people. Gough's Cave has produced more than 7,000 flint blades of Creswellian type. (J.E. Hancock)*

attributed to the Mousterian industry. In shape they have a rather flat butt, and are sometimes known by the French name, *bout coupé*. Examples are known from the Ipswich area, Little Paxton (Cambs) and Christchurch (Hants). Flake tools predominated in the Mousterian industry and are very similar to Acheulian and Levallois material.

As has already been said, there seems to have been a gap between the lower palaeolithic and the upper palaeolithic at a time when the Devensian glaciation was at its height. Some time after 15,000 BC settlement was resumed by modern man, *Homo sapiens sapiens*, who lived almost exclusively in cave sites. It should however be pointed out that occupation was not deep inside caves, where artificial light would always be required and damp conditions would have been a continual health hazard. A shelter just inside the cave mouth was favoured, where fires could be lit, and light windbreaks constructed from branches and skins (fig. 4). Dressed in furs as protection against the long icy winters, folk also ornamented themselves with bangles and necklaces made from perfor-

Fig. 4 *Overhanging cliffs provided rock shelters, often occupied by extended family groups. Here they slept, fed and prepared tools and skins used in their daily life.* (Tracey Croft)

ated animal teeth, carved bones and shells. Their equipment included flint tools for hunting and domestic use, including beautifully made leaf-shaped points for spears and a variety of flake scrapers, knives and gravers. An unusual object of possible ritual use was a deer antler with a hole bored through its widest end, known as a *baton-de-commandement*. It may also have signified social status or been used merely to straighten spear shafts. Amongst caves occupied at this time were Gough's Cave at Cheddar (Somerset) (plate 1), the Hyena Den at Wookey (Somerset), Kent's Cavern, Torquay (Devon), Victoria Cave (Settle, N. Yorks) (plate 2) and a number of sites at Creswell Crags (Derbyshire).

Flint work at the end of the upper palaeolithic consists largely of backed blades usually referred to as Creswellian after the Creswell Crags caves. These razor-sharp flakes had one long edge blunted, presumably for easier handling. A variety of bone tools which included harpoon heads were also being produced. At Robin Hood's Cave (Derby) a piece of rib bone was uncovered, engraved with the forequarters and head of a wild horse resembling the modern day Przewalskii's horses from Mongolia. A stylized human figure engraved on a reindeer rib and fish-like sign on an ivory point came from Pin Hole Cave (Derby). These are almost the only

Plate 2 *The massive entrance to the Victoria Cave near Settle in Yorkshire. Its three chambers were occupied in the upper palaeolithic and mesolithic periods. (J. Dyer)*

examples of palaeolithic art yet known in Britain: no cave paintings have ever been found (fig. 5).

The mesolithic period

At the end of the last glaciation, about 15,000 BC, the ice sheets retreated north from Scotland, and during the next 5,000 years made their way slowly towards their present-day limits in Scandinavia. The effects were decisive. The tundra and steppe which prevailed in northern Europe were slowly replaced by forest, and the herds of reindeer, bison and horse which had been the quarry of the palaeolithic hunters now retreated northwards, red deer, roe deer and wild oxen taking their place.

Palaeobotanists have worked out the long history of forest development during these early centuries, largely by analysing the pollen which has survived in peat bogs, where it was blown from neighbouring forest areas. Pollen is almost indestructible and survives in these waterlogged and acid soils. Specimens can be extracted, identified and counted under a microscope, where the pollen of each tree type may be seen to be unique. From the amount of each tree pollen

Fig. 5 (below) *Upper palaeolithic art consists of simple sketches on pieces of antler and bone. Left: Horse from Robin Hood's cave; right: man from Pin Hole cave; both from Creswell Crags, Derbyshire.*

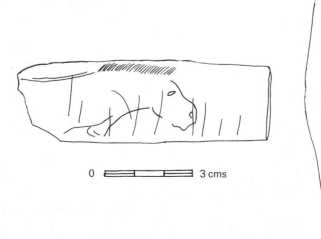

0 ⊏▭▭▭▭⊐ 3 cms

Plate 3 *Changes in sea level led to raised beaches, such as these at Great Cumbrae Island, Bute. (Cambridge University)*

present it is possible to reconstruct the original vegetation.

Between 12,000 and 9,000 BC tundra conditions prevailed throughout Britain and the adjoining areas of the continent. The soil was completely frozen except for the top metre during the summer. Plants were small and stunted and consisted of mosses and lichens and dwarf birch. By about 8,500 BC a sudden marked rise in temperature, giving warm, dry conditions, allowed the ground to thaw and fully grown birch forests spread across north-west Europe. This period is known to archaeologists as the pre-Boreal phase and it merged

Plate 4 *Replicas of dug-out canoes such as would have been used by mesolithic folk to move along the rivers and lakes of post-glacial Britain. (Ray Pettit)*

into the full Boreal period about 7,600 BC. The countryside was covered with pine forests for a time, and these then gave way to hazel and eventually mixed forests of oak, elm and lime. Changes in forest cover were clearly linked to temperature changes and by 5,000 BC when the wetter Atlantic period was well advanced the climate was noticeably warmer than today (by 2.5°C/4.5°F according to Paul Mellars).

Climatic changes also affected the sea levels around Britain. Once the ice sheets and glaciers melted the water level rose 50 m. or more, submerging thousands of hectares of land. But at the same time the weight of the ice, which had been compressing the land surface, was removed and in places the land rose well above sea level. These changes varied from one part of Britain to another. In the south from Land's End to the fens of East Anglia familiar hunting grounds were lost beneath the rising sea, whilst in Scotland and northern Ireland new lands and raised beaches arose from the waters to be colonized by plants, animals and man (plate 3). By Boreal times the area of the North Sea was

almost entirely covered with pine forests, but not later than 6,500 BC the trees were submerged under water which flowed up the English Channel and broke through the Straits of Dover to separate England from Europe. The land bridges which had allowed people and animals to walk from the continent to Britain were finally broken. At first the new straits were narrow and marshy with tidal rivers flowing through them, but as the sea level rose so eventually the Channel began to take on the shape more familiar to us today. It is worth remembering that even in the last century large areas of land, such as the Goodwin Sands, were still exposed at low tide. In the west the North Channel had already formed many centuries before, allowing the Irish Sea to divide Britain from Ireland. From now on water transport would be required to move from one island to another (plate 4).

The changes of vegetation and climate would have made the inhabitants adapt their way of life and methods of food gathering. The great herds of migrating animals of glacial times were now replaced by generally smaller creatures to be hunted through the widspread forests. The rivers and marshes were well-stocked with fish, wild fowl nested along their banks, and on the sea-shore fish, marine mammals and molluscs occurred in abundance. The melting ice sheets had left extensive marshes which impeded movement and the dense woodlands were often impenetrable without the use of a hafted axe, a tool which came into its own at this time, enabling not only the clearing of trees but also the construction of boats to conquer the water-ways. Deposits of charcoal associated with the expansion of hazel forests at places like Iping Common (W. Sussex) have led to the sugges-tion that mesolithic people may have practised forest clearance by burning on a small, localized scale, perhaps in an effort to clear areas to allow room for fruit and nuts to flourish, and grass-land to become established to encourage the expansion of herds of deer for hunting. A series of linked clearings would lead to the develop-ment of tracks through the forest.

The years between 8500 bc and 3500 bc are conventionally called the mesolithic period, meaning Middle Stone Age, and the aborigines are frequently referred to as the 'hunter-fisher folk'. With Britain joined to the continent at the beginning of the period one great territory of forest and plain, broken by rivers and marshes, stretched from Ireland in the west to Denmark and France in the east and south. A study of flint tools made by people living across this large area shows that, as one might expect, they are all broadly similar, and represent an extensive band of people we call Maglemosians, after a marshy site in Denmark.

The number of mesolithic sites identified in Britain is still relatively small, but it is now possible to see them falling into two distinct groups dated by pollen analysis and radiocar-bon dating. Those falling between 8500 bc and 6500 bc are known as *early* mesolithic, and those after that date (6500 bc to 3500 bc) as *later* mesolithic. All the tools produced in the early period are broad blade microliths, that is to say that they are constructed from very small blades of flint, seldom more than 50 mm (2 in.) long and 12 mm (0.5 in.) wide. These blades have obliquely blunted points and convex blunting along one edge. Some are shaped in isosceles triangles and trapezoids.

The microliths must originally have been fitted into wooden or bone hafts to form the composite tips and barbs of arrows or harpoons. Resin was used to glue the blades into position. Wooden spears with bone points, barbed along one edge, were also part of the hunting equip-ment. Their efficiency is demonstrated by the skeleton of an elk excavated at Poulton-le-Fylde in Lancashire which had been killed with barbed bone points and flint-tipped weapons that penetrated its skins, flesh and muscle. Maglemosian bows, about the height of a man, with a carefully shaped hand-grip are known from Holmegaard in Denmark, and were cer-tainly used in Britain. Larger implements of the period include heavy flint axes and adzes with transversely-shaped cutting edges, almost cer-tainly developed to deal with the spread of forests, and the construction of shelters and dug-out canoes.

Later mesolithic flint material evolved after Britain separated from the continent and rep-resents an insular design, though it retained many of the early shapes. In addition it included much narrower geometric microlithic blades, often with straight retouching on one or even two sides, scalene triangles, rhomboids and rectangles. Pointed microliths also appeared

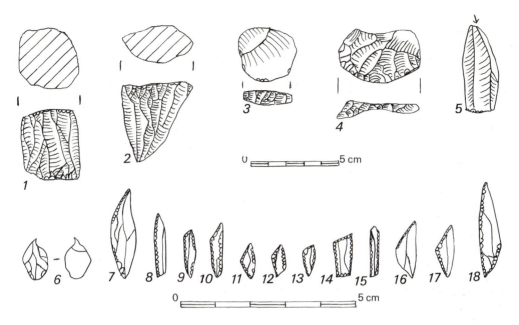

Fig. 6 *Examples of later mesolithic flintwork.*
1–2 Bladelet cores; 3 Core tablet; 4 Tranchet
axe-sharpening flake; 5 Burin; 6 Micro-burin;
7–18 Narrow blade microliths. (After Robin
Holgate, 1988)

with their lower edges worked to a point, curve
or hollow (fig. 6).

The mesolithic people seem to have spread
fairly quickly across Britain from the start of the
Boreal period, and by its end had reached parts
of Scotland. Star Carr, near the present Yorkshire coast, and closest to Denmark, has been
dated to around 7500 BC. Further south, at
Thatcham, Berkshire, slightly earlier dates
close to 7800 BC are recorded. It is legitimate to
see small nomadic Maglemosian hunting
groups making their way backwards and forwards across the undulating plains now lying
beneath the North Sea, crossing the wide rivers
and marshy lakes in search of deer, wildfowl and
fish. Only with the formation of the English
Channel did this regular movement cease, and
the mesolithic inhabitants left residing in
Britain begin to develop in isolation.

Mesolithic settlement

We can best build up a picture of the early
mesolithic population if we examine some of
their scanty settlements. A couple of kilometres
west of the Berkshire village of Thatcham is an
area of reed swamp. In the pre-Boreal period
this was a narrow lake with gravelly beaches,
surrounded by birch and pine forests, with
willows at the water's edge. Perhaps arriving by
boat the mesolithic people cleared the trees
from the lakeside with their flint axes and made
a small settlement, with huts possibly built of
branches and reeds, or wigwams with timber
frames and skin coverings. No trace of structures has survived except for hearths in shallow
pits surrounded by domestic rubbish. The
forest provided shelter for red deer, roe deer
and pig, all of which were caught and eaten.
Dogs were kept to help with the hunting. Other
animals, such as beaver, pine marten, fox and
hare, were probably hunted for their furs. Their
sinews were used for sewing skins together, and
their bones would have made the needles and
awls. Antler and bone were worked into sharply
pointed spear and arrow heads, pins for clothing
and chisels for domestic use. Although flint for
tools could be obtained from the gravel beaches,
better quality material outcropped in the chalk
some miles away and seems to have been
preferred. The Thatcham settlement was not
permanent. It was visited seasonally from time

to time over many centuries, and radiocarbon dates suggest that this occurred around 7800 BC.

At Greasby (Merseyside) a tent-like structure was excavated in 1988. It had a rectangular floor 21 m. (23 yd) square, made of sandstone slabs and pebbles. Along the centre were three large ridge poles, perhaps 2 m. (6.6 ft) high, which may have supported a covering of wood and skins. This seems almost certainly to be the earliest dwelling found in Britain. It can be dated to about 8000 BC.

Britain's best-known mesolithic site, Star Carr, was examined by Professor J.G.D. Clark between 1949 and 1951. It lay on the western edge of the Vale of Pickering, about 3 km south of Seamer (Yorks), on the shore of a former lake that is now filled with peat (fig. 7). The lake had been surrounded by birch trees, and some of these had been cleared and used to build a rough platform of branches and brushwood, on to which lumps of turf and stones had been thrown. The surface was too eroded to leave any trace of dwellings, but these were probably built of skins over a framework of poles or woven reeds. By recording the density of waste material such as bones and flint flakes it was possible to estimate the approximate area occupied, something like 200 m. (219 yd) square, and it was deduced that this would have been utilized by four or five families, perhaps two

Fig. 7 *Star Carr. This seems to have been a minor lake-side platform, not the main camp for the area, from which everyday activities such as hunting, fishing and preparing food and skins was carried out.* (Tracey Croft)

dozen people. The site was probably an activity area visited from time to time by folk primarily engaged in the food quest, hunting, fishing and gathering wild plants, as well as manufacturing tools and weapons and working skins for clothes.

Examination of the bones found shows that red deer were the main animals hunted, followed by roe deer, elk and wild oxen. There is evidence to show that the animals were selectively culled, perhaps to preserve the strength of the stock. Wild pig also contributed to the diet of the inhabitants; water birds played a small part, and almost certainly fish, though their bones have not been preserved. The bones of a small dog were also found. Plenty of evidence for the use of the bow and spears was present in the form of pointed microliths and barbed bone and antler points. Red deer antlers had been utilized in various ways. Many had deep V-shaped grooves cut into them with sharply pointed flint burins to provide longitudinal splinters which were then carved with barbed points along one edge for harpoons.

The fronts of a number of deer skulls with parts of the antlers still attached seem to have been worn by the men as hunting masks. Holes were cut into the frontlets for attaching to the head and the insides had been hollowed-out to make them light to wear. Whether they were used as decoys, or for magical, ceremonial purposes, perhaps as still remembered in the Abbotts Bromley horn dance, we are unlikely ever to know. Objects identified as 'mattock heads' were manufactured from elk antler. A high proportion of flint scrapers for cleaning skins suggests that clothes of animal fur were almost certainly worn, and Star Carr has provided beads of perforated amber, lias and deer teeth as decoration.

The waterlogged nature of the site allowed the preservation of bracket fungus, possibly used for tinder, and rolls of birch bark, perhaps used to make containers or as a source of resin. A wooden paddle (or spade?) suggests that canoes were available, although none were found at the site. Such a canoe is known from Friarton in Perthshire dated to about 6500 BC. The radiocarbon date for Star Carr is around 7500 BC.

Professor Clark saw Star Carr as a winter base camp from which the hunters made their way to the high moors in summer. Today specialists think it more likely to have been used only temporarily between late spring and early summer, and to have been only one of many encampments in that part of east Yorkshire. It is likely that hunting groups travelled 80–160 km (50–100 miles) during the year, following the movements of herds of red deer, and camping at familiar stopping places beside crags or streams, that were used time and again, year after year. The length of their stay at each camp was dependent on the amount of food available, not only to man, but to the animals he hunted as well. Excavation of moorland sites shows the same familiar range of microlithic tools, though the heavy axes are usually missing, probably reflecting environmental differences to the lowland areas. In southern Britan a few rock-shelters were occupied, typified by the site at High Rocks in Sussex. As people followed their traditional routes paths formed, fording places were established and sources of raw material were exploited. Gradually a network of well-worn trackways emerged which were ancestral to those of later prehistoric times.

Changes to smaller microlithic shapes in the middle of the Boreal period around 6500 BC, at roughly the same time as Britain's separation from the continent, heralded the gradual transition to the later mesolithic period. A much larger range of flint shapes appears, many of them forming the barbs and points of projectiles, each chosen for its ability to bring down its particular quarry, much as a modern fisherman chooses the appropriate fly.

A group of mesolithic people originating in France and Belgium are known as Sauveterrians. They lacked the flint axes of the Maglemosians, but produced many geometric microliths including hollow-based points. There is some question as to whether they spread to Britain, but if there was no actual physical movement, at least some of their technological ideas reached this country, if only second-hand, and mixed with Maglemosian traditions, as can be seen, for example, in material from Cherhill in Wiltshire (about 6100 BC). It is clear that materials were exchanged between areas, especially surface flint from the chalk downlands of Wessex, Kent and the Chilterns. Presumably supplies of stone were renewed whenever hunting groups passed through a suitable area.

During the later mesolithic period traces of people are found in the form of shell middens ranged along the post-glacial shoreline of Scotland and, to a lesser extent, along the southern coasts of England and Wales. Sites were first found in Oban in Argyll and lie thickly around the tiny island of Oronsay. Vast quantities of the shells of edible shellfish mixed with animal and bird bones lie beneath grass-covered mounds on Oronsay where they have been investigated since the 1880s. This is the waste material discarded by the Obanians some 6,000 years ago. Thousands of tons of limpet, whelk and oyster shells suggest a plentiful food supply, but it must be remembered that they each contain very little meat, and were probably also a vital late winter and early springtime resource when all else failed. The limpets may also have been used as a bait for fishing.

Of the many sea birds, gulls, cormorants, gannets, guillemots and the extinct great auk are known, but fish provided the main food source with saithe or coalfish predominant (over 90 per cent of total fish), and conger eel, bream, ling, wrasse and haddock together with crab and lobster were all exploited. Few mammal bones were present on Oronsay but large quantities of red deer antlers suggest that they were brought to the island as tools. Grey seals were butchered on the island in the autumn. A few bones of whale and otter are also known. The only plant remains to have survived are thousands of hazel nut shells.

The middens consisted of layers of loose shells, separated by occupation layers of more compact material containing charcoal, artefacts and food refuse. Rectangular stone limpet hammers, bone and antler mattocks, fish hooks and awls and harpoon heads with barbs on both edges were all found. At Cnoc Coig (Oronsay) two circles of stake holes 3–3.5 m. (3.3–3.8 yd) in diameter with hearths at their centres suggest the use of light tents or windbreaks. Tiny hollows close by may have been part of a food preparation area. All the middens were occupied seasonally, often for long periods between November and April. For the rest of the year the people would follow the game. We get a picture of families living in squalor amongst and on top of their rubbish heaps. In the heat of summer the smell and flies would have made life very unpleasant, and this is perhaps another reason why the inhabitants left them during those months for inland pastures.

Burials of mesolithic date are practically unknown in Britain. Cave sites on Mendip such as Gough's Cave (Cheddar) and Aveline's Hole have produced human remains dated to about 7100 BC, and a male skull from the River Yare at Strumpshaw (Norfolk) is likely to be rather more recent in date. We have to turn to Denmark for greater information. Burials from inside a fishing settlement at Vedbæk near Copenhagen, dated around 5000 BC, are particularly illuminating. Seventeen scattered graves were excavated containing the remains of 22 individuals, five of them children. All the men were buried with working tools such as flint knives and axes whilst the women had 'jewellery', once stitched to their dresses, in the form of teeth and shells. Red deer antlers had been buried with some of the men. One grave contained the skeleton of a 20-year-old woman, and her new-born baby lying on a swan's wing. Nearly all the corpses had been sprinkled with red ochre at the time of burial, a custom seen as an attempt to bring back a 'living' colour to the dead.

Chapter Two

Agriculturalists and Monument Builders

The first farmers

The first European farmers had settled in Greece by 6500 BC. Two thousand years later farming had spread from there by way of the loess lands of the upper Danube through western Europe to Britain (fig. 8). There is much debate as to whether this represented a movement of people or simply of ideas: it is very probable that the native inhabitants of Europe saw their eastern neighbours cultivating the soil and breeding animals, and copied the idea. Sometimes the agriculturalists needed new land and physically moved further west, or their expanding families moved off in search of new areas to cultivate. Prospectors and traders also moved west in search of new sources of raw materials.

By the middle of the sixth millennium Britain had become an island with a shore line not too different from that with which we are familiar today. The nature of the landscape – the chalk and limestone ridges, the clay vales, the high

Fig. 8 *A generalized map to show the spread of farming from the Near East to Britain in years before Christ.*

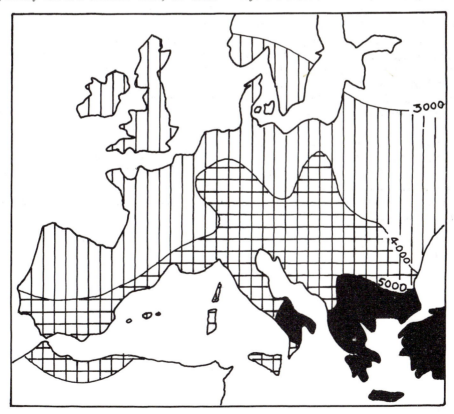

moorlands and low fens, each with its natural vegetation – has influenced the distribution and settlement of human population. More than 60 years ago Cyril Fox drew attention to a natural division of Britain into highland and lowland zones divided roughly along a line from the Tees to the Exe. Although we no longer put so much emphasis on this division, it will be seen time and again that the pattern which emerges in the lowland south-east contrasts markedly with that of the highland north and west. The south-east presents a low-lying easily accessible shore line to the continent of Europe. The Thames and many smaller rivers are waterways that stretch deep into the forested hinterland. Opposite in France, Belgium and the Netherlands great rivers such as the Seine, Meuse, Rhine and Weser penetrate hundreds of miles deep into Europe. For some these rivers were routeways, leading from inland Britain to deep inside Europe; for others they were barriers.

What seems to be clear is that by the fourth millennium BC people using a primitive farming system were established in these river valleys of western Europe. They kept sheep and cattle, grew wheat and barley and made pottery. In settlements like Elsloo in the Netherlands and on the Aldenhoven plateau in north-west Germany, villages and hamlets have been excavated where people lived in long rectangular timber houses, usually divided up into a number of sections, some of which were occupied by animals. There is no doubt that some of these people farmed on the continental shores of the English Channel and fished in its waters. Seeing the coast of Britain on the western skyline when they went out fishing, they may well have been tempted to seek shelter there on occasions and became familiar with its potential for settlement. Reconnoitring parties would have explored and found their way up the British rivers to the small clearings made by the mesolithic inhabitants. Having made a deliberate decision to colonize, they would perhaps have transported cattle for grazing and seed corn for cultivation in small, garden-sized plots, leaving one or two of their number to tend to them. Once established, more of their families would move to Britain to create a permanent settlement. These were the pioneers who would take a century or two to adjust to their new land.

It is worth noticing that some archaeologists believe that this process took place in reverse: mesolithic inhabitants of Britain crossed to Europe, saw the farmers there and borrowed their ideas, transporting cattle and seed back to Britain. This is a technical point which will continue to be debated for years to come and need not concern us deeply.

Movement for the first farmers was difficult due to thick forest cover and marshes. Wheeled transport was unknown in western Europe though heavy loads could have been moved using land-sledges or slide-cars. Water provided the best means of transport and in all probability small skin boats like the Eskimo whaling umiak or the Irish curragh were used. Already established as fishermen, they would now make the dangerous voyage across the Channel to ferry sacks of corn and animals to the British Isles: sheep, cattle, pigs and goats are not indigenous to Britain and would have had to come from Europe, and initially from the eastern Mediterranean. We can imagine the animals' hooves being tied together to prevent them struggling and overturning the small boats. Although many of the boats were unloaded on those parts of the coast closest to Europe, other landfalls seem to have been made all round Britain and Ireland between 4200 and 3500 BC. Certainly Britain's west coast has many enticing harbourages. Radiocarbon dates show that farming was established at places as far apart as East Anglia, eastern Scotland and the coast of Sligo, all at about the same time.

Forest clearance

Pollen records show that practically the whole of Britain was covered with deciduous woodlands. Even the granite uplands of Dartmoor were forest-covered. Tall trees with high, thick canopies produced dark, cathedral-like voids beneath. The varying subsoils supported different densities of undergrowth between the trees. On the escarpment edges of the well-drained chalk and close to the water in the river valleys it was easier to move amongst the trunks, and it was there in particular that the first farmers began to make their clearings. Using sharp polished stone axes, trees were felled to provide cultivation patches and grazing areas (plate 5). A polished stone axe, professionally used, can cut down an average tree (the thickness of a telegraph pole) in about 30 minutes. In 1954

Plate 5 *Neolithic polished stone axes mounted in replicas of ancient wooden hafts, being used to fell a small tree. (Forhistorisk Museum, Moesgard)*

experiments by the Dane Johs. Iversen suggested that one man could clear a hectare of forest in five weeks. Iversen used flint axes mounted in modern hafts in the manner of surviving prehistoric examples, and chopped the trees at knee height. Trees more than 35 cm. (14 in.) in diameter were ring-barked and left to die. Selected trunks and bigger branches would be trimmed and stored for building purposes. Small branches and leaves could be heaped around the bases of tree trunks and burnt. It was found that larger, unwanted trunks had to be stacked before they could be burnt.

The resultant cleared areas would be rough, with large stumps sticking out here and there, but a covering of rich ash would encourage the growth of crops once the seed had been scattered and raked with branches. Unfortunately the nutrients in the ash would be washed out after a few heavy rainfalls, and the clearings would only produce crops for five or six seasons before the yields began to fall. At first only digging sticks were used to break up the soil until the tree roots rotted away; after that it was possible to bring in a simple plough called an ard, which cut a single furrow.

Clearings were expanded as time went by, and if abandoned were temporarily prevented from regenerating by grazing animals, who would in turn refertilize the area with their manure (fig. 9). Linking trackways and expanding clearings gradually led to long stretches of open countryside, especially on the chalk and limestone hills, where ridgeways such as the Icknield Way came into being, facilitating long distance travel and the opening of the interior.

Evidence for early agriculture exists in various forms. In Wiltshire ard-marks were found criss-crossing the land surface beneath the South Street long barrow. Impressions of grain found baked into the clay of pottery and carbonized seeds tell us that two types of wheat, emmer and einkhorn, were grown in the south of England, with lesser quantities of barley. In northern Britain barley appears to have been

Thick woodland with undergrowth.

Woodland clearance by burning.

Crops grown amongst stumps and ashes.

After some years stumps have rotted. Animals manure
the land. It can be ploughed with ard.

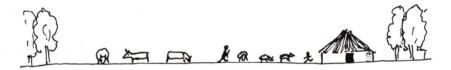

Fig. 9 *The effects of forest clearance.*

much more common. The ears of grain were cut
using flint sickles or plucked by hand and the
seeds were ground into flour on flat blocks of
stone known as saddle querns.

The arrival of the first farmers marks the
approximate beginning of the period which
archaeologists have traditionally referred to as
the neolithic period or New Stone Age. It
can conveniently be divided into two phases.
The earlier neolithic period from about
4200–3500 BC was the period when plain pottery
bowls were produced and causewayed enclosures, chambered tombs and earthen long barrows built. The later neolithic period from

3500–2100 BC is marked by decorated pottery,
cursus and henge monuments and smaller long
and round barrows.

Settlements of the earlier neolithic period are
elusive and less than a dozen house structures
are known from Britain. None of them compare
with the long-houses of Holland and Germany.
At Haldon in Devon an oblong, timber-built
house with stone footings measured 7.6 by
4.8 m. (25 × 16 ft). It seems to have had a gabled
roof and there were signs of a hearth in one
corner, separated from the main room by a
dividing wall (fig. 10). Another similar house,
but double the size of that at Haldon, was
excavated at Fengate near Peterborough in
1971. It had been of massive timber construc-

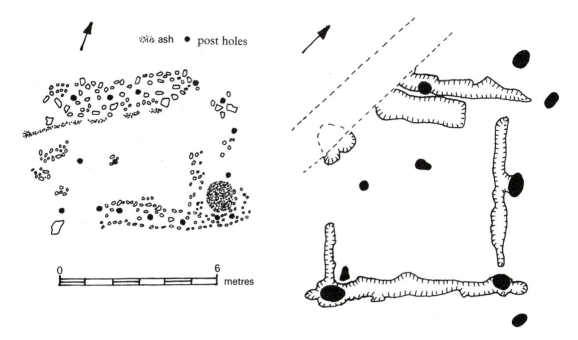

ash   • post holes

0   6
metres

Fig. 10 *Plans of rectangular neolithic houses from southern Britain at Haldon (Devon) and Fengate (Cambs).* (After Willock, 1936 and Pryor, 1974)

tion with footing trenches for plank walls. The average size of British neolithic houses seems to have been about 8 by 4.5 m. (27 × 15 ft) giving an interior area of some 36 sq. m. (405 sq. ft), roughly the size of the ground floor of a Victorian terraced house. Perhaps it would be more accurate to see the majority of neolithic houses as temporary, tent-like structures which left little trace in the ground, except for occupational debris, hearths and storage pits.

Field walking in parts of the Thames Basin by Robin Holgate has revealed scatters of flint defining areas of domestic settlement on the chalk and limestone hilltops and hillslopes, often, but not always, associated with burial monuments. Evidence of extensive settlement in the valley bottoms is not found until the later neolithic period.

It seems probable that domestic sites were not occupied for long periods but that the farmers moved around a restricted block of territory seeking out new land for grazing and cultivation as the old land became exhausted, perhaps returning to an abandoned plot after

about 20 years. Holgate has noticed that on the margin of the settled areas were the large earthwork sites known as causewayed enclosures, probably the first 'architecture' to be constructed in Britain.

Causewayed enclosures

These enclosures, of which about 50 are known, are usually roughly circular in plan and consist of one, two or three concentric rings of ditches, dug as a series of irregular pits, probably by gang labour, and separated by undug causeways of soil, rather like a string of sausages (fig. 11). The material from the ditches was thrown up ~~faced~~ into an internal bank, sometimes revetted with posts or turf, or crowned by a stockade. Many of these banks have now disappeared entirely. It was originally thought that the gaps in the ditches were entrances for driving cattle, and that gaps in the banks corresponded with them. However, it is clear that the banks were much more continuous, with only a few breaks. If entrances existed they cannot always be positively identified, but groups of post holes at Hembury, Crickley, Whitehawk and Hambledon have been interpreted as the remains of wooden gates. Little sense has been made of the interior of the enclosures, which seem to contain a mass of pits, post holes and gullies,

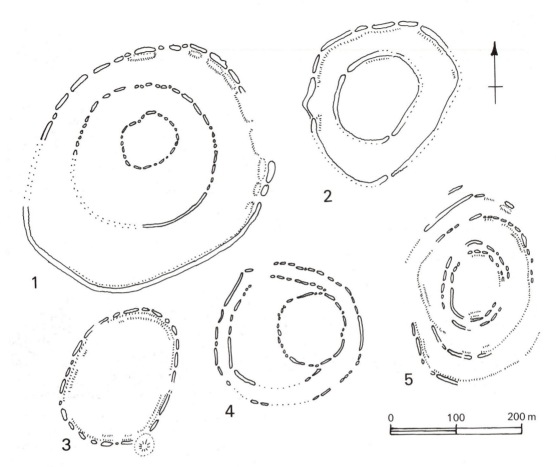

Fig. 11 *Ground plans of some typical causewayed enclosures. 1 Windmill Hill, Wilts; 2 Robin Hood's Ball, Wilts; 3 Whitesheet Hill, Wilts; 4 Briar Hill, Northants; 5 Whitehawk, Sussex. Ditch sections outlined.* (Sources: various)

perhaps indicating at least temporary settlement.

The causewayed enclosures crown rounded hills in the chalk lands like The Trundle in Sussex and Knap Hill in Wiltshire, but they are also found in low-lying valleys like Abingdon in Oxfordshire and Staines in Middlesex, and on saddles and ridges as at Combe Hill and Whitehawk, both in Sussex (plate 6). They are almost exclusive to lowland Britain and stretch from Hembury in Devon north to Alrewas in Staffordshire and Barholm in Lincolnshire, with a possible addition at South Kirby in West Yorkshire.

There is as yet little evidence that the majority of enclosures were built for defensive purposes, and the earthworks sometimes slope down the side of a hill across the contours as though deliberately displaying their interiors to the outside world. However, some East Anglian sites seem to have massive stockades inside the ditches, which might be interpreted as a form of defence. Isobel Smith suggests that they follow a 'predetermined plan carried out regardless of topography'. Size varies considerably from less than a hectare (3 acres) at Rybury in Wiltshire to over 8 ha. (20 acres) at Windmill Hill and Hambledon Hill.

Most excavation of causewayed enclosures has concentrated on the ditches which are usually some 3 m. (10 ft) wide and seldom less than 1.5 m. (5 ft) deep. Where more than one ring of ditches occurs, the outer ring is usually the deepest as at Windmill Hill and The Trundle. It is not clear if each circuit of ditch is

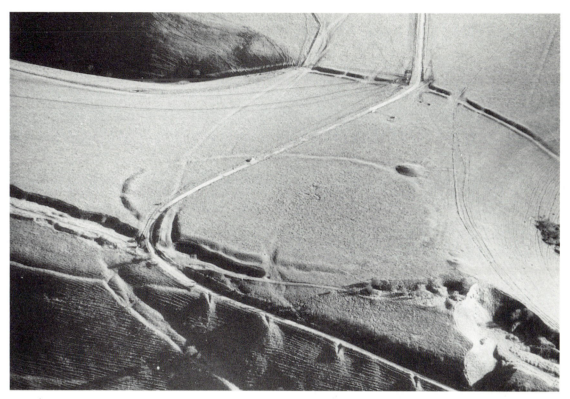

Plate 6 *An aerial view of Whitesheet Hill causewayed enclosure on the edge of the chalk escarpment in Wiltshire. A Bronze Age barrow and cross-ridge dyke also appear in the photograph. (J.E. Hancock)*

contemporary with its neighbour, and some enclosures may have increased their size as their importance grew. At Etton, Francis Pryor has suggested that only a few segments of ditch were dug at any one time. Although the ditches were basically the quarries for bank material, it is clear that they had a part to play in the activities at the site, since they were cleaned out on a number of occasions. Even so excavations show that they frequently contain large quantities of domestic rubbish. This usually consists of layers of animal bones, (especially cattle, sheep, pigs and deer), mixed with fragments of pottery, vegetable refuse and charcoal, broken flints, the occasional dead dog and human bones. Often this rubbish was carefully covered with soil as though to reduce the smell of rotting garbage.

Most of the pottery found in the ditches belongs to round-bottomed, baggy-shaped ves- ~~keel shaped~~ sels. Finer quality carinated bowls of Grimston type seem to have been of special significance. Numerous axes of non-local stone and pottery tempered with grit from Cornwall and found as far east as Gloucestershire and Sussex suggest that these objects had been brought to the enclosures from long distances. The animal bones show the cut marks of flint knives, perhaps indicating on-the-spot butchering, and some ox skulls show signs of pole-axing with a sharp flint point over the left eye.

Deserving particular attention are the human remains found in the ditches. A large number of human skulls are recorded, often lacking their lower jaws (plate 7). Some of these, at Hambledon Hill for example, seem to have been deliberately positioned on the ditch floor, as though to ward off evil spirits. Others are more casually scattered, and mixed with other human bones, suggesting that they may have been swept into the ditch in a cleaning operation. If this is the case then it is likely that they originated in the centre of the enclosure where corpses may have been exposed, perhaps on

Plate 7 *A human skull on the floor of a causewayed ditch at Hambledon Hill, Dorset. (Robin Holgate)*

platforms, and allowed to decay. Roger Mercer has written of the central enclosure at Hambledon Hill, describing it as 'a vast, reeking open cemetry, its silence broken only by the din of crows and ravens'. This implies that causewayed enclosures played a far greater part in the funeray ritual of neolithic Britain than has been realized. In Celtic Iron Age times human heads were collected as trophies and stored as prize possessions. It is perhaps worth wondering if a similar cult existed in the neolithic period.

Child burials seem to have had a special place in this ritual. At Windmill Hill the deliberate burials of two young children were found in a ditch, together with the skulls of three more. At Whitehawk the excavator found the ashes of a hearth containing fragments of five skulls, all of them of young people between 6 and 20 years. In the same ditch section was the complete skeleton of a young mother with her new-born child. Child burials also occurred in the ditches at Hambledon Hill, where they accounted for 60 per cent of the burials. Some lay crouched in the ditch bottom with cairns of flints above them. At the same site the lower trunk of a 15-

[handwritten annotation: mounds of rough stones]

year-old boy had been dragged into a ditch, perhaps by animals, whilst the flesh was still upon it. Complete adult skeletons have also been found at Offham Hill (Sussex), Abingdon (Oxon) and Staines (Middx).

Probably the best-known example of a causewayed enclosure, and first to be investigated, is Windmill Hill, 2.5 km. (1½ miles) north-west of Avebury in Wiltshire. Three roughly concentric rings of causewayed ditches circle a low hilltop. The outer ditch has a diameter of 365 m. (1,200 ft). The mean diameter of the middle ditch is 200 m. (660 ft), whilst the inner measures about 85 m. (280 ft). The ditches do not follow the contours of the hill; instead they hang lop-sidedly down the steeper northern hill-slope. They may not all be contemporary and recent excavations by Alastair Whittle suggest that the outer ditch may have been added later (plate 8). All the ditch sections are very irregular and vary considerably in size. Excavation by Alexander Keiller between 1925 and 1938 showed them to be flat bottomed, and deepest in the outer circle and shallowest in the inner ring. Only at the eastern side of the outer circle can any trace of the bank now be seen, though the excavations showed that it was present inside all the ditches. We shall probably never know if it was topped by a stockade, thus making it defensive.

Many fragments of early neolithic pottery were found in the enclosure. Nearly one-third of it had been made from Jurassic clays found some 30 km (20 miles) away around Frome and Bath. How such fragile material was carried to Windmill Hill remains a mystery. Also deliberately buried in the ditches were domestic objects such as flint scrapers, stone axes and animal bones suggesting some form of settlement, either temporary or permanent, as well as the skeletons of the two children mentioned above.

A variety of interpretations of causewayed enclosures have been offered over the years. Settlement sites and defended camps were first suggested 50 years ago, and this was possibly closer to the truth than has more recently been supposed. The large quantities of domestic rubbish in the ditches at some of these sites would support such explanations. The fact that some of the rubbish had come from some distance away led to the idea that the enclosures

Plate 8 *A section across the outer ditch of Windmill Hill, Wiltshire, excavated in 1988. (Alastair Whittle)*

were centres for periodic fairs and tribal gatherings. The wealth of animal bones was used to suggest that the sites were corrals where cattle were annually rounded up for branding, gelding or culling. Following the work at Hambledon Hill the idea of the central area of the enclosures being used as a vast mortuary for the exposure of corpses has proved most popular. There is no clear answer. It is probably wrong to try and see each site as serving the same function but the various similarities between them perhaps indicate that they were most likely ritual cult centres, where people met at certain times of the year to mourn their dead and celebrate the well-being and fertility of their crops, their animals and themselves.

Amongst the causewayed enclosures are a small group of strongly defended settlements with causewayed and continuous ditches, which tend to be sited on hill spurs. The best known examples are Hembury in Devon, Crickley Hill in Gloucestershire, Hambledon Hill in Dorset and Carn Brea in Cornwall. These sites were defended by steep natural hill slopes as well as

man-made defences. At Carn Brea a massive enclosing wall, built of boulders and 2 m. (6.6 ft) wide at the base, surrounded an area of 0.8 ha. (2 acres). The local geology precluded the digging of a causewayed ditch. Post holes indicated a number of probably domestic buildings in the enclosure, some of which had been destroyed by fire. Outside, larger enclosures were used for agriculture. More than 800 leaf-shaped arrowheads, some broken, and others amongst the boulders of the rampart, strongly suggested that Carn Brea was attacked on more than one occasion.

Crickley Hill, in its final phase, was defended by a continuous ditch and a strong stone-built internal wall topped by a stockade. Four hundred arrowheads and signs of burning again indicated a dramatic end for the enclosure. A violent end to Hambledon Hill is also seen as likely from the signs of the burning down of the stockade on top of the bank, and the skeleton of a young man with an arrowhead in his chest found there, apparently killed whilst rescuing a child from the burning enclosure.

Roger Mercer has observed that after these defended enclosures went out of use, no further defensive sites are known until the appearance of hillforts a thousand years later. It is unlikely that the causewayed enclosures were dug by the very first farmers who arrived in Britain. At first concentrated communal effort was required to establish the farming way of life with its forest clearance, house building, crop growing and animal husbandry. Only after a generation or two would there be time for large numbers of people to gather at the slack times of the year when the farming calender was not too busy, to engage in the construction of communal earthworks.

[handwritten: study of origin, structure composition etc of rock.]

Axe manufacture

We have seen that initial forest clearance had already taken place before the first farmers arrived in Britain. In the neolithic period it was accelerated by the use of the woodcutter's axe. Made of igneous or metamorphic rock or flint, and mounted in wooden hafts, these were obtained from glacially scattered surface material, from moor or mountain top outcrops or from subterranean flint mines. The indigenous mesolithic people had flint axes, but now

[handwritten left margin: volcanic]

[handwritten left margin: undergone transformation by natural agencies such as heat and pressure]

Plate 9 *The crags of Great Langdale (Cumbria). The scree on the upper slopes was the source of many igneous stone axes. (J. Dyer)*

Fig. 12 *The distribution of stone axes of Group I, Mount's Bay, Penwith; VI, Great Langdale and VII, Penmaenmawr. (After Clough and Cummins, 1988)*

[handwritten: 4 sided with no 2 sides paralell]

they were refined by being highly polished into efficient trapezoidal-shaped tools. Modern experiments by Philip Harding suggest that to make such axes required about 8 hours' continuous grinding on abrasive stone blocks. More than 30 igneous axe production factories have been identified in western Britain, of which some eight were particularly dominant. It is possible to tell from which factory many of the axes came by petrological analysis. A thin slice is cut from the axe, ground to the required thickness, usually thousandths of a millimetre, and then examined under a microscope. Because the geological survey of Britain is very good it can be matched with known geological specimens and often the source identified. Plotted on a map, information can be gained about the distribution of axes and possible distribution routes of the neolithic producers (fig. 12).

These igneous sites tend to be peaks and crags, often in difficult terrain, in such places as

Great Langdale in the Lake District (plate 9), Mounts Bay in Cornwall, Penmaenmawr in Snowdonia and Tievebulliagh in County Antrim. At Langdale in Cumbria loose rock on the dangerous lower scree slopes was avoided and the material for the axes came from the higher, less accessible peaks. The stone was split by heating the rock with fires and then applying cold water and wooden wedges to break it. The axes were roughly shaped on the spot but there is no evidence that the final polishing was done on the mountain side. It seems logical for it to have been carried out near the 'factory', to save the effort of hauling surplus stone further than necessary. Polishing stones have been found in many parts of Britain, though they may have been used mainly for resharpening axes.

It seems probable that the factories were worked by individual family groups, holding the quarrying rights and passing on their know-how over hundreds of years. We cannot tell if the manufacturers were responsible for distribution, though this might have been done during the winter months when the mountain tops were too cold and exposed for working. Those employed in full-time axe manufacture would not have had time to grow food for themselves, and so it is reasonable to assume that this was obtained in exchange for their products. Dr Isobel Smith has shown that stone axes were in use for at least 1,500 years from about 3250 BC to 1750 BC. Prior to that, surface flint or outcrops in chalk cliffs or on beaches would have been used as the source material.

As would be expected many of the axes from the various British sites finished up being used in areas close to the factories, but axes from two sources in particular, Langdale in Cumbria and Mounts Bay in west Cornwall were distributed hundreds of kilometres away, indicating that they might have been carried in bulk to distant redistribution centres in north-east England and Cambridge respectively. Axes from County Antrim have been found in the London area. It is possible that the Cornish axes were brought to Wessex and the Thames estuary by boat along the south coast by way of the appropriate river valleys.

From the thousands of axes which can be seen in museums it is clear that most of them were used for tree-felling and carpentry, but quite a large number seem never to have been used at all. They appear to have had a more symbolic significance, as perhaps did the mountains from which they were quarried. Some unused axes seem to have been deliberately buried in the great earthworks of the period, the causewayed enclosures, long barrows and cursuses, whilst others have been dredged in large numbers from the River Thames. It has been suggested that many of these were symbols of power whilst others were votive offerings generally associated with life, strength and vitality and the forces of nature. Particularly fine stone axes were brought to Britain from the continent, perhaps from Switzerland or the Italian Alps. These are of a stone called jadeite and are usually finely finished and beautifully designed. One of the best was found in Canterbury. Another, in pristine condition, was found buried without a handle beneath the Sweet Track, a contemporary wooden trackway built across a peaty quagmire in the Somerset Levels; this has been radiocarbon dated to around 3200 bc. Other jadeite axes occur in Wessex and East Anglia and at various Scottish sites. Axes of Bretton dolerite were also imported and have been found close to the river mouths of southern England.

Flint was also used for making axes and other implements. Whilst the raw material can frequently be found lying on the hillside or sea-shore in southern Britain and north-eastern Ireland, and was at first used for axe manufacture, it is usually of poor quality due to frost-fracturing, and the lumps often too small to make the sort of tools required. The best rock lies buried in seams often 5–15 m. (5.5–16.4 yd) deep which formed in the upper chalk, so mines were developed to extract it (fig. 13). When agriculture reached western Europe flint mines were quickly developed in France, Belgium, the Netherlands and Denmark. In England at least a dozen mining sites are known from Sussex (Harrow Hill (plate 10), Cissbury) and Wessex (Easton Down) to the Chilterns (Pitstone) and East Anglia (Grimes Graves). A possible site has also been located at Ballygalley in County Antrim. Radiocarbon dating shows that the earliest mines were in Sussex and must be contemporary with the first agriculturalists from 3100 to 2700 bc. The East Anglian mines at Grimes Graves span the period 2300 bc to

Fig. 13 *Map to show the principal axe factories and flint mines in Britain. Axe factories:* I *Mount's Bay;* VI *Great Langdale;* VII *Penmaenmawr;* VIII *S.W. Wales;* IX *Tievebulliagh;* XVIII *Whin Sill;* XX *Charnwood Forest. Flint mines:* I *Grimes Graves;* 2 *Easton Down;* 3 *Blackpatch;* 4 *Harrow Hill;* 5 *Cissbury.* (Sources: Clough and Cummins, 1988; Evans, 1975, with additions)

● Axe factories

▲ Flint mines

early 4200–3500

—late Ne.

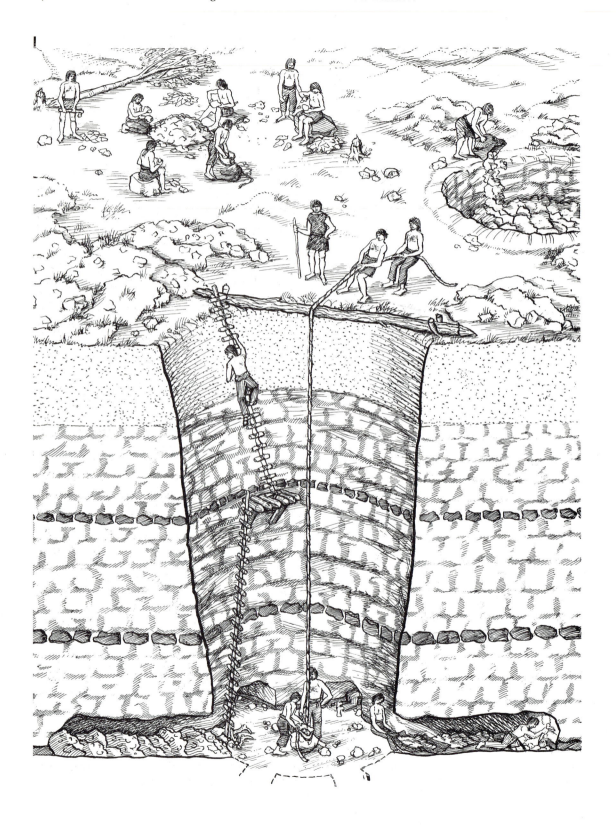

Plate 10 *About 160 filled-in flint mine shafts can be seen in this aerial view of Harrow Hill, Sussex. The rectangular enclosure was used in the Iron Age for cattle slaughtering. (Cambridge University)*

1600 bc with the greatest activity between 2000 and 1800 bc. One wonders how people knew that there was flint buried deep in the chalk. It can of course be seen outcropping in the cliffs at the seaside, and may have been encountered when ditches were dug for earthworks.

Archaeological excavations were recently carried out at Grimes Graves in Norfolk and the mines are typical. In a number of places the flint outcropped in narrow bands and could be quarried by opencast working which might involve only a few days' digging. Where the seams of flint dipped deeper into the chalk, shafts had to be sunk from above. There are more than 340 of these deep shafts close together at the site. They are from 5 to 12 m. (5.5 to 13 yd) in diameter and can be as much 15 m.

Fig. 14 *A flint mine at Grimes Graves. Material for a new shaft was back-filled into a disused one. Exhausted galleries were also back-filled. The freshly mined flint was hauled to the surface where it was roughed-out into the shape of required implements. (Tracey Croft)*

(16.4 yd) deep, depending on the depth of the best seam of flint. The stone occurs in three bands; the upper two known as the topstone and wallstone are fragmentary nodules and were not usually of much interest to the miners who made for the lowest layer, the floorstone. This seam is 5 to 10 cm. (2 to 4 in) thick.

Using pickaxes of red deer antler and shovels made of ox shoulder blades or shaped pieces of wood, the miners dug down until they reached the floorstone. Access would have been by ladder (fig. 14). Sometimes if the shaft was deep they inserted a platform about half-way down, enabling miners to descend in two stages. Occasionally small galleries might be dug to retrieve the wallstone if it seemed worthwhile but normally it was only at floorstone level that a series of galleries radiated out from the base of the shaft. These could be as much as 2 m. (6.6 ft) wide and 1.5 m. (5 ft) high at first. From these, smaller tunnels, less than a metre high, penetrated about 5 m. (5.5 yd) from the foot of the shaft (plate 11). Often the galleries of one mine communicated with those of an adjoining abandoned shaft, the whole area being honeycombed with hundreds of tunnels (fig. 15).

The miners worked lying on their sides in the galleries, removing the chalk with their picks and levering out the blocks of flint which lay buried beneath them. They passed the material

Plate 11 *A view of the galleries at Grimes Graves, Norfolk. Flint floorstone can be seen at the base of the chalk on the right. (British Museum)*

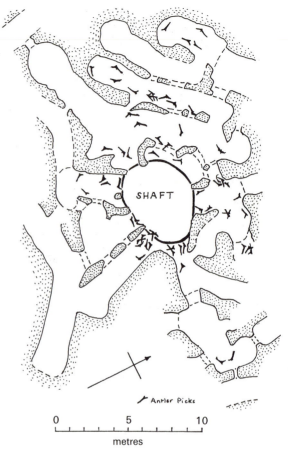

Fig. 15 *Plan of the galleries at Pit No. 2, Grimes Graves (Norfolk), ranged round the central access shaft. The position of deer antlers used in mining have been indicated. (Source: Armstrong, 1926)*

back down the tunnel and other workers removed it into baskets which could be hauled to the top of the shafts. Galleries and shafts already cleared were back-filled with rubble. The galleries would have been hot and stuffy with limited air supply. Although we have no evidence for this, the miners must have worn protective clothing, especially for the hands, since the flint is razor sharp and the chalk very abrasive. Lamps, made by hollowing out a block of chalk and filling it with animal fat, have been found in a number of British mines, though not at Grimes Graves. It is possible that daylight reflected from the white walls was sufficient when the miners' eyes became accustomed to it, providing the galleries were not too long. In the Sussex mines, where soot marks have been found on the roofs and ashes on the floor, faggots or tapers were also used for lighting.

It is likely that about a dozen men worked at each mine. A new shaft was dug every one or two years, though the actual digging time may have been only about two months. An average mine produced a total of around 45 tonnes (44.3 tons) of flint. This would have been roughly trimmed and shaped close to the top of

the shaft. The rough-outs were then transported to would-be customers who we imagine were responsible for shaping the finished tools. These would include not only axes but adzes, arrowheads, scrapers, knives and sickles (fig. 16). Men engaged in mining may have had little time for agriculture unless the quarrying was carried out after the harvest. Perhaps they exchanged their flint for a large part of their food supply?

[handwritten annotation: a tool for cutting away the surface of wood, like an axe with an arched blade at right angles to the handle]

From the number of axes, adzes and other woodworking tools produced it is clear that carpentry was a major craft in neolithic Britain.

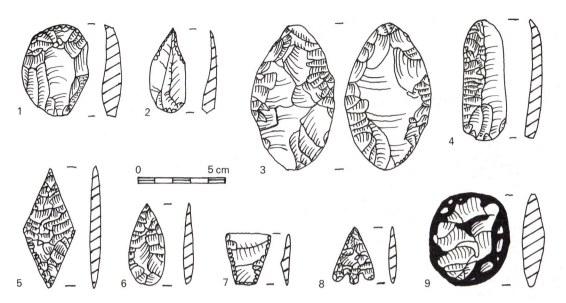

Fig. 16 *Typical neolithic flint implements.*
1 Scraper; 2 Piercer; 3 Ovate; 4 Knife;
5 Lozenge-shaped arrowhead; 6 Leaf-shaped
arrowhead; 7 Petit tranchet arrowhead;
8 Barbed and tanged arrowhead; 9 Ground-edged
knife. (Source: Robin Holgate, 1988)

Fig. 17 (below) *A reconstruction of the neolithic trackway across the Somerset Levels known as the Sweet Track.*

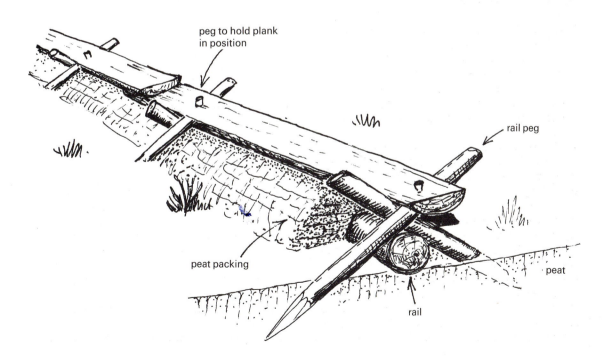

peg to hold plank
in position

rail peg

peat packing

peat

rail

Unfortunately since wood has seldom survived we have little idea of carpentry skills, though obviously this included the construction of houses and cult buildings, furniture, wooden bowls and domestic goods, handles for tools, hunting weapons and boats. Only on waterlogged sites in the Somerset Levels has wood such as ash, oak and hazel survived in sufficient quantities for us to see some of its uses. Here, many metres of timber trackways dating from 3200 bc have been uncovered stretching across the marshland, composed of thousands of tree trunks, many split into planks and jointed together with traditional carpentry joints (fig. 17). Wooden artefacts found from the Levels include bows of hazel, arrow shafts, paddles or spades, digging sticks, an ash figurine, handles, pins, a spurtle or stirrer, a mallet and a child's toy 'tomahawk'. Reeds and rushes from the marshes would also have been used to make baskets, some of which probably suggested the design on decorated neolithic pottery.

Pottery

The need to cook and store food led to the invention of pottery. Skin vessels, clay-lined baskets and hollowed-out wooden containers were almost certainly used, but pots of clay seemed most satisfactory. The earliest pottery consisted of simple round-based pots, cups and bowls, two variants of which are known as Grimston and Lyles Hill wares (fig. 18). It first appeared around 3500 bc and was in use throughout Britain with little change for the next thousand years. There was little decoration, though the vessels might have a slight shoulder or a gentle 'S' profile. As time went by regional groups appeared, characterized by distinctive local features. In the south and west of England Windmill Hill and Hembury styles were common, with bag-shaped bowls, often with protruding lugs to help lift them. These pots are usually undecorated though some Windmill Hill vessels have vertical slashes on the shoulders. In Yorkshire, Heslerton and Towthorpe bowls are found. Simple decoration occurs on three southern regional styles, Abingdon from the upper Thames area, Mildenhall from East Anglia and Whitehawk from Sussex. Some of the finer Hembury ware pots were made of gabbroic clay found only on the Lizard peninsula of Cornwall. This suggests they were made by full-time potters whose wares were distributed all over the south-west and eastwards to Wiltshire 300 km. (185 miles) away. Even if packed carefully the vessels would have been difficult to carry through the forested terrain; perhaps water transport was involved.

Fig. 18 *Examples of early neolithic pottery. A–B Bag-shaped Windmill Hill style pots; C Mildenhall style bowl; D Specialized bowl from Grimston. The Grimston bowl is about 30 cm. (11.8 in.) in diameter.*

Chapter Three

The Cult of the Dead

Collective burial

Throughout the western seaboard countries of Europe during the neolithic period there was a tradition of collective burial of the dead. From Scandinavia, through Britain to Spain some social or religious cult required that its members be buried together in a tomb, either individually, one at a time, or as a group. The origin of this burial custom is one of the great problems of western archaeology to which no satisfactory answer has as yet been found. Like farming, the ideology of the cult probably spread by word of mouth rather than by folk movement and tombs developed in different, although essentially similar, ways in each country. In the north and west of Britain stone-built burial vaults which could be entered whenever desired followed distinctive regional styles, for example the Cotswold-Severn tombs, the Clyde cairns and the Medway megaliths. In the south and east, where stone was usually lacking, long barrows were constructed of earth over sealed wooden or turf burial chambers. Similar examples are also found in eastern Scotland. Incidentally, mounds built mainly of earth or chalk are called barrows while the term cairn is reserved for mounds of stones.

About 260 earthen long barrows are known, mainly from the chalk hills of Wessex, Lincolnshire and eastern Yorkshire (fig. 19). They are rectangular or wedge-shaped mounds of earth averaging 60–90 m. (66–98 yd) in length and about 3 m. (10 ft) high, flanked by quarry ditches on either side. It seems likely that the smaller mounds are earlier than the largest ones. Frequently they are built on poorer quality marginal land and when possible they are sited prominently on the skyline, with one end higher than the other. There is a tendency, where the terrain allows, for them to lie approximately east to west, possibly aligned on the rising moon. In spite of the length of the mound burials are usually confined to a small area under the higher end. An average of six burials is normal although the number could be as high as 50, or in a few cases none at all. It is clear from most of the skeletal remains that have been found that the flesh had rotted away from the bones before the corpses were buried and that in many cases they had been stored elsewhere before being transferred to the barrow. This storage may have been in causewayed enclosures, or in specially constructed mortuary enclosures, such as one excavated on Normanton Down in Wiltshire in 1959. This was an oval area of ground enclosed by a causewayed ditch measuring 40 m. by 22 m. (43 yd by 24 yd). It contained no human remains since these had presumably been removed to a long barrow near by.

In many cases the mortuary enclosure was eventually incorporated in the long barrow mound. At Wayland's Smithy (Oxon) a tent-shaped mortuary hut had been constructed by erecting two massive tree trunk halves 5 m. (5.5 yd) apart, probably with a ridge pole between them. Against this roof-timbers had been laid to form a hut. Inside were the remains of 14 persons. One skeleton was articulated whilst the others lay as a jumble of bones in the middle of the chamber. Sarsen stone slabs were later placed against the outer walls of the hut and the whole structure then buried under a mound of chalk quarried from two flanking ditches. A very similar ridged building lay under the Dalladies long barrow in Kincardineshire, Scotland.

The Nutbane long barrow (Hants) had a much more complicated series of enclosures beneath it. In its final phase this consisted of a free-standing roofed hut measuring some 12 m. (13 yd) by 6 m. (6.6 yd) with a fenced mortuary yard on its eastern side in which lay four burials.

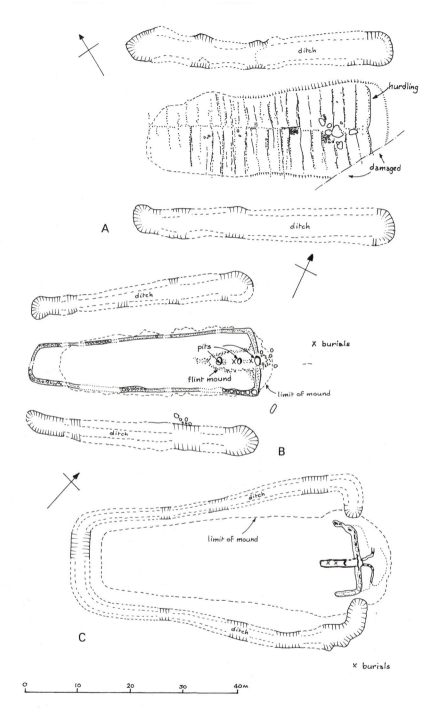

Fig. 19 *Three earthen long barrows. A South Street, Wilts, contained no burials but the interior was divided up into many sections with hurdling.* (After Smith and Evans, 1968); B *Fussell's Lodge, Wilts. The pits may have* supported a roofed mortuary structure which covered the burials.* (After Ashbee, 1966); C *Foulmire Fen, Cambs. The burials were contained in a massive oak mortuary chamber.* (Hodder and Shand, 1988)

drink offering

This yard was eventually filled with chalk, after which the adjoining hut was set on fire. As it burnt more chalk from side ditches was piled on to the smouldering remains and built up into a barrow 52 m. (57 yd) long and 23 m. (25 yd) wide, lying east to west.

A rectangular mortuary chamber constructed of massive oak posts with a flat plank roof and measuring approximately 7 m. (7.6 yd) long, 1.5 m. (1.6 yd) wide and 1.3 m. (1.4 yd) high, lay at the eastern end of the Foulmire Fen, Haddenham (Cambs) long barrow. It contained the partially articulated remains of at least five individuals. Later the mortuary chamber was partially dismantled and burnt. It was eventually covered by a mound of turf and soil measuring 50 m. (55 yd) by 16 m. (17.5 yd). The Foulmire Fen long barrow can be compared with the neolithic cairn excavated at Street House (Cleveland) where a similar mortuary structure was burnt before it was covered by a trapezoidal cairn.

Not all mortuary chambers were of wood. Turf was sometimes employed as at Royston in Hertfordshire. In other cases no trace of a chamber was detected at all though this may have been due to unscientific barrow excavation in the past which failed to notice the signs. A disadvantage of wooden chambers is that they were inclined to decay after about 50 years. Whilst the building was free-standing rotting timbers could be replaced from time to time, but once it was covered with chalk it was sealed for good and could not be renewed, nor could further burials be placed inside it. Consequently the wooden structure is likely to have stood as the main feature at the centre of repeated ceremonial activity for as long as possible before eventually being buried under a mound. Compared with stone chambers, to be discussed shortly, this suggests that the life of an earthen long barrow was relatively short. There must have been some kind of oral tradition that said that eventually the chamber would be covered, since those who built it would have been long dead before this was finally done.

In the body of the barrow mound and in the side ditches deposits of animal bones, often whole joints of oxen and pig and traces of fires with sherds of broken pottery, suggest the holding of funeral feasts from time to time.

Small pits containing black earth perhaps contained libations. Numerous finds of ox skulls might indicate a belief in the power and strength of the bull to watch over the tomb.

Only one Lincolnshire long barrow has been totally excavated under modern conditions. The Giants' Hills long barrow at Skendleby is 65 m. (71 yd) long. It was almost totally surrounded by a ditch and the mound demarcated by a rectangle of wooden posts. At the east end was a slightly concave facade of massive half-logs. The body of the mound was divided up into compartments by short lengths of hurdling. The disarticulated remains of seven adults and a child lay on a chalk platform under the mound. It is probable that the rectangle of posts around the sides of the mound originated as a mortuary enclosure. This certainly seems to have been the case at the East Heslerton barrow (E. Yorks), where a mound 124 m. (135.5 yd) long and 9 m. (9.8 yd) wide was similarly bounded by a large post enclosure which had been destroyed by fire. Any burials had been removed by nineteenth-century lime digging.

It is likely that East Heslerton belonged to a group of about a dozen long barrows where cremation was practised – found mostly in Yorkshire. First observed by Canon Greenwell in the last century, they seem to have contained narrow rectangular wooden chambers in which the jumbled remains of human corpses were incinerated. This was well illustrated by the excavation of the Willerby Wold long barrow which measured 37 m. (40 yd) by 10 m. (11 yd). Beneath it was a trapezoidal mortuary enclosure. At its eastern end was a concave facade of posts as at Giants's Hills, but at Willerby Wold they had been burnt down before the mound was built. At the eastern end of the barrow lying axially behind the facade was the cremation deposit, a fused mass of chalk, flint, human bones and charcoal, apparently once enclosed in a wooden chamber some 6 m. (6.6 yd) by 1.5 m. (1.6 yd). There can be little doubt that the human remains had been exposed for some time and were disarticulated before the burning; the incineration was only the final stage of a long ritual which it is impossible to recover.

On the Yorkshire Wolds, round barrows, sometimes extremely large, were also constructed over neolithic inhumation burials which were often accompanied by elaborate grave goods. The skeletons were frequently those of older men, and the barrows might have been built to a great size to mark individual achievement. Cremation of collective burials also occurred under round barrows in Yorkshire at this time.

Ceremonial monuments

Cursuses are in some ways the most unusual monuments of the neolithic period and the least understood. They consist of two long parallel ditches with internal banks, running for some distance across the countryside, and vary in length from the Dorset cursus at 9.8 km. (6 miles) to examples more akin to long barrows at around 100 m. (109 yd) (plate 12). They are never wide compared to their length; for example the Stonehenge cursus is 2.8 km. (1.7 miles) long and only 128 m. (140 yd) wide. The ends tend to be squared-off but rounded ones are not uncommon. High banks seem to be a feature of the sites, the ditches being mere quarries; entrances are few and often non-

existent. Little is known about the interiors but at Springfield (Essex) a timber circle has been excavated at the eastern end, and a similar one may have existed at Dorchester-on-Thames (Oxon). Traces of fires are common, and pits containing burnt animal bones and pebbles at the Essex site may indicate sacrificial ceremonies.

Whilst a few cursuses are sited on the chalk hills many more lie on the gravel terraces of major rivers of southern Britain. In view of the great diversity of size their function may have varied considerably. It is a fact that some are connected with long and round barrows, mortuary enclosures and henge monuments. At least six long barrows impinge on the Dorset cursus, one being built into the bank of the monument and another on Gussage Down lying across its axis. There are suggestions that this cursus is sited upon the latter barrow, and that it post-dates it. The Stonehenge cursus terminates in a false long barrow at its eastern end. Round barrows concentrate around the southern end of the Rudston A cursus (Yorks) and close to that at Dorchester-on-Thames. The latter site, which is at least 1.2 km. (0.75 miles) long, was associated with three mortuary enclosures and a group of henge monuments. At Thornborough (Yorks) the central henge was not built until the ditches of the cursus over which it lay had silted up.

Plate 12 *An aerial view of the Dorset cursus. Its parallel ditches (marked by arrows) run for almost 10 km. (6.2 miles) across undulating downland. The Roman road Ackling Dyke is crossing the picture from top to bottom. (J.E. Hancock)*

Most cursuses were very long, narrow, banked enclosures, often running through obscuring woodland and looking far from impressive. What went on inside was not for ordinary eyes; it was part of the ritual of the dead, perhaps controlled by a priesthood. It is possible that entrances were immaterial since the cursuses may have been processional ways and spirit paths for the exclusive use of the dead. As such they deserved the enormous communal effort involved in constructing them.

Linked to cursuses and earthen long barrows are a small group of late neolithic bank barrows found in Dorset. They are characterized by their length which varies between 180 m. (197 yd) and 550 m. (600 yd). The longest is at

Fig. 20 *The portal dolmen of Dyffryn Ardudwy, Merioneth. The original dolmen is left of centre. Later the tomb was enlarged by the addition of the eastern chamber and rectangular mound. The smaller drawings show cross-sections of the west and east chambers. (After Lynch, 1969)*

Maiden Castle where it overlies, and is therefore later than, a causewayed enclosure. In spite of its great size it seems only to have covered the remains of two small children.

It is clear that only a small proportion of the neolithic population was buried under long barrows. Who these rather special individuals were we shall never know. It is possible that they represented a tribal elite, which would justify the enormous effort of hundreds of hours involved in the contruction of the barrow and hundreds more in the accompanying ritual. Men, women and children were interred, and we might see these as members of a ruling household. However, sometimes, as at the South Street long barrow (Wilts) or West Rudham (Norfolk) no trace of any burials has been found and we are left with the possibility of cenotaphs constructed to the memory of people whose mortal remains were not available for burial.

We must briefly consider the disposal of the remaining dead, who did not reach the long

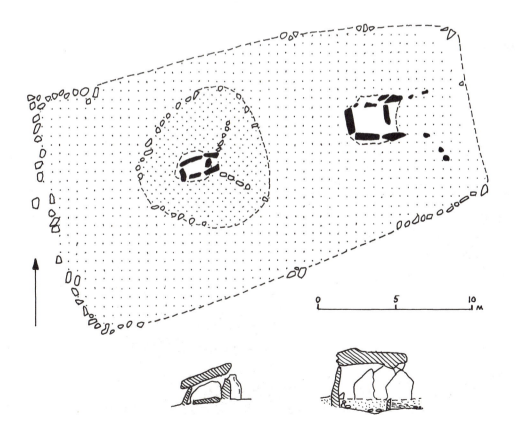

barrows. The evidence of human remains scattered in causewayed enclosures suggests that many corpses may have been exposed on the ground or on platforms within the enclosures until the flesh had rotted or been pecked away by carrion crows and scavenging dogs. Perhaps once the flesh had left the bones they lost their religious or magical significance and were no longer of great concern to the living. The scattering of ashes at a cremation was also a possibility. At Etton (Cambs) cremated remains were excavated, and may have formed part of a rite centred on East Anglia.

Megalithic tombs

In the west and north of Britain the place of the earthen long barrows with wooden chambers was taken by megalithic structures utilizing the local building stone – megalithic means 'great stones'. The earliest tombs were probably portal dolmens. These are usually small, free-standing stone chambers with few or no circular mounds or stone cairns around them. The chambers are rectangular, becoming lower and narrower towards the rear. A sloping roofstone rests on two portal stones which mark the entrance and project beyond the chamber to form a porch. Between these two stones is a third septal or blocking slab, which often reaches up to the roofstone and acts, in theory at least, as a door. In parts of west Wales tombs can be found in which these features are no longer very obvious, suggesting that the type has a long uninterrupted history of devolution.

Today most portal dolmens are in a ruinous state. Sweyne's Howe North in Glamorgan has all the typical components but the capstone has slipped backwards and the blocking slab has fallen forwards. Modern excavations have taken place at Trefignath and Din Dryfol in Anglesey and at Dyffryn Ardudwy in Merioneth. At the latter site a complete portal dolmen with a V-shaped forecourt was examined (fig. 20). In the disturbed chamber only one cremation burial remained, whilst in a pit beneath the forecourt were many fragments of plain-bowl style neolithic pottery. The whole tomb was originally enclosed in an oval cairn of stones. Some time later a new and larger rectangular burial chamber, measuring 2 m. (2.2 yd) by 1.5 m. (1.6 yd) and not dissimilar to a portal dolmen, was constructed 10 m. (11 yd) east of the first. (Its

[handwritten margin note:] Ig flat stone laid on upright ones

[handwritten margin note:] separating compartments in a burial chamber

contents had been robbed before the excavation.) Eventually, when access to neither burial chamber was required, a rectangular cairn of stones 30 m. (33 yd) long was constructed to enclose both tombs.

The Whispering Knights near the Rollright Stones in Oxfordshire is a ruined portal dolmen, as is Kit's Coty House, an outlier in Kent. Related but not exactly similar tombs can be found in Cornwall where they are sometimes called Penwith chamber tombs, and of which Trethevy Quoit is the best example (plate 13).

Plate 13 *Trethevy Quoit at St Cleer in Cornwall is a portal dolmen of localized Penwith type. It stands more than 3 m. (3.3 yd) high on its southern side. (J. Dyer)*

It has been suggested that whether built of wood or stone the burial chambers imitate the houses of the living, and that in them not only would the remains of the dead lie in perpetuity but also their spirits could dwell and watch over the living. Indeed the position of many of the tombs on hilltops might be a clue as to the location of neolithic settlement. It is dangerous to suggest modern parallels but perhaps the majority of tombs served a function more akin to medieval parish churches, in that they provided a structure in which to perform religious ceremonial and at the same time were the burial places of a small, selective group of the parish dead, added to only occasionally over hundreds of years.

Broadly speaking the chambered tombs of Britain can be divided into two groups, first recognized by Glyn Daniel, and known as gallery and passage graves. The gallery graves consist of long stone passages either divided into sections with cross (septal) slabs, or with chambers on either side. They normally occur in rectangular mounds. Passage graves have longish passages, opening into a round or rectangular chamber at the end; there is usually a circular covering mound. These occur mostly in western and northern Britain.

The Cotswold-Severn tombs

Amongst the most impressive stone-built tombs are a large group found on both sides of the Bristol Channel from the Gower to the Severn estuary, concentrated in the Black Mountains, the Cotswolds and the chalk hills of north Wiltshire. Known as the Cotswold-Severn group, there are more than 180 long barrows, all exhibiting general similarities but none an exact copy of its neighbours. The group can be broadly divided into three tomb types. Most have a rectangular or wedge-shaped covering mound. Inside this the burial chambers can consist of either lateral chambers, that is chambers entered from the long sides of the mound; simple terminal chambers, that is a single chamber entered from the higher 'business' end of the mound; or transepted terminal chambers, which is a central chamber entered from the higher end of the barrow with side chambers leading off like the transepts of a Christian church (fig. 21).

The chambers are usually built of large slabs of stone called orthostats, with any gaps between them filled by dry-stone walling. The mound is composed of stone gathered from the surrounding area or dug from quarry ditches on either side. It is usually retained either by a stone wall or by a kerb of larger stones placed on edge. As with the earthen long barrows there is a tendency to orientate the mounds with their higher and broader ends facing very roughly east. The higher end of the barrow is also often cusp-shaped with two protruding rounded horns, between which is the entrance to the terminal burial chamber. Even in the case of the lateral chambered barrows a dummy doorway

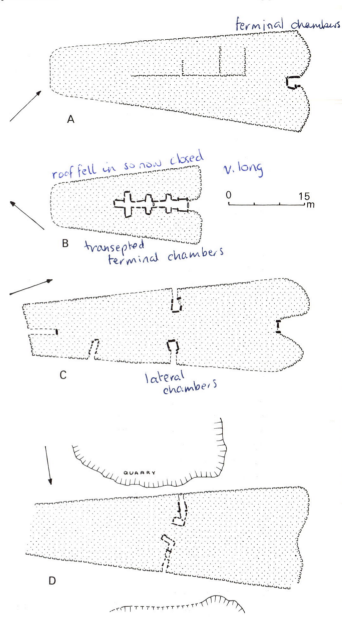

Fig. 21 *Tombs in the Severn-Cotswold tradition. A Randwick, Glos; B Stoney Littleton, Somerset; C Belas Knap, Glos; D Hazleton North, Glos. (Saville, 1984)*

(margin note: originally a stone house + forecourt)

or false portal may be built between the horns. It is this funnel-shaped area between the horns and in front of the entrance that is known as the forecourt, and in which funerary ceremonies took place.

In some cases the burial chamber seems to have been built first as a free-standing structure, usually on some high prominence, making it visible for a considerable distance. It may have remained in this state as a stone 'house' for many years, receiving fresh burials from time to time, and being a place of frequent pilgrimage. The forecourt is likely to have been established at the same time as the chamber and ceremonies involving making hearths, preparing ritual feasts and the smashing of pots after libations could easily have taken place. Eventually the time came to enclose the chamber in a mound of stones. Sometimes this seems to have been done in stages and excavation has shown the mound built as a series of cells, perhaps for greater stability, or simply representing the amount of construction possible by a small gang of work-

men in a particular season. This was well represented at Hazleton North (Glos) and Ascott-under-Wychwood (Oxon), two sites excavated in recent years.

There has been much debate as to which type of Cotswold-Severn tomb came first. Some current thinking suggests those with lateral chambers may have been followed by the simple terminal chambers, with the more complex and larger transepted chambers completing the development. But these may be no more than regional variations in tomb types since the sequence is by no means certain. Earlier thinking saw the simple terminal chambers built first, becoming more elaborate with transepts, and then degenerating to lateral chambers and false portals. Until we get many tombs accurately dated by radiocarbon methods, the sequence will remain unclear.

What is certain is that the tombs almost invariably contained deposits of human bones in the chambers, passageways and occasionally in the forecourts. Whilst these were sometimes complete articulated skeletons, more often they were a jumble of bones suggesting either that they had been placed in the tomb from elsewhere after the flesh had rotted, or alternatively that they had been laid complete in the tomb but

Plate 14 *The facade of stones at the eastern end of the West Kennet long barrow (Wilts). The transepted burial chamber was entered from behind the largest stone. (J. Dyer)*

had been swept aside after a while to make way [appease]
for later burials. Sometimes the bones were
arranged in the vault according to type, age or
sex. At Lanhill the long bones were at the back
of the chamber and half a dozen skulls at the
side. Certainly many bones are missing altogether and may have been taken away to serve
magical or propitiatory purposes, as at West
Kennet where at least 46 burials were found,
and Pont y Saer (Anglesey) with 54 persons,
there being at both sites many lacking long
bones and skulls. It was suggested that some of
the West Kennet skulls might be those found in
the excavation of the causewayed enclosure
nearby at Windmill Hill. There is evidence that
some burial chambers were cleaned out at
various times during their active life, and this
makes it difficult to assess how many corpses
were deposited altogether in any particular
barrow. As mentioned above, 46 burials could
be accounted for at West Kennet, but we have
no record of how many more were removed by
Dr Toope and other diggers in the seventeenth
and eighteenth centuries. Like the earthen long
barrows the maximum was probably about 50.
The excavation showed that West Kennet had
been open and in use for about a thousand years
(plate 14). During that long period of time the
central passage in the tomb had been accessible
and may have been frequently entered in order
to undertake various ritual functions, and also
on occasions to polish stone axes on the orthostats (though these may have been used for
polishing before the tomb was constructed) or
to shelter from inclement weather. Eventually
the tomb was deliberately filled with chalk
rubble and refuse, probably gathered from the
adjoining barrow ditches, where the remains of
feasting, ceremonial and more mundane, everyday events had left sherds of pottery, animal
bones and flints.

Most of the early pottery from this group of
tombs belongs to the sub-styles of 'plain-bowl'
wares. At West Kennet the Windmill Hill style
was represented, but because of the long life of
the tomb it extended to include the later neolithic Peterborough and grooved-ware styles.
Small finds tend to be rare, flint arrowheads,
knives and scrapers being the most common,
with a few items of jewellery such as beads and
pendants of bone, shale or jet.

The construction of the Cotswold-Severn
[soft finely stratified rock which splits easily]

tombs and other stone monuments in Britain
engaged large numbers of people for many
hours. It is easy to forget that they were also
farmers as well as builders of megaliths. Suitable local stones were dragged to the chosen site
on rollers or grass sledges. The ground surface
was cleared of obstructions: at South Street
(Wilts) it was part of a ploughed field. Shallow
holes were dug with antler picks, and into these
the wallstone orthostats were set, their weight
often being relied on to keep them in place.

The capstones of the burial chambers were
usually the heaviest stones to be utilized. It has
been estimated that the roofstone of Tinkins-
wood (Glam), which weighs 50 tons, would
have required 50 to 100 people to move it.
Lligwy in Anglesey is half that weight, and had
to be slid into position over the burial chamber,
probably by hauling it on rollers up a ramp. The
chamber may have been temporarily filled with
soil at the time to stop the wallstones collapsing
inwards. This filling would subsequently be
removed, the weight of the capstone being
relied on to keep the orthostats in position.

The Hazleton North (Glos) barrow, now
destroyed, was a wedge-shaped mound a little
over 52 m. (57 yd) long and 20 m. (22 yd) wide at
its higher (unusual) west end. Midway along its
length on either side were two lateral chambers
consisting of narrow passages 4 and 5 m. (4.4
and 5.5 yd) long, leading into rectangular chambers 1.5 and 2.5 m. (1.6 and 2.75 yd) long and
about 1 m. (1.1 yd) wide. Both passages were
very low and anyone entering to deposit a
corpse would have had to crawl with great
difficulty. Both chambers were intact when
excavated; the passage walls of the northern one
had collapsed whilst the tomb was still in use.
The floor of the chamber was littered with
jumbled bones but the passage itself was empty.
The last two burials to be added to the tomb lay
near the entrance outside the area of collapse
and were both articulated. One of them was
accompanied by a quartzite hammerstone and a
core. On the south side the whole of the passage
and chamber were filled with scattered bones,
whilst some of the skulls had been placed round
the walls of the chamber and the long bones
stacked beside them (plate 15). The bedrock
had been quarried on either side of the barrow
to provide the mound material which had been
built as a series of cells along a central spine,

Plate 15 *The southern burial chamber at Hazleton North (Glos), showing the disarticulated human remains. (A. Saville)*

Plate 16 (below) *The false portal at Belas Knap (Glos) recessed into a funnelled forecourt. The lower part of the dry-stone walling is original. (J. Dyer)*

copying design of a similar artefact

eventually all joined together. There was a forecourt between horns at the western end, but no trace of a false entrance or portal.

The Gwernvale long cairn in Brecknock was in many ways similar to Hazleton North, although it had been very badly damaged prior to excavation in 1977–8. It had two lateral chambers placed midway along its north and south walls, with one, and possibly two, additional lateral chambers on the south side. Insufficient traces of human remains were left in the barrow to be informative. Radiocarbon dates obtained using charcoal from blocking material in the chamber entrance fall between 2640 and 2440 bc. The barrow had a deep, funnel-shaped forecourt with, at its apex, a false portal closed by a damaged block of sandstone.

The barrow with the classic false portal is Belas Knap (Glos) (plate 16). Today it is a carefully restored tomb 52 m. (57 yd) long and 18 m. (20 yd) wide. It contains three lateral

chambers, all of which may once have been enclosed in circular cairns, which were later incorporated into the wedge-shaped mound. The barrow contained at least 35 burials. The false portal stands between deep dry-stone horns. A pair of upright stones and a lintel frame a flat door slab which guards no burial chamber of any kind. Its significance can only be ritual, a skeuomorph of an entrance to a real chamber. We can only speculate as to its function. Did religious ceremonies at the forecourt require the physical presence of a door? Did it allow the spirits of the dead to enter and

Fig. 22 *The passage grave of Bryn Celli Ddu, Anglesey. A buried stone circle and decorated stone behind the burial chamber suggest that the latter may once have been free-standing, before it was enclosed in a kerbed cairn of stones. An ox burial was found in a small pit in front of the tomb entrance.*

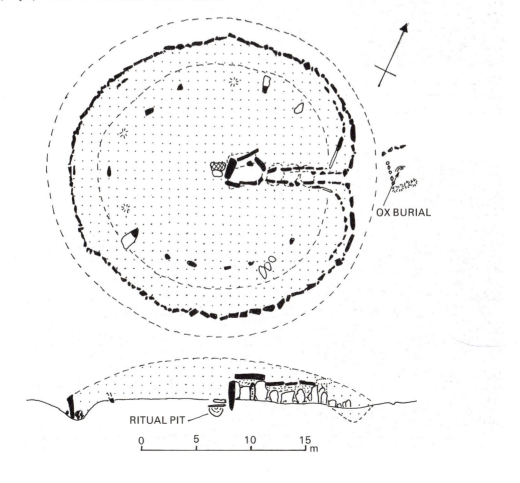

OX BURIAL

RITUAL PIT

0 5 10 15 m

Plate 17 *The decoration on stone 22 of the burial chamber at Barclodiad y Gawres, Anglesey. (H. Senogles)*

leave the tomb? Did it serve to conceal the burial chambers from those who were not intended to see them (those who were not elders of the tribe) or did it serve to fool potential tomb robbers as to the whereabouts of the real burial chambers? Such a reason might lead us to speculate on the stealing of relics of the ancestors, and its effect on the well-being of the tribe.

In Anglesey are the sites of Bryn Celli Ddu and Barclodiad y Gawres, two of about half a dozen passage graves built in the tradition of the Irish Boyne valley tombs (fig. 22). Circular mounds enclose passages leading to oval central burial chambers. Four of the stones of Barclodiad are decorated with sinuous spirals and chevrons making abstract patterns beyond interpretation (plate 17). Bryn Celli Ddu seems to

have been built over an earlier henge monument, suggesting that it was constructed later in the neolithic period.

The northern barrows

An important group of chambered tombs exists close to the coast in south-western Scotland and is known as the Clyde cairns. Although there are great variations amongst them these tombs tend to have a long narrow burial gallery divided into segments by high sill-stones and with side slabs which overlap each other like the scales of a fish. Quite often the gallery opens out into a forecourt which is marked by a crescent-shaped facade of upright stones with dry-stone walling between them. The whole is set into a cairn which can be circular, oval, rectangular or wedge-shaped.

Like some of the Cotswold-Severn tombs a few of the Clyde group began as simple rectangular chambers. Two chambers in neighbouring tombs at Mid Gleniron in Wigtownshire were set in circular stone cairns which were later incorporated into wedge-shaped mounds. At Cairnholy I, (Kirkcudbright) the initial rectangular chamber measured 2 m. (2.2 yd) by 0.5 m. (0.55 yd) (fig. 24). A high septal stone sealed and separated it from its neighbour, which opened onto a spectacular forecourt through two very high portal stones (plate 18).

More typical in shape is Beacharra in Kintyre, with a burial gallery 6 m. long, divided into four segments, with low overlapping side slabs. The roofstones are missing. The straight dry-stone facade is not typical. Monamore in Arran also has the overlapping side slabs and three compartments, with a slightly concave facade of orthostats alternating with dry-stone walling in what is called 'post and panel' technique. The Clyde cairns can contain up to 40 burials, normally disarticulated, with skulls and long bones sorted as in the Cotswold-Severn tombs. Cremations are not unknown. Pottery found in the tombs is always round-bottomed and baggy and includes the local Beacharra ware with decorated bowls with prominent shoulders and contracted mouths. Other grave goods are rare, but arrowheads and knife blades of flint, and implements of pitchstone, probably from Arran, are known.

Further north in Scotland are other groups of tombs that must be briefly considered: the

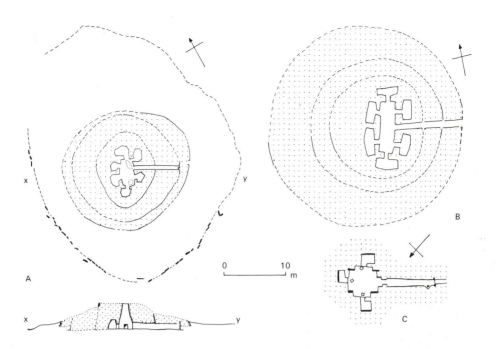

Fig. 23 *Maes Howe type tombs of Orkney.
A Quoyness; B Quanterness; C Maes Howe
(chamber only), all to the same scale. (A and C:
Henshall, 1963; B Renfrew, 1979)*

Plate 18 *Cairnholy I (Kirkudbright) viewed
from behind. In the foreground is the earliest
burial chamber, with behind it a later cist opening
between the tall stones of the forecourt. (J. Dyer)*

Plate 19 *Looking along the passage of the great stalled cairn of Midhowe on Rousay in the Orkney Islands. More than 23 m. (25 yd) long, the passage is divided into 12 compartments, in some of which lay numerous burials. (J. Dyer)*

Plate 20 *The interior of the chambered tomb of Quoyness on Sanday (Orkney) which still stands 4 m. (4.4 yd) high. The pit contained the partial remains of about 15 adults and children. (R.C.H.M. Scotland)*

Hebridean group, the Orkney-Cromarty group and the Maes Howe group.

In the Outer Hebrides, Skye, and the western edge of Inverness and Argyll are about four dozen simple passage graves, usually consisting of a short passage opening into a small rectangular or oval chamber, the whole covered by a circular cairn of stones. Barpa Langass on the moors of North Uist may be taken as typical (fig. 24). Inhumation burials were placed in the chambers, accompanied by pottery and evidence of fires.

In the most northerly part of the Scottish mainland and the Orkney Islands are tombs containing rectangular burial chambers, divided into compartments by protruding wall slabs creating segments or 'stalls', and usually entered from a side passage (plate 19). In the round cairn of Isbister on South Ronaldsay, the chamber is divided into five segments, and is

[handwritten: emblem of a clan / a hierarchy]

entered from a narrow passage on the eastern side. Excavation produced the remains of 340 skeletons. All had been exposed before burial and brought into the tomb as individual deposits of bones, together with animal and fish bones, pottery, flints and simple beads. The remains of a number of sea eagles could suggest a totemic element in the funeral ritual. Built around 3150 BC, the tomb was in use for about 700 years.

Maes Howe gives its name to a small group of tombs found in the Orkney Islands (fig. 23). Only about a dozen have been recognized, and Maes Howe and Quanterness are fine examples. The cairns are round with a long low passage entering the chamber at right angles to its axis. The main chamber is usually large and squarish with three or more side chambers leading from it (plate 20). Maes Howe is the most sophisticated monument of its kind in Britain, if not in

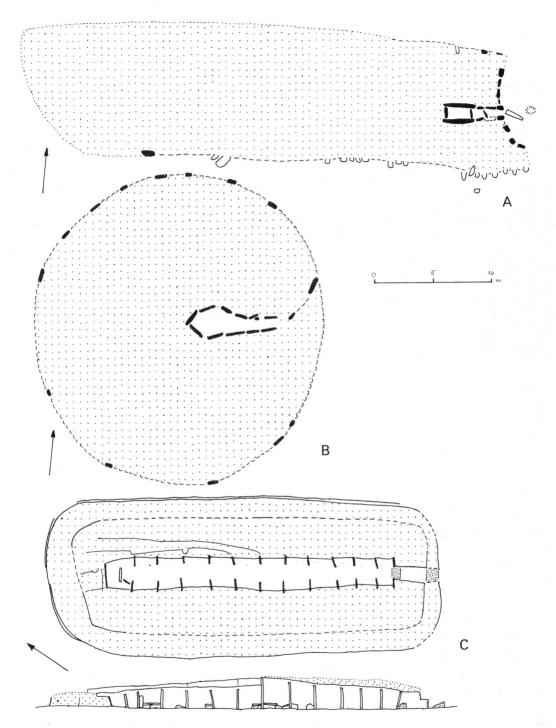

Fig. 24 *Chambered tombs in nothern Britain.*
A Cairnholy I (Galloway) belongs to the Clyde cairn tradition (Piggot and Powell, 1948);

B Barpa Langas, North Uist is a simple passage grave (Henshall, 1972); C Midhowe, Orkney is a stalled cairn (Henshall, 1963).

western Europe. Built of carefully shaped blocks of stone to a symmetrical design, it is a triumph of the mason's art. Inside a broad circular ditch stands a grass-covered mound 7.3 m. (8.2 yd) high and 35 m. (38.3 yd) in diameter. A passage 9 m. (10 yd) long leads into a chamber 4.5 m. (5 yd) square, and originally about 4.5 m. (5 yd) high, with a square corbelled roof vault. On each side a small square opening leads into a side chamber averaging 1.7 m. (1.9 yd) by 1.3 m. (1.4 yd) in size. Any burials that the tomb contained have long since disappeared. The entrance passage to Maes Howe faces south-westwards. At midwinter the rays of the setting sun shine along the passage and fall on the rear wall of the central chamber. In Ireland the sun at midwinter sunrise also illuminates the burial chamber of the great passage grave of New Grange.

Quanterness was excavated in 1972–3. In many ways similar to Maes Howe, though lacking its architectural quality, its central chamber had six cells leading off from it. In these were the remains of about 150 persons of both sexes and all ages. Radiocarbon dates associated with the use of the tomb are between 3550 BC and 2300 BC.

Finally we should mention an isolated group of chambered barrows in Kent known as the Medway tombs. With a small stone chamber in a rectangular mound, this type is reminiscent of the dysse and hunebeden of Denmark, Germany and the Netherlands. The geographical position suggests that they could have represented a genuine cultural link with Europe.

Chapter Four

The Growth of Ceremonial

The rise of territories

The neolithic appears to have been dominated by its major monuments, the causewayed enclosures, barrows and mines. Their massive size has been mainly responsible for their survival. The simple domestic sites, mostly small farmsteads, are still largely unknown. Consequently we get an unbalanced picture of life between 4200 and 2500 BC.

Clusters of long barrows surrounded by causewayed enclosures in Wessex suggest that territories were forming in that area, centred on the calcarious uplands, for example, Cranborne Chase, the Marlborough and Berkshire Downs, Salisbury Plain and the Dorset Ridgeway. In the later neolithic these peripheral sites were replaced by central henge monuments. In other parts of the country similar territories can be observed, for example the Yorkshire Wolds, the Sussex Downs and the Orkney Islands. If these territories are real then they pose certain questions which we must try to answer. Since the monuments seem to be the key we must ask why and by whom they were built. The population must have been strongly motivated to come together and dig out 10,000 cubic metres of chalk to build a typical long barrow. Since the barrows only contain the burials of selected members of the community some kind of class system must have emerged. In view of the emphasis on funeral monuments surely sectarian beliefs, with priests or shaman in charge, were developing with some religious fervour.

Colin Renfrew has seen the long barrows as territorial markers. We have already drawn an analogy with medieval parish churches, and in spite of the danger would use it again. The church was the only permanent building in most villages, surviving for worship and burial for hundreds of years. In it were the tombs of

the most important ancestors and the cumulative ambience of prayer left by successive generations. The church was constructed, cared for, and added to, by the villagers over the centuries, the embodiment of corporate effort. Its building dominated the settlement and everyone knew the extent of its territorial influence. We suggest that the long barrows of the earlier neolithic period fulfilled a loosely similar function, a place where the local inhabitants came time and again to commune with their ancestors and invoke their gods. In spite of regional differences there are so many similarities between the collective tombs around Britain that we can speculate on broadly mutual religious beliefs being held. The content of those beliefs we shall never know but we can guess that they involved the well-being of the individual and the group, the crops and animals, resources and weather.

It seems fairly certain that by the middle of the third millennium BC major changes had taken place. To suggest that this was the outcome of some kind of intertribal warfare may be stretching the evidence to its limits. Signs of burning and many arrowheads marked the end of the settlements at Crickley Hill, Hambledon Hill and Carn Brea. Occasional burials containing arrowheads have come from the tombs, but thousands of other arrowheads from all over Britain and spanning a thousand years in time can be explained as a requirement of everyday farming life. There is little doubt that many causewayed enclosures were passing out of use around 2500 BC, or that numerous chambered barrows were finally blocked-up. With abandonment came regeneration of woodland in some areas. This may have led to a temporary check on the amount of arable land in use and a greater concentration on pastoral farming with increased pig production or an increase in

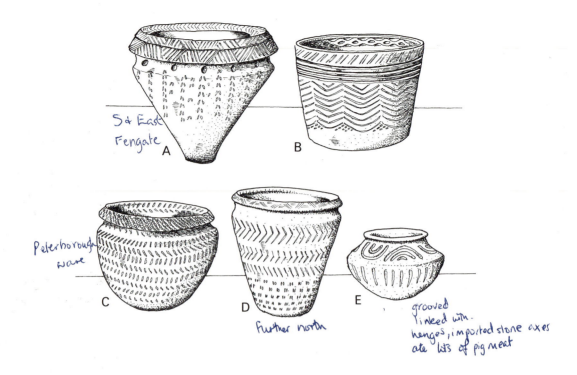

S & East Fengate (handwritten annotation near A)

Peterborough ware (handwritten annotation near C)

further north (handwritten annotation near D)

grooved, linked with henges, imported stone axes, ate lots of pig meat (handwritten annotation near E)

Fig. 25 *Examples of late neolithic pottery:*
A *Fengate style from West Kennet 20 cm.*
(7.8 in.) high; B *Grooved ware from Clacton;*
C *Peterborough style from Hedsor, Bucks;*
D *Rudston style from Humberside and*
E *Beacharra ware from south-west Scotland*
(Kintyre).

arable land in the valleys at the expense of some upland areas.

Pottery still remained round-bottomed and baggy but it developed into thicker decorated styles with heavy rims. Generally known as Peterborough ware, it can be divided into regional styles. In the south and east these are known as Mortlake, Ebbsfleet and Fengate wares (fig. 25). Further north Meldon Bridge and Rudston styles are common, and in Scotland Unstan ware and other localized forms are found. An entirely new style of pottery known as grooved ware also appeared and was frequently associated with the elaborate henge monuments of the period. Where it occurs on a very small number of settlement sites it is frequently found with imported stone axes, and

there are indications that large amounts of pig meat were consumed. This pottery tends to be tub-shaped, with a flat bottom and deeply incised decoration. Some authorities refer to it as Rinyo-Clacton ware.

The earlier neolithic leaf-shaped arrowheads were replaced by new transverse types. These had a broad sharp blade replacing the pointed tip.

Henge monuments

Henge monuments, found exclusively in Britain, make their appearance around 2500 bc. Various features of their structure, particularly interrupted ditches in some sites, suggest that they replaced the causewayed enclosures. This is particularly noticeable in Wessex where Avebury can be seen to replace Windmill Hill, Rybury and Knap Hill, and Robin Hood's Ball was supplanted by Durrington Walls and Stonehenge, for example. Henges consist of an open circular area, surrounded by a bank and internal ditch. Two main groups can be recognized, Class I with a single entrance and Class II with two or more (fig. 26). They can vary in

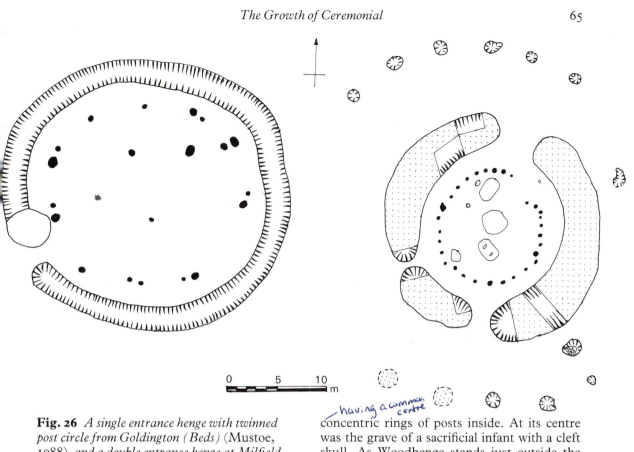

0   5   10
m

Fig. 26 *A single entrance henge with twinned post circle from Goldington (Beds) (Mustoe, 1988), and a double entrance henge at Milfield North (Northumberland) which enclosed a circle of 30 small pits, and was surrounded by at least 13 shafts that may have held posts.* (A.F. Harding, 1981)

diameter from about 42 m. (46 yd) at Bally-meanoch (Strathclyde) to Durrington Walls (Wilts) in excess of 450 m. (492 yd). The Class I henges tend to be smaller and more circular than the second group (plate 21). A number of even smaller sites are known as mini-henges and have diameters as small as 10 m. (11 yd) at Fargo Plantation (Wilts) and 15 m. (16.4 yd) at Dorchester-on-Thames (Oxon).

Most henges occur on low-lying land close to streams or rivers. Often they form part of a cluster of related sites including cursuses and ring-ditches. The interiors are frequently empty, but any of them can contain settings of posts, stones or pits. A lack of domestic refuse suggests that they were sanctuaries used for some special purposes, most probably religious or ceremonial. Amongst the first to be excavated was Woodhenge (Wilts), a Class I site with six

— having a common centre

concentric rings of posts inside. At its centre was the grave of a sacrificial infant with a cleft skull. As Woodhenge stands just outside the southern gate of Durrington Walls it is probably part of the same complex.

In Norfolk pioneering aerial photography revealed Arminghall in 1929. Here a horseshoe-shaped ditch enclosed eight massive wooden posts almost a metre each in diameter, with their bases sunk 2.3 m. (2.5 yd) into the ground. Unlikely to have formed part of a building, these great trunks may have been carved like totem poles. The site is radiocarbon dated to 3230 bc.

In Derbyshire Arbor Low is a Class II henge. Concentric with the inner edge of the ditch stood a circle of 39 large limestone blocks, whilst at the centre seven more stones formed a box-shaped setting, sometimes known as a cove – a human skeleton was found in that feature. The site is unusual, being on a plateau. There is a large round barrow adjacent (Gib Hill).

In Yorkshire three Class II henges lie in a row stretching over 2 km. (1.2 miles) at Thornborough. Excavation showed that the bank of the central site had been coated with gypsum brought from some distance to give it a white

Plate 21 *This henge monument at Goldington (Bedford) had a single entrance (far left) and contained a ring of paired upright timbers, perhaps decorated like totem poles. (Beds C.C.)*

appearance, perhaps imitating the chalk of the south country. One of the circles overlies a cursus monument.

Stonehenge

There can be little doubt that the best-known example of a henge is Stonehenge itself, which indeed gives its name to the whole group. It is a very complex monument with a development spreading over 1,700 years into the early Bronze Age. It seems logical to discuss its complete history at this point. There is some disagreement amongst experts as to the precise order of construction but Professor Richard Atkinson's scheme is generally accepted (fig. 27).

Stonehenge (Period I) began as a causewayed circular ditch 115 m. (126 yd) in diameter with an internal bank. It was broken on the north-eastern side by a single entrance. Some 20 m. (22 yd) outside this stood the Heel Stone, a 25

ton block of unshaped sarsen stone. Inside the bank a ring of 56 pits called the Aubrey Holes were dug, and almost at once refilled. They may have held wooden posts for a brief period. It is also possible that a timber setting stood at the centre of the site, but if it did almost all trace has been destroyed by later disturbance. Stonehenge I probably involved about 11,000 man-hours of work. The approximate date for all this is around 2800 BC. Some 500 years later at least 25 cremations were inserted into the filling of the Aubrey Holes which must still have been visible.

Period II of Stonehenge saw the entrance slightly realigned so that from the centre it faced approximately towards midsummer sunrise, and in the opposite direction to midwinter sunset. An Avenue of two parallel banks with external ditches was laid out for about 530 m. (580 yd) towards Stonehenge Bottom. Four small stones known as the Station Stones were set up on the inner edge of the ditch, two of them enclosed by small ditches of their own. At this stage it was decided to erect a double circle of stones in the centre. The material chosen was

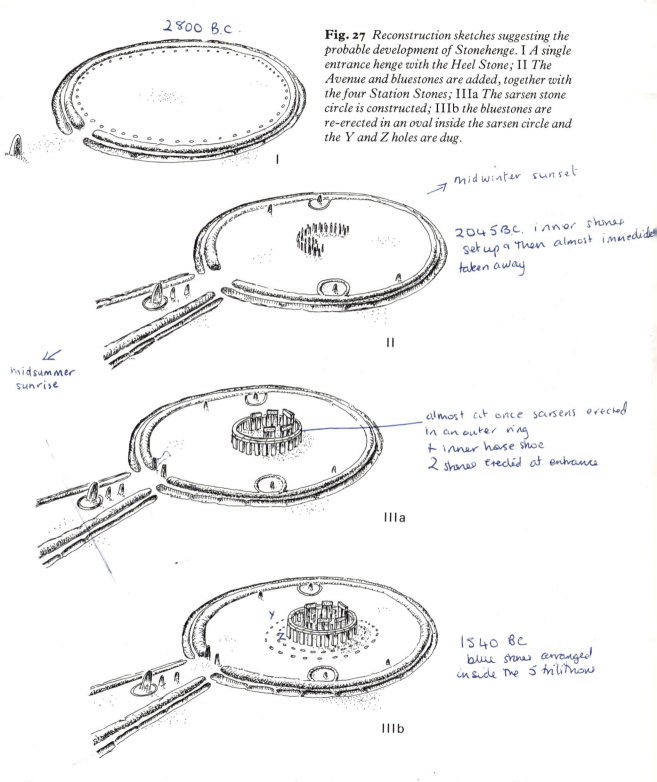

2800 B.C.

I

Fig. 27 *Reconstruction sketches suggesting the probable development of Stonehenge. I A single entrance henge with the Heel Stone; II The Avenue and bluestones are added, together with the four Station Stones; IIIa The sarsen stone circle is constructed; IIIb the bluestones are re-erected in an oval inside the sarsen circle and the Y and Z holes are dug.*

→ midwinter sunset

2045 B.C. inner stones set up a then almost immedide taken away

II

midsummer sunrise

almost at once sarsens erected in an outer ring + inner horse shoe 2 stones erected at entrance

IIIa

1540 BC blue stones arranged inside the 5 trilithons

IIIb

1075 BC. extension of the Avenue.

spotted dolerite, commonly known as blue-stone, of Welsh origin. About three-quarters of the circle was set up, but a change of plan brought the work to a sudden halt. The stones were cleared away and the holes refilled. This took place about 2045 BC at the beginning of the Bronze Age. It has been estimated that it took about 360,000 man-hours to construct.

Period IIIa: Almost at once great sarsen stones were dragged to the site from the Marlborough Downs and set in an outer ring of 30 uprights, with inside it a horseshoe of five trilithons (literally three stones) all crowned with sarsen lintels (plate 22). Two further stones were erected at the entrance to the Avenue, of which one, the Slaughter Stone, though fallen, still survives. An estimate of

1,750,000 man-hours for constructing this phase is unlikely to be an exaggeration. Period IIIb: About 1540 BC an oval of bluestones was arranged inside the five trilithons, and two rings of holes labelled Y and Z were dug, probably to hold the remaining bluestones. However this project was abandoned and the bluestones were rearranged in the horseshoe and circle setting which partially survives today. One final event (Period IV) was the extension of the Avenue from Stonehenge Bottom to the River Avon at West Amesbury, making its entire length 2.5 km. (1.5 miles). This happened around 1075 BC (fig. 28).

There are many remarkable things about Stonehenge, not least the source of the bluestones. For 60 years it was believed that they had been dragged 320 km. (200 miles) to Stonehenge from the Preseli Mountains of north Pembrokeshire. This was based on a petrological examination carried out by Dr H..H. Thomas in 1923, which showed that most

Plate 22 *The carefully shaped lintels of the outer ring of sarsen stones at Stonehenge (Wilts). The smaller stones (centre foreground) are the bluestones that originated in Wales. (R.J.C. Atkinson)*

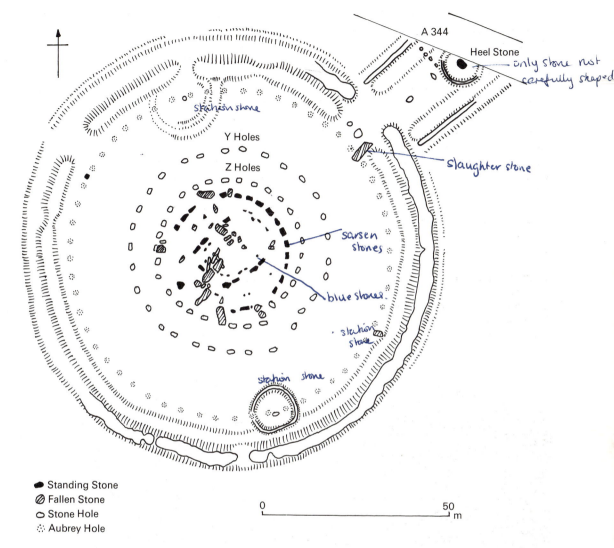

A 344

Heel Stone — *only stone not carefully shaped*

station stone

Y Holes

Z Holes

slaughter stone

sarsen stones

blue stones

station stone

station stone

● Standing Stone
◍ Fallen Stone
○ Stone Hole
∴ Aubrey Hole

0   50
                      m

Fig. 28 *A plan of Stonehenge as it survives today.*

of the rocks of which the bluestones are composed – spotted dolerite, rhyolite and volcanic tuffs – all occurred together around Carn Meini. In 1971 G.A. Kellaway suggested that the source was correct, but that the stones had reached Salisbury Plain by the movement of glaciers or ice sheets during the Ice Age. Recent discoveries show that the great Irish Sea Glacier would have crossed Pembrokeshire on its way eastwards, plucking up and redistributing erratic boulders along its course. Evidence for its presence has been clearly found on the Mendip Hills only 45 km. (28 miles) west of Stonehenge.

In 1982 Hilary Howard showed that at least some of the bluestones made of welded tuffs do not occur at Preseli at all, and are more likely to have come from Snowdonia. From the many chippings of bluestone in the Stonehenge area, it is clear that they were not shaped until they reached the site. It would seem odd that the stones, with all this excess weight and awkward shapes, should have been dragged all the way from Wales. If, however, ice movement had brought them from Presili or Snowdonia to somewhere on the western side of Salisbury Plain, then such action would be less surprising. The glacial theory would also help to explain how one block of bluestone got into the Boles long barrow near Heytesbury (Wilts) which predated Stonehenge by at least 500 years.

A convenient glacial deposit of at least 60 stones, each weighing between 6 and 7 tons, could have been moved with levers on to land sledges. Experiments have shown that this could have been achieved over flat grassy ground using the strength of about 32 young

Fig. 29 *The lintel stones at Stonehenge were dovetailed together* (top) *and attached to the upright stones by mortice and tenon joints* (below).

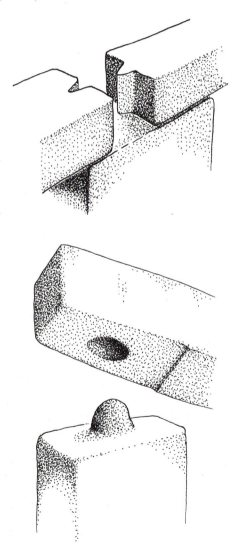

men. Alternatively, using wooden rollers, the number might be reduced to 14 haulers, though others would be needed to return the rollers.

Other large-scale stone movements were required for the much bigger sarsen stones brought from the Marlborough Downs. Here the distance was about 42 km. (26 miles) but the weight of each of the stones was nearer 50 tons. Again experiments suggest that between 100 and 150 people would be needed to haul them, depending on the steepness of the ground.

It seems likely that the bluestones did not come immediately to Stonehenge but may have first been set up somewhere else. This could have been near the western end of the Stonehenge cursus, where many chippings of bluestone have been found. Certainly all the stones at Stonehenge, with the exception of the Heel Stone, were carefully shaped. Four thousand years of weathering have given them their present rugged appearance. All the upright sarsen stones were smoothed into rectangular blocks using balls of stone as hammers. Each upright had an entasis or swelling half-way up. That is a sophisticated device used by architects to counteract the effects of perspective. All the lintel stones have groove and tongue joints and are attached to the uprights by mortice and tenon joints (fig. 29). This suggests that the builders were copying the work of carpenters with which they were more familiar. These remarkable architectural refinements are not found on any other contemporary monuments in western Europe.

A number of the stones carry carvings of metal axes and one has a hilted dagger. These may be mason's marks, or even the graffiti of the day. However serious consideration should be given to them as symbols of an axe cult surviving from earlier neolithic times. Stone axes are known from a number of henges, for example Llandegai (Gwynedd), and at Stonehenge and Woodhenge imitation axes made of chalk have been found.

In Period II Stonehenge was approximately aligned on midsummer sunrise and the midwinter sunset and the four station stones were set up to mark the corners of a rectangle whose short sides also point to the rising sun at midsummer and the setting sun at midwinter. Similarly the long sides of the rectangle point to the most southerly rising and most northerly setting of

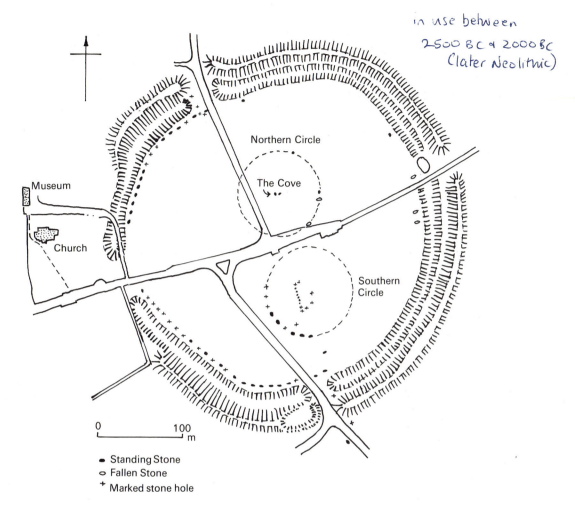

in use between 2500 BC & 2000 BC (later Neolithic)

- Standing Stone
○ Fallen Stone
+ Marked stone hole

Fig. 30 *A plan of Avebury henge and stone circles, Wiltshire.*

the moon, events which happen every $18\frac{1}{2}$ years. These observations go some way to suggest that Stonehenge was a sanctuary deliberately aligned to predict certain dates in the farming calendar. Alternatively we may be looking at an example of the sun or moon worshipped as a sky god. The true purpose will always remain unclear. (It is worth remembering that most Christian churches are aligned east to west but are not deliberately pointing to the rising sun at the equinoxes.) Certainly some very strong driving force must have existed to involved so many people from a very wide area, in building and using such an elaborate monument for so many centuries.

Wessex

In Wessex there are four extra large Class II henge monuments – Avebury, Durrington Walls and Marden, all in Wiltshire, and Mount Pleasant in Dorset. A fifth site, Waulud's Bank in Bedfordshire, may be related.

Avebury, at the foot of the Marlborough Downs, is an enormous earthwork (fig. 30). A circular bank still 4 m. (4.4 yd) high, surrounds a ditch that was originally 9 m. (9.8 yd) deep. (plate 23). It has been estimated that 150,000 tons of chalk were dug out of the ditch and piled up to make the bank, which stood slightly back from the edge of the former. Four entrance gaps passed through the earthworks at the cardinal points; an area 365 m. (400 yd) in diameter was enclosed. Around its edge stood an outer circle of 100 unshaped sarsen stones, each weighing about 15 tons. Within this were two smaller

4 main points of the compass

Plate 23 *The excavated ditch of the Avebury henge monument, showing its steep chalk-cut sides. The silt is almost 7 m. (7.7 yd) deep. (H. St George Gray)*

stone circles, the northern containing three massive sarsens in a box-like formation called a cove. In the southern circle are an enigmatic line of smaller blocks. Many of the stones are now missing; some were broken up for building and others destroyed by farmers clearing the land for cultivation in the eighteenth century.

There is no dating evidence to show if all the features at Avebury are contemporary. Burl suggests that the two smaller circles pre-date the earthwork and outer circle by 200 years, but as yet this cannot be substantiated.

From the southern entrance an avenue of two parallel rows of standing stones ran south then east to the Sanctuary on Overton Hill, a distance of 2.4 km. (1.5 miles). The Sanctuary was a complex site consisting of three successive and expanding rings of posts, followed by concen-

tric stone circles which linked to the avenue and Avebury. A second avenue, now destroyed, almost certainly ran from the west entrance of Avebury towards Beckhampton and the Longstones (fig. 31).

Avebury seems to have been in use between 2500 and 2000 BC in the later neolithic period. Objects found were so few that the excavators suggested that the ditches had been deliberately kept clean. A few pieces of Windmill Hill pottery, and scraps of Peterborough and grooved ware, together with flint arrowheads and scrapers, are almost all that are known. Burials at the foot of two stones in the Avenue contained late neolithic beaker pots.

Close to Avebury is the great mound of Silbury Hill (Wilts) (plate 24). Its purpose is uncertain but in all probability it covers a burial chamber. It was built in three stages, each of

Fig. 31 *Major monuments in the locality of Avebury, Wiltshire.*

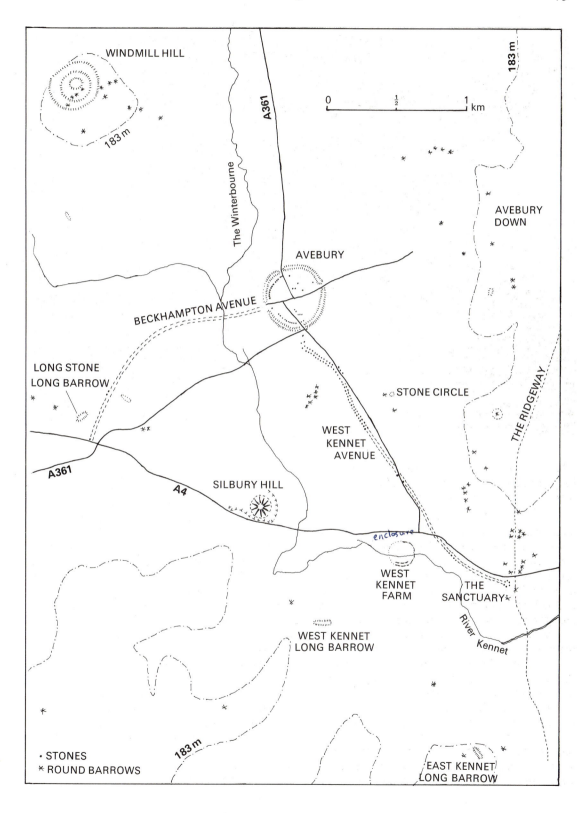

WINDMILL HILL

183 m

A361

183 m

0   ½   1 km

The Winterbourne

AVEBURY

AVEBURY DOWN

BECKHAMPTON AVENUE

LONG STONE LONG BARROW

STONE CIRCLE

THE RIDGEWAY

WEST KENNET AVENUE

A361

A4

SILBURY HILL

enclosure

WEST KENNET FARM

THE SANCTUARY

River Kennet

WEST KENNET LONG BARROW

183 m

EAST KENNET LONG BARROW

• STONES
✳ ROUND BARROWS

Plate 24 *An aerial view of Silbury Hill. The great quarry for its chalk can be seen in the shadow on the right and to the left of the mound. (J.E. Hancock)*

which increased its size to its present height of 40 m. (44 yd), with a base covering 2 ha. (15 acres). It has been estimated that its construction occupied 4 million worker hours.

Also close to Avebury at the hamlet of West Kennet was a double ring-shaped enclosure, consisting of two concentric circles of posts 700 m. (766 yd) and 540 m. (591 yd) in circumference. The inner post holes were 2.5–3 m. (2·7–3·3 yd) deep and must have supported massive tall timbers. Like Avebury and the Sanctuary the Kennet enclosure was probably used for both religious and secular activities.

Limited excavation at the other three Wessex henges – Durrington Walls, Marden (with a large round barrow inside) and Mount Pleasant – shows a common feature in the presence of concentric rings of post holes, apparently indicating large circular rings of upright timbers as at Woodhenge (and Arminghall). It has been suggested that these were tribal meeting places,

perhaps like those of the Creek and Cherokee Indians of the south-eastern United States in the eighteenth century. A word of caution is needed: the rings of posts might be forerunners of stone settings that culminated at Stonehenge, in which case they were not roofed over.

Excavations and geophysical surveys at Durrington Walls show that it contained a number of these circular timber settings, one 38 m. (42 yd) in diameter, constructed of massive oak posts. Unlike the other henges, it was noticeable that the ditches contained much domestic refuse including large quantities of grooved ware, and much smaller amounts of Windmill Hill and beaker pottery.

Stone circles

We have seen that some of the henge monuments contain stone circles. It seems fairly clear that the function of both henges and circles was related and may have been to some extent complementary. There is a tendency for henges to have a southern and eastern distribution in Britain, whilst stone circles are found to the west and north, although there is a certain amount of overlap.

The earliest stone circles were quite large,

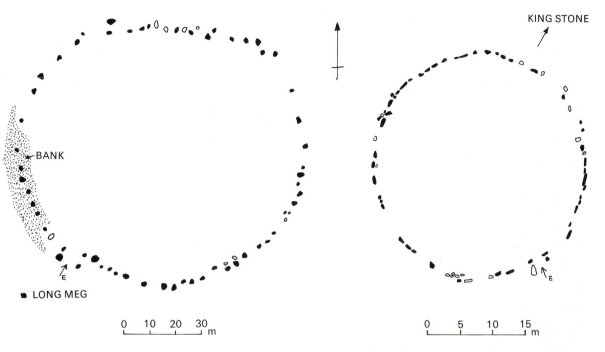

Fig. 32 *An early stone circle* (left), *the oval Long Meg and her Daughters (Cumbria) – Long Meg is the outlier to the south-west; and the later true circle of Rollright (Oxon). The arrows point to the entrances.* (After Burl *et al*)

Plate 25 *Rounded glacial boulders form one of the largest stone circles in Britain: Long Meg and her Daughters (Cumbria) consists of an outlying column of sandstone, and a ring of about 66 stones. (J. Dyer)*

over 30 m. (33 yd) in diameter, and usually true circles, probably laid out from a central stake hole. Dated to between 3400 BC and 2700 BC they are found mainly in northern Scotland and the Lake District. The stones tend to be closely spaced, with a clear entrance gap, often marked by extra portal stones.

Long Meg and her Daughters (Cumbria) stands on a sloping sandstone terrace above the River Eden (fig. 32; plate 25). It measures 109 m. (119 yd) across and contains about 66 stones, the heaviest of which weighs some 25 tons. On the south-west side an entrance is marked by two extra stones. Facing this is the outlying megalith called Long Meg decorated on its side with three incised spirals, and aligning on midwinter sunset. Not far away at Keswick the Castlerigg circle also has an outlying stone, but it is not in its original position. There is a curious rectangular setting of stones within the circle which has produced traces of charcoal: its function is unknown. Aubrey Burl has observed that Cumbrian circles tend to lie

Plate 26 *The recumbent stone circle of Easter Aquorthies (Gordon) consists of nine upright stones, a recumbent with smoothed face, two flankers, and two supporters in front of the recumbent. (Aubrey Burl)*

12 to 16 km. apart and that they may represent local tribal centres.

In the late neolithic period (2700 to 2000 BC) and on into the early Bronze Age, some of the biggest stone circles were constructed. We have already mentioned Avebury, 400 m. (437 yd) across, and in Avon, Stanton Drew stands 113 m. (124 yd) in diameter. Smaller constructions around 18 to 30 m. (20 to 33 yd) in size were much more normal. The Rollright Stones (Oxon) are 33 m. (36 yd) in diameter, and consist of a closely spaced ring of gnarled limestone blocks, with a possible entrance on the southeast (fig. 32). The outlying King Stone was set up some centuries after the circle and is unlikely to be connected with it. A few regional traits were appearing: in north-east Scotland circles tended to be composed of 10 stones whilst in the Lake District 12 were more popular. This may imply a certain numeracy on the part of the builders, but it need not support the notion that all of the circles embodied complicated geometrical constructions in their layout or involved sophisticated astronomical observations. As O. Neugebauer has written, 'The mathematical requirements for even the most developed economic structures of antiquity can be satisfied with elementary household arithmetic which no mathematician would call mathematics.'

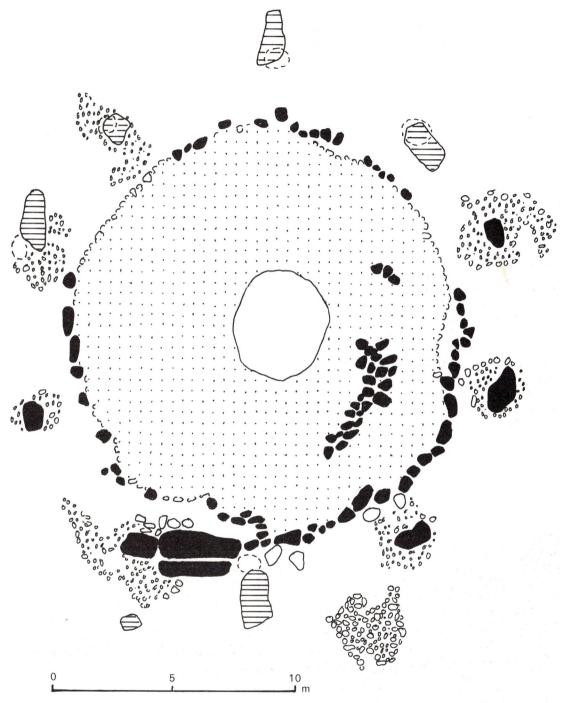

Fig. 33 *The recumbent stone circle of Loanhead of Daviot (Aberdeen). Eight standing stones graded in height, two flanking stones and a horizontal recumbent stone surround a central ring cairn, in the centre of which pottery and cremated human bone were found. The eight standing stones each stood in a small cairn.* (After Kilbride-Jones, 1935)

Professor Alexander Thom has shown that some circles were planned with a precision that suggests that a standard unit of measurement was used in some parts of Britain. Such a standard was possibly based on a human pace, and Thom has called it a megalithic yard. It measures 0.829 m. (2.72 ft). A small number of circles seem to be aligned on the rising or setting sun or the moon at the solstices. How much of this is the result of accurate planning and how much pure chance is open to debate.

The later stone circles in Britain are usually associated with burials. One obvious group is that of the recumbent stone circles of Aberdeenshire (plate 26). There, about 100 circles have been recognized on hillside terraces, often commanding wide views, and orientated towards the south-west. Loanhead of Daviot may be taken as typical: the circle consists of a ring of ten stones, graded in height, with the two tallest at the south-west, standing on either side of a horizontal or recumbent block weighing 12 tons (fig. 33). In the centre is a low cairn of stones covering a burnt area which may have been added to the circle at some time after its initial construction. The burnt material included pottery, wood and human bone, amongst it children's skull fragments. It is possible that there may have been a small wooden mortuary hut under the cairn. On one of the stones of the circle a vertical line of five cup-marks can be seen. These enigmatic egg-cup shaped hollows are often found ground into the stones, especially on burial monuments, but their purpose and exact date remain obscure. The pottery from Loanhead of Daviot suggests that it was in use for many centuries, eventually going out of use at a time when beaker pottery was flourishing, perhaps about 2000 BC.

Possibly related to the recumbent circles are a group of about thirty tombs found on the south side of the Moray Firth usually called the Clava tombs. These are small passage graves with entrances, like the circles, facing south-west, often surrounded by a ring of upright stones (plate 27).

The last stone circles were small and irregular in shape. They stood on marginal land from Devon to the Western Isles. In the north-east of Britain 'four-posters' were set up: rings (or squares?) of only four stones, often with a cremation burial at their centre. Cup marks

again occur as a related feature. Stone circles in the Peak District have their bases embedded in a bank of stone rubble, as at the Nine Ladies circle on Stanton Moor. Much more dramatic is the small circle at Callanish on the Isle of Lewis, with its close-set tall pillars and rows of stones radiating to the cardinal points (plate 28). At its centre is a small chambered tomb which contained scraps of human bone when examined in 1857.

Stone rows are found in the south-west, mostly on Dartmoor and Exmoor and in Caithness and Sutherland. On Dartmoor the row on Stall Moor and Green Hill is over 2 km. (1.2 miles) long. Rows can consist of single, double and sometimes triple lines of stones, almost always running from a large terminal stone up to a burial cairn. The majority of the stones are very small, some less than 30 cm. (1 ft) high, and for this reason are unlikely to have served any astronomical purpose as has often been suggested. Instead they may represent the highland equivalent of the lowland cursuses, being processional ways to lead the spirits across the moors to the resting places of the dead.

Settlements

The Orkney settlements of Skara Brae and Barnhouse (Mainland), Rinyo on Rousay and the Links of Noltland (Westray), represent small villages of the later neolithic period and exhibit many similarities. Skara Brae is the most complete (fig. 34). Dug into the midden of an earlier settlement it consists of six single-roomed stone-built huts of roughly square or rectangular ground-plan, each about 4.5 m. (5 yd) square internally. Their single, low doorways face on to a narrow, roofed passage which links them together. The walls are of dry-stone masonry which still stands 3 m. (3.3 yd) high in places. How they were roofed is uncertain but rafters of whalebone or driftwood covered with turf or thatch is most likely. Because it was built of the local, easily split flagstone, the main furniture of each house has survived. A large two-shelf dresser facing the door dominates each room (plate 29). In front of it is a rectangular stone-lined hearth for burning peat, which at Rinyo was flanked by small clay ovens. On each side are box beds which were once filled with heather or bracken and covered by a canopy of animal skins. The larger bed was

Plate 27 *The south-western cairn at Clava (Inverness) is a passage grave with surrounding circle of stones. Fragmentary pots and cremated bones were excavated about 1928. (J. Dyer)*

Plate 28 (below) *At Callanish (Lewis) an avenue, or double line of stones, leads up to a circle of 13 stones. The bottom 1.5 m. (1.6 yd) of the site was covered with peat until 1857. When it was removed a small chambered cairn was found inside the circle. (Colin Ramsay)*

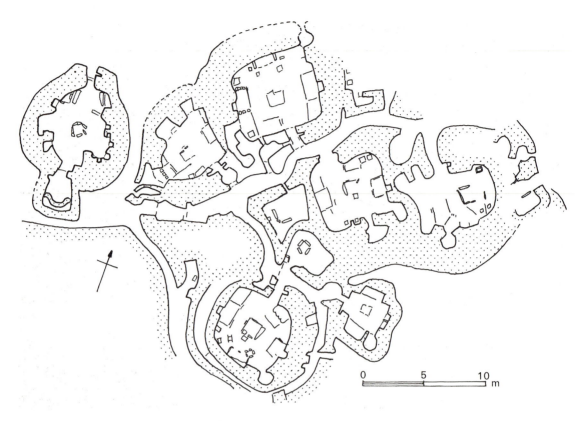

Fig. 34 *A plan of the neolithic village of Skara Brae on Mainland, Orkney.*

presumably for the master of the house, the smaller for women and children. Let into the floor are a number of clay-lined stone tanks which may have held fresh water, shellfish, or limpets softening for fishing bait. In the walls were numerous small cupboards and hiding holes. Each hut had one or more circular cells which may have been storerooms, but since they often have drains leading from them they are more likely to have been lavatories. One hut (No. 8) at Skara Brae stands apart from the others, and lacks a dresser and beds. It seems to have been used as a workshop and contained the debris left by a flint worker. Skara Brae was deserted in a hurry, perhaps at the approach of a storm, and the excavators found a trail of beads scattered in the passage by a fleeing villager.

The settlements, submerged in their rubbish middens, must have been dark and filthy, the air filled with acrid peat smoke and the stench of sewerage. Most of the houses are so similar to

each other that they remind one of a group of prehistoric council houses. Radiocarbon dating suggests that Skara Brae was occupied from about 3100 BC to 2450 BC.

The Orkney villages are unique, and it is tempting to transcribe their details to other parts of Britain where evidence for later neolithic dwellings is lacking. This could be dangerous since settlements are adapted to fit into their appropriate geographic environments, and the windswept northern isles bear no comparison to the more hospitable lands of the south. In western Europe the communal long-house was the most common type of dwelling, but in Britain such buildings have proved elusive. Only one possible long-house at Balbridie (Aberdeen) has been recognized, with radiocarbon dates between 3000 and 2900 bc. It was a large rectangular structure 26 m. (28.5 yd) long by 13 m. (14.2 yd) wide, divided into three compartments. More of a great hall than a house in formation, its function was possibly more akin to the circular structures in the southern henges (fig. 35).

Plate 29 *A house at Skara Brae (Orkney) with stone dresser, box beds, central hearth, stone water tank and quern stone. In the wall are cupboards and hiding holes. The roof was probably of driftwood and turf. (J. Dyer)*

In the highland areas of Britain houses are few and largely rectangular. In the Isle of Man a house beside Ronaldsway airport measured 7.5 m. by 4 m. (8.2 × 4.4 yd). It was slightly subterranean with a curved entry passage on the south-west. The roof was supported by an irregular double line of posts. In the centre was a square hearth. Large quantities of pottery, stone tools and bone indicate long occupation.

At Mount Pleasant in south Glamorgan a rectangular house was found beneath a Bronze Age burial cairn. Measuring 5.7 m. by 3.3 m. (6.2 × 3.6 yd), it had a pitched roof, and its walls were composed of sandstone slabs. Unlike Ronaldsway it contained no domestic refuse, possibly indicating a ritual function – or simply that they kept the floor clean and dumped rubbish outside the house!

In the south of Britain houses are almost non-existent. Single post holes associated with occupation debris may be all that is left of simple light huts which resembled Indian wigwams. Numerous finds of pits in the same areas may have been for grain storage, cooking holes or cess pits. At Honington in Suffolk dark patches adjacent to pits were interpreted as the floors of small huts or tents. The possibility of turf as a building material might be considered. Once it had decayed it would leave little trace, especially after ploughing.

One of the most extensively excavated sites is Fengate (Cambs) (plate 30). An area of late neolithic settlement was enclosed by a ring ditch 20 m. (22 yd) in diameter. Outside were a series of stock enclosures separated by ditched droveways with skilfully positioned entrances to allow the control of animals. Tracks led down to the fen edge where there were lush grazing lands, and the hunting of wild cattle and deer took place at the waterside.

Fig. 35 *An imaginative reconstruction of the great hall at Balbridie (Aberdeen), based on the excavation of Ian Ralston and N.M. Reynolds between 1977 and 1981.* (J. Dyer)

Neolithic people

With so much emphasis on burial in the neolithic it is fairly easy to form opinions about the people of the time from their skeletal remains. Generally speaking the men reached an average height of 170 cm. (5 ft 7 in) and the women around 160 cm (5 ft 3 in). They could expect to live between 25 and 30 years; only in exceptional circumstances would they reach 50. Lots of tibia bones have a deformity showing that most people squatted on their haunches a great deal. Childbirth was always hazardous for mothers and many children died at birth or in the first two years of life.

Diseases were those caused by the environment, rather than the stress-related problems of today. Osteoarthritis seems to have been the most prevalent, often occurring in very young people. Diseases like tuberculosis may have been common but few signs have been found. Dental problems included pyorrhea and abscesses. Broken limbs were common. Animals, too, were affected by disease. The wetlands would have been breeding grounds for malaria, prevalent in the fens until the last century, and devastating parasites like the liver fluke would have played havoc with flocks of sheep. Life was not easy and a great deal had to be learnt in a short lifetime, making us realize that long-term construction projects involving work spread over many years must have been passed on from one generation to another. Astromical observations over periods of 60 or 70 years, postulated for sites like Stonehenge, would have been out of the question without the use of writing, or some method of recording the passing of time.

Plate 30 *The central droveway, with ditched
stock enclosures on either side, at Fengate
(Cambs). Hedges probably grew beside the
droves. (Francis Pryor)*

Chapter Five

The Beaker Users

Invasion or exchange?

About 2750 BC there appeared amongst the thick pottery types of southern Britain a new vessel known as a bell-beaker. Finely made of thin red ware with an S-shaped profile, it was decorated with lines of twisted cord (all-over-cord beakers). These vessels were widely known on the continent from Denmark to Spain and it seemed logical to prehistorians in the past that these pots were brought to Britain by invaders, particularly as their earliest distribution is close to the south and east coasts, eastern Scotland, and on Salisbury Plain and in the upper Thames valley, all areas easily reached from the sea (fig. 36).

At the present time invasion theories are unfashionable and archaeologists have been at great pains to consider alternative explanations for the arrival of these beakers. This has re-

sulted in two schools of thought: those who still believe in a limited invasion and those who seek to explain their presence as part of a package of prestige items. The writer is more inclined to the former hypothesis, but suggests that there are further possibilities.

After the arrival of farming immigrants at the beginning of the neolithic period, contact with the continent continued with boatmen engaged in sea travel for purposes of fishing, prospecting and trade. One of the most tangible results is called acculturation, that is the interchange of ideas and beliefs and sometimes objects, which we can see broadly reflected in the design of causewayed enclosures, megalithic tombs, stone rows and pottery. These were not brought about by mass movements of people coming to Britain and reproducing exact copies of items made in their own country. Instead we have the transfer by word of mouth of interesting ideas, memorized and carried to Britain, to be mulled over and perhaps absorbed in total or part into our cultures. In the case of beakers it has been suggested that perhaps 200 continental vessels reached Britain from the Rhinelands over a century or two, and are found in graves with

Fig. 36 *Examples of beakers:* A *All-over-cord beaker from St Andrews, Fyfe (height 15 cm. (6 in.)); B Bell-shaped beaker from Wilsford, Wilts (22.5 cm. (8.9 in.)); C Long-necked example from Berden, Essex (22.5 cm. (8.4 in.)).*

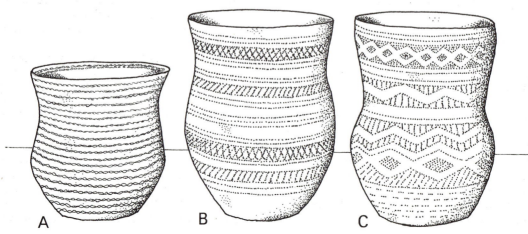

A   B   C

crouched inhumations, as well as in the blocking deposits and upper ditch fills of some
chambered tombs and the causewayed enclosures and in the lower ditch fills of a number
of henges.

If these pots were not brought by immigrants
they may represent items of value and prestige
acquired by trade or exchange, buried with the
dead to signify their personal importance or
rendered taboo by the death of their owner. It is
assumed that beakers were drinking vessels, and
a specimen from Ashgrove (Fifeshire) contained traces of mead. It is conceivable that
these vessels might have been no more than the
appropriate accompaniment to a new drink
which swept the country – mead, barley or fruit
wine, or even something with hallucinatory
powers – the sherry or brandy glass of the later
neolithic period.

The traditions of collective burial in chamber
tombs and round barrows of the earlier neolithic period had changed. Cremation had been
practised in the north for centuries, and by
2750 BC it was widespread thoughout Britain,
especially in the henges like those at
Dorchester-on-Thames. A few individual inhumations were placed in the megalithic tombs
and round barrows, and it has been argued that
these occurred before the appearance of the
first beakers in Britain. A closer look suggests
that they are broadly contemporary. The
chambered tombs were finally sealed and inhumations under round barrows, or cremation,
were introduced. In some parts of Britain collective burial continued but under round
barrows, where multiple interments both of
inhumations and cremations occurred under
the same mound.

The beaker burials consisted of a crouched
skeleton in a pit or stone cist with a bell-beaker,
possibly accompanied by barbed-and-tanged
arrowheads, small metal tools and gold ornaments. The burial, which could be a man,
woman or child, was normally crouched on its
side in the natural position of sleep, or foetal
position, with knees drawn up to the chin.
Many such burials are found with no grave
goods of any kind. It could be that objects
placed with the dead were of perishable
materials now decayed. It may suggest im-
poverishment, that there was no beaker available to accompany them. In time the native

British potters began to make their own regional
styles of beakers, following a mixture of their
own intuition and new ideas from the Netherlands. The bell-beakers changed shape, having
first a short neck and later a long neck, both with
more adventurous zones of patterning. A study
of beaker burials in Yorkshire shows that 83 per
cent of beaker bodies lie east to west, with males
facing east to the sun and females west to the
moon.

It is difficult to explain why inhumation
burial under a round barrow became the dominant burial practice. One cannot help feeling
that a new religious experience was introduced
that was strong enough to alter the practice of
centuries. At first it seems to have run in
opposition to the old beliefs. Alasdair Whittle
has observed for example that early beaker
burials are not found in close proximity to
Stonehenge and the larger henges. Only when
they are well established in the country and
perhaps new beliefs are accepted do later beaker
burials occur close to these monuments. At the
same time major building changes at Stonehenge were taking place in Periods II and III
(p. 66ff).

Early beaker burials are usually found under
small low barrows or cairns, though they can be
found without any visible surface feature.
Sometimes a number of graves are covered by
the same barrow. At Roundway Down (Wilts)
in 1855 William Cunnington found a deep oval
grave pit beneath a low mound. In it was the
crouched skeleton of an old man 183 cm. (6 ft)
tall, with a bell-beaker standing at his feet. Near
his chest was an archer's bracer or wristguard,
beside it was a bronze, racquet-headed pin and
by his left hand a broad, flat, copper dagger.
Close to the skull was a barbed and tanged
arrowhead.

In 1976 a small barrow at Barnack (Cambs)
produced a primary male burial lying on its
back, with knees drawn up. He was between 35
and 45 years old and again had a bell-beaker at
his feet. A splendid wristguard of central European affinity made of green schist, with nine
gold-studded perforations was beneath his left
wrist. Close to his right hand was a small copper
dagger, and the grave also contained an unusual
bone pendant, possibly used as a dress fastener
(plate 31). The Barnack barrow was later enlarged at least twice, eventually becoming a

Plate 31 *A bell-beaker from a grave at Barnack (Cambs), together with a gold studded wristguard, bone pendant and copper dagger. (British Museum)*

bell-barrow, to which 22 burials were added.

A bell-beaker burial from Crichel Down (Dorset) had a large oval opening on the left side of the skull showing that it had been the subject of prehistoric brain surgery or trepannation. By cutting a roundel of bone from the head with a flint knife it was probably thought that pressure would be released curing epilepsy, madness, convulsions or severe headaches. Many people surprisingly recovered in spite of the dangers of haemorrhage, infection and shock. One person from Denmark survived until the fourth operation. The earliest known dated trepanning operations have been found in France.

Multiple burials

In the Pennines and parts of southern England a number of beaker inhumations and cremations might be placed together in the same grave. A complex example of a multiple burial was examined by William Greenwell in 1869 at Rudston G62 in Humberside (fig. 37). This barrow, on the chalk Wolds above Holderness, was 20 m. (22 yd) in diameter, but only 1.4 m. (4.6 ft) high, having been damaged by ploughing. Although the barrow must have been built in neolithic times, it had been disturbed late in

the same period, when a circular shaft 2.8 m. (3 yd) in diameter was dug down through the mound and 3 m. (3.3 yd) into the solid chalk beneath, destroying any earlier burials. At the bottom of the shaft two rectangular stone cists or boxes were constructed. In one of them the body of a man had been laid, and near his legs were the skeletons of two small children. At his head was an unusual beaker decorated with grooved lines, and a piece of burnt ironstone. In the other cist were the cremated bones of two men and a few pieces of ox skull. In the corner was a second beaker containing 'some dark coloured matter'. Between the two cists was another male cremation and a third beaker. The grave shaft was filled with earth which contained the mixed up bones of a man and child, probably disturbed when the shaft was dug. Above this was a layer of large sandstone slabs and more earth and chalk rubble.

After some time the surface of the refilled shaft had subsided, leaving a weed-filled hollow a little over a metre deep in the top of the barrow. The area was burnt clean and then the body of a young woman aged between 18 and 24 was laid on the bottom accompanied by a fourth beaker and a flint knife. Almost immediately above her the body of a man was placed and covered with soil. He, in turn, was disturbed when the corpse of an old woman was interred, together with a fifth beaker and two bronze awls. Lastly a young child was added to the shaft, before it was sealed by a layer of burnt earth and charcoal, perhaps representing a scouring of the surface. The barrow now contained at least a dozen burials.

In the early Bronze Age two further interments were made to the surface of the barrow, a woman with a bronze awl and pottery food vessel, and an unaccompanied middle-aged man. When the barrow was re-examined in 1968 four more crouched, secondary burials were found in the mound. None of these was accompanied by grave goods. Other barrows close by covered similar multiple burials, indicating intense activity in an area rich in neolithic ceremonial remains, which include three cursuses and the Rudston monolith, the tallest standing stone in Britain at 7.8 m. (8.5 yd) high.

Close to the River Nene at Irthlingborough (Northants) lies a group of ceremonial monuments which include four round barrows. One

a small pointed tool used for piercing holes

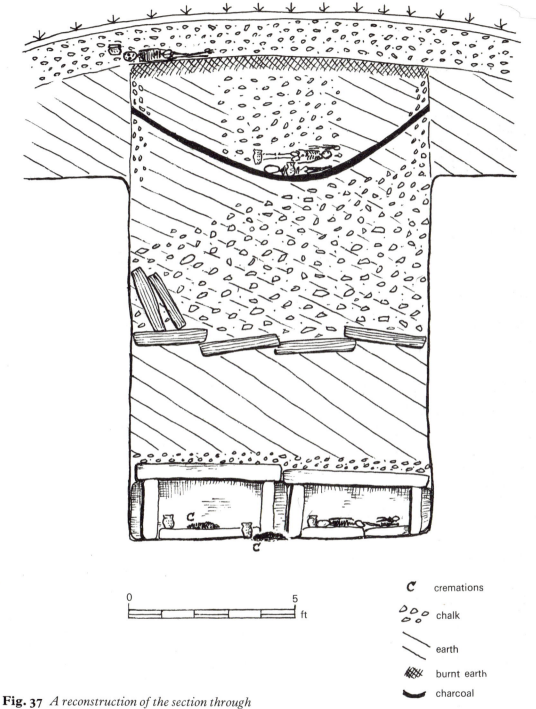

Fig. 37 *A reconstruction of the section through the Rudston G62 barrow (Humberside), excavated by Canon Greenwell in 1869 and based on his description.*

Plate 32 *Barrow No. 1 at Irthlingborough
(Northants) looking south-east. The ditches
represent the subsequent enlargements of the site.
(English Heritage)* [handwritten: legs drawn up under the chin]

barrow covered a flexed male burial orientated
south-west to north-east (plate 32). At his feet
lay a long-necked beaker, five conical V-
perforated jet buttons, a flint dagger and an
amber ring. The grave goods also included an
archer's wristguard, a whetstone, a triangular
bifacially worked point (which was possibly a
blank for a barbed and tanged arrowhead), nine
flint flakes (some retouched as knives and
scrapers), a boar's tusk, three bone spatulae and
a sponge-finger stone – items which make up an
archer's equipment and a craftsman's tool kit.
The smaller grave goods may have been
wrapped in a bundle.

[handwritten margin: for sharpening; 2 faces?]

The burial appeared to have been in a wooden
coffin roofed by timber beams, and a small
limestone cairn was raised above it. The cairn
was partly composed of, and overlain by, about
1,000 fragments of animal bone representing
more than 200 skulls, the majority those of
cattle. Their weight eventually caused the coffin

lid to collapse and stone and bone to descend
into the grave. Cattle seem to have played a
special part in funeral ceremonies, being an
important symbol of status and wealth. During
the construction of tombs it was customary to
slaughter a great number of animals, and the
number of skulls deposited was in direct re-
lation to the importance of the dead person.

The Irthlingborough barrow, enclosed by a
ditch 15 m. (16.4 yd) in diameter, eroded and
was twice enlarged (enclosed by ditches 24 m.
and 32 m. (26 and 35 yd) in diameter). A cremation in a food vessel and several other cremations, including an urned cremation accompanied by a riveted bronze dagger, were
added to the site during construction.

Personal ornament

From a study of burial mounds men's graves
can be most reliably identified. These tend to be
'warriors' buried with flint or metal daggers or
knives, arrows (and presumably bows, now
decayed) and perhaps battle axes of Cornish or
Preseli stone. Graves of 'craftsmen' include flint
knives, stone polishers, a bronze awl and antler
spatulae probably for leather work, and polish-

Fig. 38 *Bronze Age costumes, based mainly on preserved examples excavated in Denmark.* (Tracey Croft)

ing stones and a possible beaver tooth engraver for metalwork. Shale and copper beads with a small beaker from Beggar's Haven (Sussex) probably belonged to a woman. Bronze awls and gold hair trusses that could be women's are also found in men's graves.

Woven woollen fabric for clothing was certainly in use by the time beakers appeared (fig. 38). Sheep were clearly being bred for their wool, as well as to provide milk and meat. A beaker barrow at Kelleythorpe (Yorks) produced cloth 'under the entire length of the skeleton' and three jet buttons at the throat. At the Manton barrow (Wilts) the fabric which extended above the head of the burial left an impression still visible on a metal axe blade. A rock-cut tomb near Skara Brae in Orkney in 1989 produced a large piece of felt material, perhaps beaten bark. Animal skins were also used for clothing, as they had been in earlier times. Buttons of jet, shale and bone were probably used for securing garments. A middle-aged male burial from Acklam Wold, Yorkshire had a pair of jet buttons at the outer side of each ankle suggesting that he wore gaiters or buttoned boots. Buttons at the neck suggest the fastening of a jumper or cloak. Copper and bone pins may also have secured clothing, and examples often found behind the skull in women's graves must have held hair in a bun.

[handwritten: Projection on the blade by which the blade is held firm in the handle]

Bracers or wristguards found in the men's graves are still used in archery to protect the wrist from the recoil of the bow string. Some men were buried with a dagger clasped in their hand, its blade protected by a wooden scabbard lined with fur; other blades seem to have been wrapped in moss or cloth. Two male graves are recorded containing hawks' heads, suggesting that falconry was practised, one near Buxton (Derby) and the other at Kelleythorpe (Yorks).

If these objects indicate a belief in a life after death then, as Canon Greenwell observed in 1877, it must have been considered similar to the life just ended or there would have been no need for weapons, implements and ornaments.

Plate 33 *Gold collars or lunulae were probably* *[handwritten: crescent shaped bronze age ornament]* *symbols of status passed from one generation to another. This example was found at Blessington in Co. Wicklow. (British Museum)*

The coming of metal

Triangular copper daggers with a tang for attaching a wooden or bone hilt seem to be amongst the earliest metal objects to reach Britain around 2700 BC. Analysis shows that some of them came from central Europe and others from Ireland. Basket-shaped gold hair trusses like those from Radley were also derived from the continent, and there is a clear link with beaker influences reaching Britain at that time. Gold discs, which were possibly button covers, and flat copper axes were typical of Irish workmanship and were at first probably imports, but soon local manufacture developed. This concentrated on the production of daggers, knives, awls, jewellery and a few flat axes.

Copper is found in south-western Britain, as well as Wales and Scotland. Recognizable by its purplish-brown or green stains, it occurs, for example, at Mullion on the Lizard peninsula. It

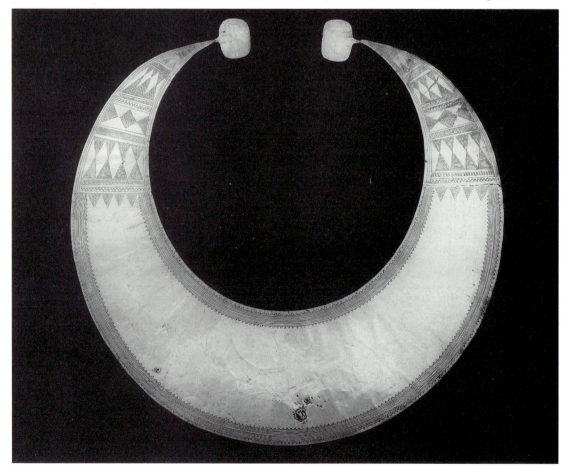

was probably dug out of the face of the cliffs since there is little indication that mines were sunk at this time, although they are known from central Europe and Mount Gabriel in West Cork, Ireland. Metallurgy probably spread slowly towards Britain from south-east Europe. At first the native copper was hammered into shape but later it was found that heating it made it less brittle or liable to crack. Eventually it was discovered that at a temperature of 1,100°C/2012°F it would melt and could be cast into numerous desirable shapes.

Gold is easier to work and outcropped at a number of Irish sites, and may have been worked in Carmarthenshire, and perhaps the Sutherland goldfield of Kildonan in Scotland. Crescent-shaped gold collars called lunulae are contemporary with the bell-beakers, and are found in southern Scotland and Cornwall (plate 33). Joan Taylor has suggested that examples from Harlyn Bay in Cornwall and Côtes-du-Nord in France were the work of the same craftsman. As the lunulae are not found in graves it has been suggested that they were communally held, perhaps the symbol of rank of a local dignitary.

Yorkshire jet and Dorset shale were utilized in making conical buttons, beads and so-called pulley-rings, the latter functioning as belt fasteners.

Fig. 39 *Using a saddle quern to grind corn.* (Tracey Croft)

Although dense scatters of flint artefacts, occasionally associated with broken beaker pottery, have been found from time to time, convincing evidence of houses and domestic sites is rare. This has led to the assumption that most beaker users were itinerant and may have lived in tent-like structures leaving little trace in the ground. It is more likely that erosion has simply destroyed traces of any structures. A possible oval house was excavated at Flamborough (Yorks) and two more convincing superimposed circular huts were excavated at Gwithian (Phase I) (Cornwall) in 1960. The first was 4.5 m. (4.9 yd) in diameter with a central post and free-standing entrance porch. There was an off-centre hearth. Fifty years later a second hut 3.6 m. (3.9 yd) in diameter was built on the same site, with a porch on the south side and a central

hearth. As well as sherds of pottery and animal bones, fragments of a saddle quern (for grinding grain) were found (fig. 39), together with a Cornish stone axe, a copper awl and pottery ring. There were possibly contemporary ploughed fields close by.

At Northton on the Isle of Harris (Hebrides) Derek Simpson excavated two oval structures. The better preserved measured some 8.5 m. by 4.2 m. (9.3 × 4.6 yd) and consisted of stone revetting outlining a pit which may have been covered by a tent or upturned boat.

At Belle Tout (Sussex) a rectangular enclosure partially excavated in 1968–9 was associated with numerous sherds of beaker pottery and flint implements. Close by in the bottom of a dry valley at Kiln Combe a beaker occupation site was recently excavated, though no settlement features were recognized.

Chapter Six

Into the Bronze Age

Climatic changes

At the end of the neolithic period and into the ensuing Bronze Age the climate was drier than today, with long, warm summers. Much of Britain was still forested. At the start of the neolithic period there had been a gradual decline in elm trees due to the insect-spread Dutch elm disease. Between the forests were large irregular areas of arable land intermixed with grassland and heath used for grazing. Perhaps because of soil exhaustion some communities chose to move to new areas, and land once cleared gradually became forest once more.

Cattle, sheep, goats and pigs remained the basic farm animals, and excavation shows that walls, fences and ditches lined by hedges were used to enclose them in fields. By the end of the neolithic period pig bones feature prominently in faunal assemblages from henge monuments and pit groups, rubbish pits near Dunstable (Beds), for example, producing 60 per cent pig bones as against 23 per cent oxen and 17 per cent sheep or goats. Barbed and tanged arrowheads show that hunting continued to be practised, especially of deer, though probably more for the use that could be made of their antlers than their meat. Wild oxen (aurochsen) were also exploited and precautions had doubtless to be taken so that they did not mix with domestic cattle and crossbreed.

Circular timber-framed huts with wattle and daub walls and thatched roofs were almost certainly being built, surrounded by small fields and separated by droveways that lead to watering places by suitable streams. Dean Bolton on the Marlborough Downs (Wilts) and Gwithian in Cornwall may be cited as examples.

Round barrow burials

More easily recognized on the less productive marginal land are the hilltop round barrows and riverside ring ditches marking burial places. In use since the later neolithic period, particularly in northern Britain, round barrows now came into their own. The simplest are known as bowl-barrows and consist of a mound formed by throwing soil inwards from the surrounding ditch. Sometimes where the subsoil was too hard and rocky for a ditch the mound was simply scraped together from the surrounding countryside, or built of stacked turves. In such cases a small retaining fence of stakes, or enclosing ring of stones might occur, suggesting that the original monument was more drum-shaped than it is today. Both usually covered burials, although in highland areas cairns may be nothing more than piles of stones cleared from once ploughed land.

Also in the highland parts of Britain a series of stone-built monuments occur known as ring cairns. These consist of a circular stone bank or wall surrounding a flat central burial place. If this central area is filled up with soil it is known as a platform cairn. Other localized variants will also be found.

Sometimes in southern Britain a circular ditch was dug and the material raised into a bank outside it. The area inside remained flat but was used for burials. This is now known as a ring ditch. Archaeologists also identify barrows that have been destroyed by ploughing, leaving only their ditches, as ring ditches. Beneath the barrow the first burial, known as the primary, usually occupied a pit at the centre. Other burials made at the same time, and sometimes in the same grave pit, are often called satellite burials (fig. 40). The barrows seem to have retained their sanctity for hundreds of years, and further burials might be added to the mound at a much later date. These are known as secondary burials.

The corpses were often crouched inhu-

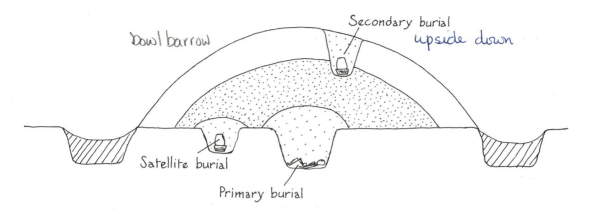

Labels on diagram: bowl barrow · Secondary burial · upside down · Satellite burial · Primary burial

Fig. 40 *Diagram to show the position of primary, secondary and satellite burials in a round barrow.*

mations, but cremations were just as common, and some barrows contained both. At Eaton in Leicester four successive burials had alternated from cremation to inhumation then back to cremation and inhumation again. The human remains might be placed in a wooden coffin, a hollowed tree-trunk, a wicker basket or a woollen shroud. The tree-trunk coffins often had a wooden prow resembling a boat and have been likened to a ship of the dead.

At Loose Howe in north Yorkshire what appeared to be three dug-out canoes were found in the barrow. Two had been fitted together as the base and lid of a tree-trunk coffin. This contained a few fragments of a skeleton buried with a bronze dagger, traces of linen foot wrapping and part of a leather shoe. The corpse had been laid on a bed of reeds or rushes with a straw pillow beneath its head. The coffin also contained hazel husks, suggesting an autumn burial.

Cremations might be placed in cinerary urns, *an urn for holding the ashes after a cremation* or simply wrapped in a cloth bundle and placed in a hole. One Wiltshire barrow had been thrown up over a cremation pyre. Alternating layers of charred logs still lying at right angles to each other were clearly visible. Careful modern excavation often reveals a wealth of information about the burial ritual.

At Cassington in Oxfordshire, for example, a circular ditch was dug and the soil from it piled up to make an inner bank. This enclosed a ritual area 40 m. (44 yd) in diameter, at the centre of which a pit a metre deep was dug. On the bottom was laid the body of an adult man, crouched on his right side with a flint scraper at his knee. Burning flowers or twigs were then dropped into the grave before it was half-filled with gravel. At this point the crouched body of a 5-year-old child was placed in the grave pit, which was next filled to the top with gravel. A ring of a dozen pointed oak stakes was driven into the top of the grave filling, with an additional stake at the centre of the circle. These seem to have formed a miniature hut about a metre in diameter, possibly with an entrance on the west, and with a thatched roof. The hut may have been shaped like an old-fashioned straw beehive, and it is tentatively suggested that the central stake supported a small table on which offerings were placed. About 2 m. (2.2 yd) north of the burial pit areas of burnt wood ash and scraps of bone were found. Close by were three small pits, one holding the cremated bones of a child of about 5 years old, probably originally contained in a leather bag; another held a small pottery urn filled with the burnt bones of a 6 month-old baby; whilst the third pit held a mixture of hawthorn charcoal and fragments of a burnt human foetus. From the large spread of ash it was clear that all the children were cremated on the spot. In the general area of burning there were also the charred remains of part of an adult skeleton. As this was incomplete it may have been brought to the site in a decayed state from a storage place elsewhere. Whether all the cremations took place at the same time or over a period of weeks is unknown. The ritual next involved the burning of the central hut, perhaps the spirit home of the corpses buried beneath. Once this was completed a new encircling ditch was dug and the material thrown up to build the covering barrow.

Many ceremonial sites of the neolithic continued in use into the Bronze Age, often undergoing structural alterations which suggest that beliefs were changing. At Mount Pleasant in Dorset the four-entrance henge monument underwent major changes. A circular timber setting similar to that at Woodhenge was replaced by a rectangular cove of stones, and a massive timber palisade was set up around the hilltop, enclosing some 4 ha. (10 acres) inside the henge. The timbers which were complete tree trunks were placed closely side by side and may have stood some 6 m. (6.6 yd) above ground level. Two extremely narrow entrances were detected. The structure has every appearance of being defensive and was ultimately destroyed by fire. The excavator, Dr G. J. Wainwright, estimates that 1,600 oak posts would have been required for the palisade, cut from about 364 ha. (900 acres) of forest.

The Wessex elite
These were not the only changes at henge monuments; development at Stonehenge (Phase III) has already been outlined. The population was being organized to create massive structures. The impetus for such a drive is unknown but certainly involved distinctions in social class. Whilst the majority of the population belonged to the working classes, an elite clearly existed that could give orders and expect them to be carried out. Whether this elite represented an aristocracy, a military dictatorship or a priesthood, or something of each of them, we cannot tell. Nor do we know if their energizing power was one born of serfdom and slavery, or whipped up by religious fervour or national pride. We do know that in Wessex, and a few other localities in southern England, a small number of burials are found with rich objects, and these may be the graves of this elite band. These objects differ according to sex. For men beautifully made grooved bronze daggers and polished stone battleaxes predominate; for women necklaces of jet and amber, pendants, bronze awls and small knives are common. In both cases it is the quality of workmanship that makes them special. In addition to these more normal objects are a few exotic items in a dozen

Wessex barrows fashioned from gold and amber. The most famous burial was found by William Cunnington in 1808 in a small bowl-barrow called Bush Barrow, a kilometre south of Stonehenge (fig. 42). There the skeleton of a well-built man was accompanied by three daggers, one with a hilt finely decorated with hundreds of minute gold nails, a flat axe, a polished stone mace-head, its handle decorated with cylindrical bone mounts (fig. 41), and three sheet-gold plates which once decorated the clothing of the deceased. The Upton Lovell barrow (G2e), also in Wiltshire, was probably a woman's grave despite containing a bronze dagger, since it also housed a complex amber necklace with spacer-plates, cylindrical gold beads, a bronze awl, various gold ornaments and an accessory vessel, a grape cup – a small pottery vessel covered all over with tiny round nodules of clay, resembling grapes. A barrow at Wilsford (Wilts) contained a bone flute. It must be stresed that these graves were exceptional and a well-made dagger, battleaxe or beads were the more normal accompaniments.

Most of the richer materials found in the Wessex graves do not occur naturally in that area, though the objects may well have been made there. Amber came from the coast of East Anglia if not, in some cases, from Scandinavia. The gold probably came from Ireland or Scotland. Stone for the battleaxes and maceheads originated in highland Britain. Shale is found at Kimmeridge in Dorset and jet at Whitby (Yorks).

Fig. 41 *Possible reconstruction of a mace or sceptre from Bush Barrow, Wilts.*

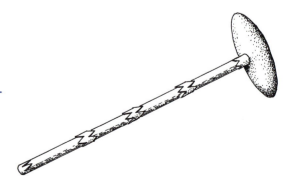

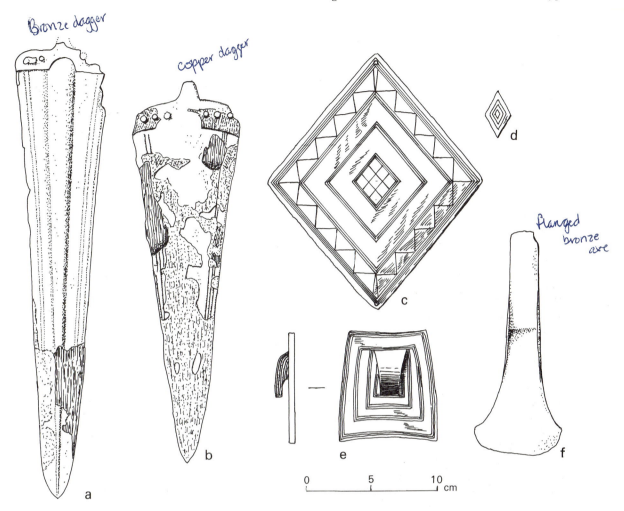

Bronze dagger

copper dagger

d

flanged bronze axe

a

b

c

e

f

0   5   10 cm

Fig. 42 *Objects excavated from the Bush Barrow (Wilts), found with a well-built warrior in 1808. a Bronze dagger; b Copper dagger; c Lozenge-shaped plate of sheet gold; d Small lozenge-shaped plate of sheet gold; e Belt-hook of hammered gold; f Flanged bronze axe.* (After Annable and Simpson, 1964)

increase power wealth rank

Links between the Mediterranean, Brittany and Britain during the period of Wessex aggrandisement have been long suspected. Blue glazed beads known as faience may have originated in central Europe. They may have reached Britain in return for amber, much prized in the eastern Mediterranean. They are found in Egyptian graves dated as late as 1450–1400 BC and in some Wessex graves. Bone mounts, similar to those on the shaft of the Bush

Barrow mace, and amber space-beads, are found in the Aegean about 1600 BC. Amber discs bound in gold and dagger pommels decorated with minute gold nails can also be seen as continental links. These items could all have reached Britain as gifts obtained from far-travelled seamen; they might even have been exchanged by traders for northern animal furs needed to trim costumes. In total they number less than 100 items and could all have arrived in the same cargo.

Wessex barrows

The Wessex burials occur under quite ordinary bowl-barrows, but also under a variety of 'fancy' round barrows, again restricted mostly to Wiltshire and Dorset, with a few outliers as far afield as Cornwall and Norfolk. The largest

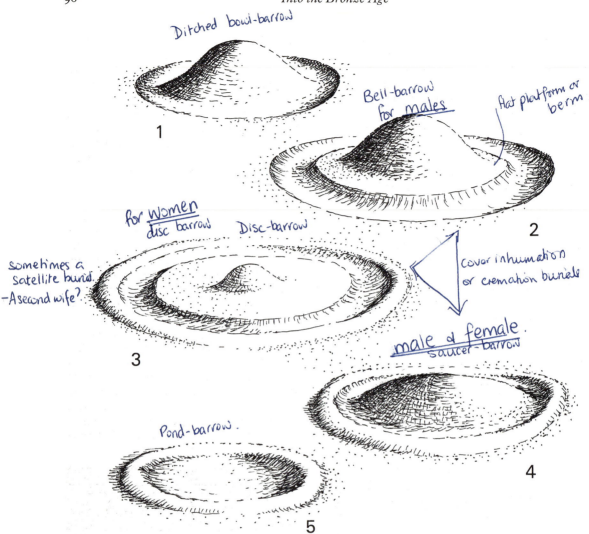

Ditched bowl-barrow [handwritten]

1

Bell-barrow for males [handwritten]

flat platform or berm [handwritten]

2

for women disc barrow [handwritten]   *Disc-barrow*

sometimes a satellite burial. — A second wife? [handwritten]

cover inhumation or cremation burials [handwritten]

3

male & female. saucer-barrow [handwritten]

Pond-barrow. [handwritten]

4

5

Fig. 43 *Typical round barrows of Wessex:*
1 *Ditched bowl-barrow;* 2 *Bell-barrow;*
3 *Disc-barrow;* 4 *Saucer-barrow;*
5 *Pond-barrow.*

more than one wife [handwritten]

Wessex barrows are bell-barrows consisting of a great mound of earth separated from a surrounding ditch by a flat platform or berm. Sometimes there is a bank outside the ditch (fig. 43). In disc-barrows the surrounding ditch and external bank encloses a flat area with a tiny burial mound at the centre, and occasionally a second off-centre mound for a satellite burial. Saucer-barrows are low circular mounds stretching out to the inner edge of the enclosing ditch. These three barrow types cover inhu-mation or cremation burials. Analysis of the contents of excavated examples by Leslie Grinsell suggests that bell-barrows were the exclusive tomb for male burials, disc-barrows contained females and saucers (like bowls) either. They could also cover child burials. Second mounds in a disc barrow might indicate polygamy. A final enigmatic 'fancy' barrow called a pond-barrow is in fact an embanked hollow in the ground. Some examples have contained cremations, but they have not been much studied and may be adjuncts to the funerary ritual rather than actual burial places. We must also notice that the size of the barrow was no indication of the wealth of its owner. A small bowl-barrow like Bush Barrow (Wilts) may cover a rich burial and a large bell-barrow contain only an unaccompanied skeleton.

Whilst in some parts of the country Bronze Age barrows occur in isolation or small groups, in Wessex and the Middle Thames they tend to form cemeteries, often along ridges, and sometimes containing 30 or 40 monuments. Andrew Flemming has suggested that some of these large groups were built in the summer months on pastureland by people practising transhumance, and that they do not represent the burial places of local residents. The suggestion remains speculative. One of the best documented of these cemeteries is at Snail Down, near Everleigh in Wiltshire (plate 34). It was almost totally excavated in the 1950s following serious damage by the military. Prior to the establishment of the cemetery there had been a beaker settlement on the Down, and a maze of stake and post holes were found, which may have been connected with a flimsy tent-like structure.

Plate 34 *An aerial view of the great barrow cemetery on Snail Down (Wilts). Bell-, disc- and saucer-barrows can be seen, together with numerous bowl-barrows. Holes left by eighteenth-century barrow diggers can be seen in the top of many of the mounds. (Ashmolean Museum)*

[handwritten: seasonal moving of livestock to a different region]

Probably the first barrow to be built was a scraped-up bowl-barrow (G3a) without a ditch. The mound, originally about a metre high, had been retained by a circle of posts, 15 m. (16.4 yd) in diameter. Beneath it were three pits, only one of which contained the cremated remains of an adult, including a trepanned disc of skull. The excavators suggested that a row of five small scraped bowl-barrows were next built, to the west of the first, mostly to cover cremations. After that the order of building is uncertain.

One bowl-barrow seemed to have a wooden platform at its centre. Perhaps the corpse was exposed here until the flesh had decayed. The bones were then burnt. A collared urn, usually for holding the ashes of the dead, was placed in a central pit and ritually broken before the cremation was placed on top of it. The barrow mound was then built.

There were six impressive bell-barrows at Snail Down. One of them (G8) covered an adult male who had been cremated on the spot. His ashes had then been collected and buried in an urn at the centre of the barrow, which had afterwards been covered by a stack of turf. When the ditch was dug, the excavated chalk was piled over the turf stack to cap it. A double

Plate 35 *The excavation of a disc-barrow with two mounds on Snail Down (Wilts). It had previously been opened by William Cunnington in 1805 or 1806. (J. Dyer)*

bell-barrow also had two mounds built of turf and held in place by wooden posts. One covered a loose cremation, and the other a coffin containing burnt bones, a bronze dagger and a pin of German origin.

Two disc-barrows were examined (plate 35). In one a cremation was found, but the other had been robbed in the past, making it impossible to comment on the suggestion that disc-barrows were for women. The only saucer-barrow in the Snail Down cemetery covered two pits. One contained the cremated remains of an adolescent with a trepanned skull disc, and the other a cremation accompanied by two small vessels of unknown use known as incense cups, and a bronze awl. V-shaped ditches 1.5 m. (1.6 yd) deep were dug round the cemetery to prevent the local Bronze Age farmers from intruding into sacred ground.

In examining barrows in Britain, pits are found, some empty, others containing bodies, both human and animal. Concentric rings of posts or stones are uncovered. Post holes suggest enigmatic huts or platforms. All conceal a hidden ritual. They have involved hours of construction which we can recognize, but there were also hours of ceremonial use which we can never understand. Each site gives different clues but we can only guess at dancing, singing, chanting, feasting, incantations and prayers. Animal bones suggest sacrifices, and stains indicate the pouring of libations and the burning of purifying fires. Ceremonies may have taken days or weeks to complete, and may have involved groups of people gathering at the barrow whenever the omens were propitious. Some bodies were exposed elsewhere and brought to the barrow as loose bones while others were trussed and bound as complete corpses. Some bodies may have been brought to such a traditional burial place from afar. A burial at Dorchester-on-Thames (Oxon) which contained traces of a possible sledge and a Wessex-type beaker may have been dragged from as far away as the New Forest. In some cases the barrow contains no corpse at all and we may ask if the ritual actually required a burial, or on the other hand whether burial simply needed a ritual?

flange = a projecting flat rim, collar or rib, used for strengthening or attachment.

The bronze smiths

Bronze is an alloy of about 90 per cent copper and 10 per cent tin. When it appeared in Britain around 2300 BC it could offer a harder and sharper cutting edge than copper and soon became by far the more popular metal for making tools and weapons, which were still based on the earlier copper types. Flat axes, and knives and daggers with rounded butt ends, remained in fashion. The axes had the beginnings of flanges on their long sides cast to stiffen them, and to prevent them twisting in their mounts. All these types continued to be made alongside the elaborate Wessex metalwork produced between 2000 and 1600 BC, which has already been mentioned, and riveted and grooved daggers of Bush Barrow type, all clearly linked to central European examples (fig. 44).

By 1600 BC smiths in southern and eastern England, working in what is known as the Arreton tradition, were producing new cast flanged axes, some decorated with simple hammered designs. New daggers appeared with an ogival outline, grooved blades and two or three plug rivets. Two types of spearhead were fashionable, one with a tang, pierced for a rivet, and another with a hollow socket – both devices for attaching the head to a wooden shaft. A famous example from Snowshill in the Isle of Wight is a hybrid of the two. By the end of the early Bronze Age the fully socketed spearhead was in production. Amongst minor bronze work innovations appear tanged 'lollipop-shaped' razors, a series of dress pins with various head shapes, and slender bronze chisels.

Beakers remained in use until about 1950 BC. Before that date other pottery types had been

Fig. 44 *Examples of Bronze Age metalwork around 1600 BC. a Flanged axe; b Ogival dagger, with cross section showing rivets for attaching to a wooden or bone hilt; c Tanged spearhead; d Socketed spearhead.*

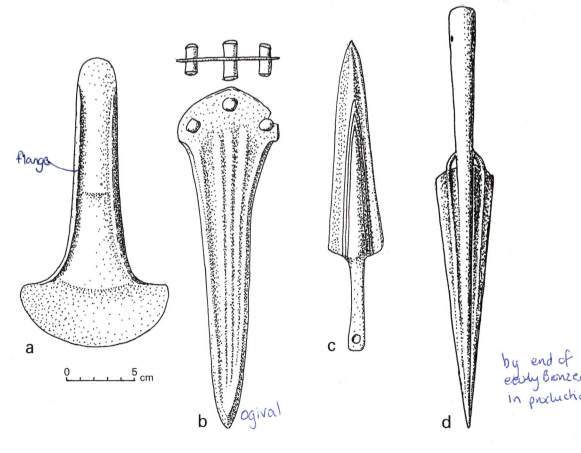

flange

a

0 ___ 5 cm

b   *ogival*

c

d

by end of early Bronze Age in production

Beakers 2750 BC – 1950 B.C. = 800 yrs

some use domestically mostly for cremations collared urn

Fig. 45 *Examples of Bronze Age pottery. A Food vessel from Garton Slack, Yorks: B Collared urn with decoration based on example from Warminster, Wilts: C,D,E Pygmy cups; C Grape cup, Wilsford, Wilts; D Incense cup, Winterbourne Stoke, Wilts; E Aldbourne cup, Durrington, Wilts.*

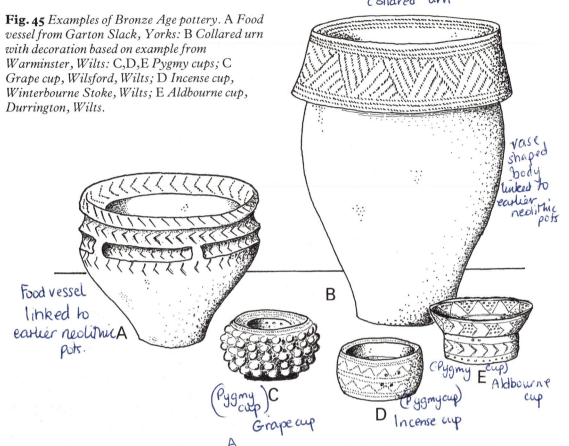

vase shaped body linked to earlier neolithic pots

Food vessel linked to earlier neolithic pots. A

B

(Pygmy cup) C
Grape cup

(Pygmy cup) D *Incense cup*

(Pygmy cup) E *Aldbourne cup*

A

introduced. Food vessels were heavy squat pots with thick rims, flat bases and lots of decoration, and had clearly evolved from neolithic Mortlake and Meldon Bridge styles. They are found mainly in northern Britain where they are bowl shaped. In the south a vase form with less decoration was more popular. As their name implies these pots were almost certainly containers for grain and other dry foods. They are much more roughly made than the beakers, most of which were clearly used as drinking vessels. As time went by a number of regional styles of food vessel evolved in the north, including a large vessel with elaborate decoration around the neck, which served both for domestic use and as a container for cremations (fig. 45).

Amongst early Bronze Age ceramics mention must be made of a series of tiny vessels called pygmy or incense cups. Normally found in graves, especially female ones, and often accompanying cremation urns, they must have played some part in the funerary ritual which we do not understand. They did not contain liquids as they are normally perforated, and the nineteenth-century identification of them as incense holders may not be too far from the truth. The vessels include grape cups, open-mouthed Aldbourne cups, and examples with rectangular windows in the sides, resembling models of Stonehenge-like structures.

All over Britain in the early Bronze Age collared urns made an appearance. Whilst some were used as domestic vessels the majority were containers for cremations. As their name suggests, the main feature of the urns was a broad, heavy decorated collar, above a vase-shaped body. Like the food vessels they too derived from earlier neolithic Peterborough pottery. Many complete examples are found in round barrows. Quite often they are buried in an inverted position, sometimes with their mouths sealed with clay, presumably to keep the spirits of the dead securely in the grave.

upside down

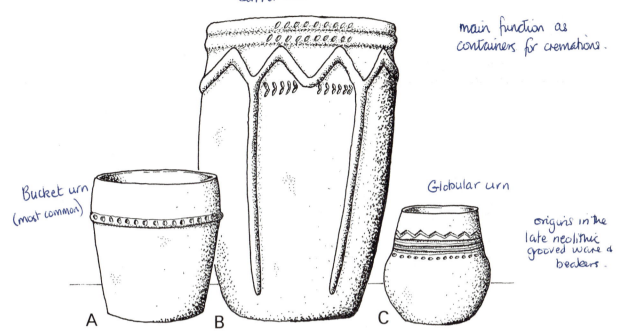

Barrel urn

main function as containers for cremations.

Bucket urn (most common)

Globular urn

origins in the late neolithic grooved ware & beakers.

Fig. 46 *Late Bronze Age pottery.*
A *Bucket urn, Collingbourne Ducis, Wilts;*
B *Barrel urn, Pokesdown, Hants;*
C *Globular urn, Bournemouth, Hants.*

Strong contacts with northern France and the Netherlands by the middle of the second millennium BC led to the appearance on both sides of the Channel of new metal types and pottery in the Deverel-Rimbury tradition. The pots were of bucket, barrel and globular shapes and had their origins in the late neolithic grooved ware and beakers (fig. 46). Their main function was as containers for cremations. Bucket urns are the most common and take their name from their shape and are usually simply decorated with fingernail impressions along the rim, or on a horizontal cordon. The barrel urns tend to have convex sides, being widest about half-way up their height. Fingernail-impressed vertical and zig-zag cordons of clay are used to decorate them. The globular vases have narrow rims and often incised decoration. In south-west England a local Trevisker style of urns can be recognized with plaited cord decoration on their upper halves, and in their earliest phase two or even four vertical looped handles on their shoulders.

By 1500 BC cremation had overtaken inhumation as the most normal method of burying the dead. The rich Wessex burials had come to an end and cremations were now placed in urns which were inserted into earlier round barrows that still retained their ancient sanctity. At Knighton Heath in Dorset, for example, 60 cremations had been placed into the top of an existing barrow, and at Latch Farm (Hants) 90 inurned cremations sprawled over the south side of a barrow. In other places large flat cemeteries appeared containing many cremations as at Kimpton in Hampshire, where more than 300 were uncovered, arranged in a series of overlapping cairns that were in use for almost a millenium. In Dorset, at Simons Ground, most of the cremations were in upright urns, but others were inverted, and some without urns at all. Often blocks of sandstone were placed above the burials as markers which could possibly be seen on the ground surface. Others may have been marked with posts. Surprisingly few cremations had been disturbed by later burials, further suggesting that their positions were known.

Collared urn burials seem to have taken pride of place, with Deverel-Rimbury vessels in subordinate positions. It was more normal for Deverel-Rimbury cemeteries to be placed on the margins of chalk land, and in the river valleys and coastal lowlands of southern, eastern and central England, where the soil was poorer. This has led to the belief that classes of society were developing with the collared urn users as dominant farmers and the Deverel-Rimbury folk perhaps as subservient cultivators. Just how real this divide was, it is hard to tell. It seems to have led to territorial divisions of land which are best seen in Wessex but can be detected in most other parts of southern Britain.

Agricultural activity

In spite of these divisions, throughout the second millennium farming continued to provide the basis for existence for the greater part of the population of Britain, which it has been suggested was then numbered at a very conservative 10,000 individuals. For reasons which are not clear this population was to expand

rapidly by 1600 BC. The country was still well-wooded except on the most exposed highlands. Large areas had been cleared for arable farming, but this clearance though widespread was patchy. On the chalk downlands of southern England, the moorlands of the south-west and in the large river valleys of the Midlands field survey and aerial photography reveal patterns of settlements accompanied by intense agricultural activity. By its very nature the dating of the evidence is not always clear but certain clues point to the middle and later Bronze Age. On the Wessex Downs linear field boundaries carefully avoid barrow cemeteries whilst some new burial mounds were built on previously cultivated surfaces.

Remains of field systems in many places give a false picture of the areas originally cultivated since modern ploughing has eradicated large sections, creating artificial blanks on maps where once there were extensive fields. Today we see only the fringes of prehistoric cultivation, often the marginal land no longer required or unsuitable for intensive farming.

Plate 36 *Low evening sunlight reveals the rectangular field system of the Bronze Age on the downs at Fyfield (Wilts). (Ashmolean Museum)*

Centuries of ploughing the richer land have destroyed the evidence of its former use.

Generally speaking, fields in lowland Britain were laid out according to preconceived patterns, usually on a rectangular basis (plate 36). People who were capable of carefully designing cursuses and henge monuments were just as capable of laying out their land. It was not done casually. Careful planning is everywhere evident. Long continuous land or field boundaries were laid out. Usually consisting of linear ditches, banks or wooden fences, they seem to have separated major land holdings. Inside these boundaries much smaller divisions were made. Fields were divided up on a broadly geometrical basis, into plots averaging around 70 m. by 50 m. (77 × 55 yd). Obviously they varied in detail depending on the local topography and geology, but normally areas of arable and pasture were clearly defined, the latter on water meadows beside a river, or on the upper downland. Woodland, too, played its part, providing fuel and building materials.

In highland Britain the picture was similar, though areas of settlement and agriculture were more limited. Uplands now devoid of settlement were once farmed, due to more favourable climatic conditions. The long land boundaries took the form of well-built stone walls, with lesser walls or stone banks and heaps separating the fields between them. On Dartmoor such walls are called reaves, and more than 200 km (124 miles) of them have been traced, often running in roughly straight lines, ignoring natural features such as rivers or steep valleys (plate 37). The soil of fields laid out on sloping ground was liable to slip and creep down hill and to pile up at the bottom against any obstacle – a fence, hedge or line of stones. This created a bank known as a lynchet, and gave some Bronze Age fields a step-like appearance (fig. 47).

In contrast with earlier periods when settlement evidence is scarce, we now know of a number of sites. Settlements consisting of circular houses built of wood or stone, together with their ancillary stables and work huts, were either scattered in isolated clusters amongst the fields or grouped together in walled or ditched enclosures. Saddle querns are invariably found, indicating the grinding of home-grown cereals. Droveways connected one settlement to another and also gave access to fields, pasture and watering places. There seems to have been little differentiation between the size of houses, suggesting that everyone was more or less equal.

On the Sussex Downs settlements have been

Plate 37 *A stone field boundary or reave near Kestor on Dartmoor (Devon). (J. Dyer)*

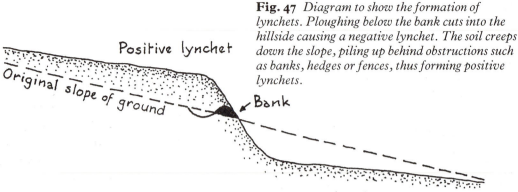

Fig. 47 *Diagram to show the formation of lynchets. Ploughing below the bank cuts into the hillside causing a negative lynchet. The soil creeps down the slope, piling up behind obstructions such as banks, hedges or fences, thus forming positive lynchets.*

excavated at Black Patch and Itford Hill. When Itford Hill was excavated it was described as a farmstead with at least a dozen huts, occupied for only a short period. Recently it had been reinterpreted as four successive settlements occupied for at least a century (fig. 48). A sunken holloway between fields led uphill to an embanked terrace on which stood two huts, one for living in with a porch, a second for food preparation, domestic chores and storage. After some years, perhaps due to an increase in family size, a second group of five huts replaced the first on a terrace to the east. The main living hut was again porched, with a cooking hut beside it. A second hut for food preparation and two store huts, one used for weaving, completed the group. Each house was set back into the chalk hillside, almost certainly with wattle and daub walls at the front and thatched roofs. Perhaps because of rotting timbers after 20 or 30 years, a third move was made a few metres to the south, where four huts were constructed in a banked enclosure, possibly topped by a hedge. Although on this occasion none was porched, two may have been living huts, one a weaving shed and the other used for storage. In its final stage the settlement was much smaller, the expanding family having probably split up and only two huts were required.

Some 160 m. (175 yd) north of the settlement was a barrow, excavated in 1971. It was unusual in containing a ring of 12 posts 5m. (5.5 yd) in diameter, set in a footing trench, with an entrance gap facing the settlement on the south side. Although the posts were substantial enough to have supported a building, the steepness of the slope on which they stood makes this interpretation unlikely and they were probably free-standing. At their centre was buried the cremation of an elderly man. On the slope outside the barrow were 14 more cremations of men, women and children, some in middle Bronze Age urns. This was almost certainly the family burial ground for the settlement. A piece of one of the cinerary urns was found in the living enclosure. The surface of the barrow was covered with knapping debris, suggesting that for some members of the community this was a favourite spot to sit in the sun and chip flints.

Examination of a similar Sussex settlement at Black Patch also produced a number of groups of huts spread amongst fields. Five adjacent houses excavated within one 'hut platform' were interpreted as two living huts, one food production hut and two store or stabling huts. Other 'hut platforms' investigated suggested a move downhill over many years. Evidence for food production indicated crop growing, animal husbandry, hunting and gathering. Barley, wheat, beans and possibly cabbages were grown. There were few animal bones, but those that survived showed cattle predominant, followed by sheep and pigs. Shells of mussels and other edible molluscs were present, as were the shells and seeds of wild fruit and berries.

In south-west England settlements consisted either of individual houses scattered amongst fields or grouped together and enclosed by a stone wall, frequently known as a pound. The best known and most accessible is Grimspound on Dartmoor. A wall 3 m. (3.3 yd) wide and 1.5 m. (1.6 yd) high encloses an oval area between two hills, through which a small stream flows. There is an imposing paved entrance on

Fig. 48 *The site of Itford Hill, Sussex as excavated in 1949 and 1953. Ann Ellison's reinterpretation is shown below, dividing the farmstead into four successive phases. Material found in each hut suggests whether it was used for living, sleeping or working.* (After A. Ellison in P.L. Drewett, 1978)

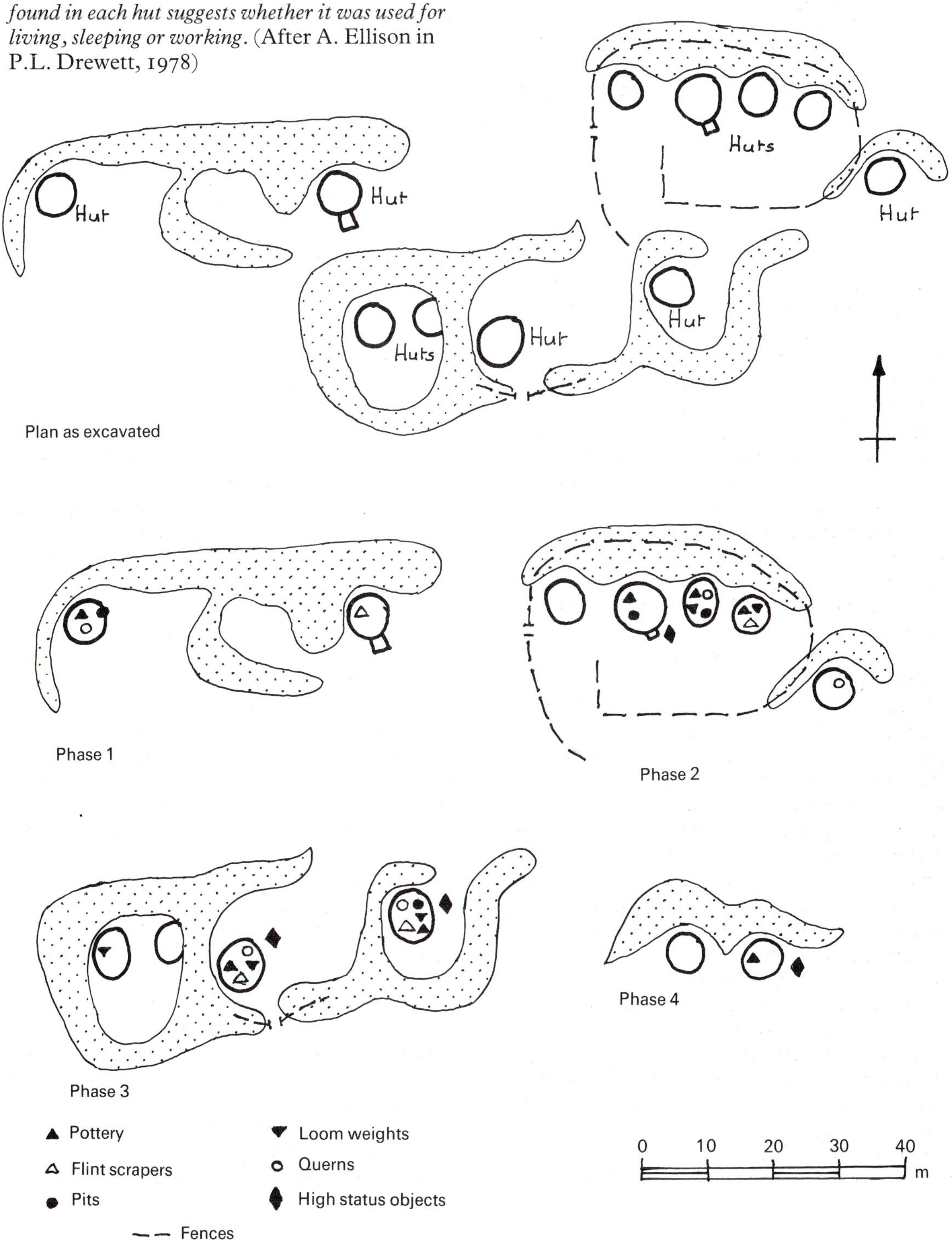

Plan as excavated

Phase 1

Phase 2

Phase 3

Phase 4

▲ Pottery   ▼ Loom weights

△ Flint scrapers   ○ Querns

● Pits   ◆ High status objects

– – Fences

0 10 20 30 40 m

Plate 38 *One of the huts inside Grimspound (Devon). It was probably roofed with reeds or turf and had a porch to screen the door from the Dartmoor winds (J. Dyer)*

the eastern side facing uphill. Inside were 16 small circular stone huts 2.5 m. to 4.5 m. (2.7–5 yd) in diameter with walls about 1 m. (1 yd) thick. Each had a conical roof thatched with reeds. Two of them had external wing walls to screen the door from prevailing winds (plate 38). Excavations last century found traces of benches and hearths. Beside the walls of the pound were five enclosures, probably used as cattle pens. It is likely that modern excavation would find traces of wooden sties and byres inside the settlement. The site is clearly non-defensive and with its enclosed water supply and entrance gate facing the upland grazing was probably mainly concerned with animal husbandry, though some cereals may have been grown in the sheltered valley to the south-east. The inhabitants may also have worked simple tin mines which can be seen on the side of the valley opposite.

Scattered lowland homesteads are represented in Cornwall by a site at Trevisker where two middle Bronze Age houses in a ditched enclosure were excavated in 1956. Both houses were about 8 m. (8.7 yd) in diameter and were built with two concentric rings of roof-supporting posts. The outer walls were probably construc-ted of turves revetted by stakes and hurdling, and the roofs would have been of thatch. One of the houses had contained the posts of a loom for weaving and two loom weights lay on its floor. The other building was most likely to have housed animals. It was later replaced by a rectangular structure with stone footings, and again it is suggested that this was used as a byre or workshed. Large quantities of domestic pottery indicate that the site was permanently occupied, with subsistence based on cereal production and the keeping of domestic animals.

No fields were found at Trevisker, but also in Cornwall under the wind-blown sand dunes at Gwithian (Phase II) near St Ives at least eight fields were found buried, associated with an enclosed farm with three wooden houses. Clear evidence showed that the fields had been cross-ploughed with an animal-drawn ard, which left V-shaped grooves in the ground. There was also evidence that wooden spades had been used in areas that the ard could not reach.

Farming, first begun in the neolithic, continued beside the fen edge at Fengate in Cambridgeshire. Herds were grazed on the fen pastures in summer and brought back to the fen edge fields in winter. Rectangular fields were laid out at right angles to the fens. These consisted of long strips often 50–150 m. (55–164 yd) wide, frequently separated by droveways (plate 30). The fields were divided by deep V-shaped ditches and subdivided by lesser cuttings with entrance gaps at most corners. Shallow wells to provide water for stock and for people occurred in some of the fields. Ditches and hedge-capped banks marked the sides of the droveways and the picture could not have looked very different from Cambridgeshire farmland at the beginning of the present century. It all formed part of a complex land-mangement system dated between the second and first millenia BC.

In Wales Bronze Age farming settlements have largely passed unrecognized. Both field systems and huts exist but are attributed to other periods. However this identification may well be incorrect. At Ty Mawr on the south-west slopes of Holyhead Mountain in Anglesey are a cluster of some 20 huts (out of about 50 recorded last century), spread out at the inter-section of cultivated land below and rough pasture above. Identified in the past as Roman, excavation and radiocarbon dating shows that they are really of late third and early second millennium date. The earliest huts were cir-cular and built of stone, like those on Dartmoor, and had walled yards or enclosures outside. Later, enlargements include bigger huts with thick stone walls and internal rings of posts to support the roof. Drains ran from the centre of one of the huts and emptied into a sump outside. The adjoining farmyard included a raised gran-ary, or stack for hay or straw, several storage pits, a stone-lined tank, an animal pen, and a midden composed mainly of animal bones and limpet shells.

The rectangular arable fields below the huts have formed lynchets on the hillside. One of those examined has accumulated 2 m. (6½ft) of soil against a bank of stones that formed the original field boundary. Plough marks running parallel to the boundary were found on the old ground surface. On the mountainside above the huts are walls marking more fields with large blocks of stone, often built in panel and post technique: large uprights with layered stones between.

In northern England evidence for farming settlements is limited. It exists in many high areas although not the most mountainous. Numerous groups of circular huts are known from the moorlands but remain undated. Large areas have been cleared of stones for ploughing, the boulders piled into innumerable stone-clearance cairns. Settlement took place on the North York Moors, the Dales and Cumbrian Fells. In Northumberland, barrows, stone clearance cairns and stones decorated with cup-and-ring marks are sufficient evidence to indi-cate mid Bronze Age activity and probable date for platforms with unenclosed timber-built houses and fields in the Cheviots and over the Borders in southern Scotland. Green Knowe in Peeblesshire, terraced into the hillsides, with nine hut platforms and finds of stone rubbers and saddle querns, is typical of this group of open settlements. Circular houses at Standrop Rigg had two rings of posts. The inner sup-ported the roof whilst the outer provided a frame for a wattle wall.

In the remainder of Scotland, on coastal plains and in the lowland areas, the pattern remains the same, with platforms cut into south-facing slopes containing the foundations of circular stone or wooden huts, and clearance cairns showing that arable cultivation took place as well as stock raising on machair and higher land. On the Moss of Achnacree in Argyll fields perhaps 200 m. square were enclosed by banks 1.5 m. (1.6 yd) wide thrown up around a stone wall core. Excavation provided a date around 1360 bc for one of them, but whether they were for arable or pastoral use is not known.

Whilst much information is available about the houses and buildings of farming settlements, some matters remain obscure. Provision of domestic water supply is a point in question. Many settlements are fairly close to streams but others on hilltops must have relied on roof-top run-off, ponds or occasionally shallow wells. Due to the lowering of the water-table streams that once flowed might no longer do so today. Cesspits are not normally identified before the Iron Age yet some sort of toilet provision would have been essential.

Bathing has recently been recognized in the form of saunas or steam baths. The sites con-cerned belong to a group known all over Britain as 'burnt mounds' and were once believed to be exclusively cooking places where meat was boiled or roasted. Large water-tight troughs are frequently found which were originally filled with water that could be heated by dropping in red hot stones. Michael O'Kelly showed that a 4.5 kg. (10 lb) leg of mutton placed in a trough of boiling water could be cooked in 3 hours 40 minutes. Roasting mutton in a stone-lined pit, also heated by red hot stones, took the same length of time. Whilst cooking was the primary function of most of the burnt mounds, it is probable that some were intended to produce hot water and steam for bathing purposes. A structure excavated at Liddle in Orkney contained a trough for heating water and half-a-dozen possible cubicles for the bathers (plate 39). Another from Cob Lane, Birmingham, had a radiocarbon date of 1190 bc (*c.* 1450 BC). Burnt mounds are often found in the proximity of barrows and stone circles which may suggest that bathing was seen more as an act of ritual purification, rather than one of hygiene. They could also have provided food for funeral meals.

There can be little doubt that the countryside

Plate 39 *The excavation of a burnt mound at Liddle (Orkney) revealed an oval hut with a central trough for cooking food by heating water and alcoves that may well have been used as sauna cubicles. (J. Dyer)*

was rapidly filling up by 1600 BC. The appearance of large numbers of weapons suggests that fighting and warfare were becoming commonplace. Perhaps as a result a few defended hilltop settlements began. Huts were surrounded by a bank and ditch on Mam Tor in Derbyshire, and a timber and stone rampart protected Dinorben in Denbighshire.

Mention has already been made of stones decorated with cup-and-ring marks and related designs. During the late neolithic and Bronze Age in northern Britain these developed into an extensive rock art. From Derbyshire north to Orkney carvings are found on living rock surfaces, mostly horizontal, but sometimes vertical, and sometimes covering several square metres (plate 40). Boulders were also decorated, as were standing stones and slabs used in burial cists. In almost all cases the softer sedimentary rocks were utilized as they were easier to carve.

Since the carvings are abstract and non-figurative it is impossible to attempt an interpretation. Cups, rings, concentric circles and rectangles, spirals and grids, all jostle for pos-

Plate 40 *Some of the finest cup-and-ring marks in Britain can be seen cut into the vertical sandstone rock surface at Ballochmyle (Ayrshire). (J. Hadman)*

ition on the rock faces. Because many designs occur on grave slabs and other ceremonial sites some would claim that they have a religious significance but it must be remembered that not all art needs to be religious and that there may be a multitude of explanations ranging from art for pleasure and prehistoric shepherd's doodles, to games and maps. Possible cup-mark stones have also been recorded in south-western Britain on Dartmoor.

The metal industry

Although farming dominated Bronze Age life, other industries and crafts also had their place. Most settlements had their local potter, leather-worker, weaver, carpenter and smith. Perhaps most important of all was the rapidly growing metal industry. The farmers were quick to realise its potential and seek new and more efficient metal tools. There was a certain amount of unrest in the countryside which required the production of new metal weapons. There was also room for innovation on the part of the smiths, who produced new vessels such as buckets and cauldrons, often incorporating pleasing ornament.

Early bronze objects were cast in matrices [a mold in which a thing is cast.] fashioned from stone or made of clay. The first were open moulds carved into a block of stone for items such as flat axes. Later two half-moulds were carved and tied together and the molten bronze poured into it. The resultant axes needed considerable forging to prepare them for use (fig. 49).

By the middle Bronze Age a new technique for casting bronze objects called the lost wax or *cire perdue* method, had come into being. A model of the object to be cast was first made in beeswax. It was coated with clay and baked in a kiln. The wax melted and was poured out, and liquid bronze was poured into the cavity. When it had cooled the clay could be broken and the casting removed, an exact copy of the wax original, ready for forging into its final shape.

By the middle Bronze Age onwards moulds

Fig. 49 *Moulds for casting metalwork. An open mould for flat axes, and a two-part mould for casting looped spearheads. The latter would need a conical 'plug' to prevent the shaft filling with solid metal.*

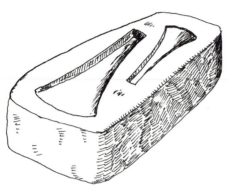

a kind of chisel made of bronze etc shaped to fit into a split handle.

fashioned in bronze became very popular in Britain. They were stronger than stone ones but could suffer if the newly poured-in hot metal welded to the wall of the mould as it cooled.

Whilst metal ores continued to come from Cornwall, Wales, Ireland and northern Britain, much reliance was placed on melting down old and broken bronzes. The scrap metal was probably collected by localized itinerant smiths or tinkers trudging from one settlement to the next exchanging new goods for old. In order not to have to carry the scrap for long distances they often buried it beside a trackway or barrow with the intention of retrieving it on their return journey. This they sometimes failed to do, and their cache is found today in what are called founders' hoards. On occasions the scrap metal was buried for safe keeping close to the smith's working place, as at Isleham in Cambridgeshire.

Other types of metal hoards found in Britain include merchants' hoards, consisting of good quality items ready for exchange; and personal hoards representing the wealth of an individual and buried for safe keeping. It is also possible that some hoards were buried as votive offerings, like the six bronze shields found lying in a circle at Luggtonridge in Ayrshire in 1780. A lot of scrap metal was brought to Britain from the continent, and in return ingots and finished objects of copper, tin, bronze and even gold

were distributed to those parts of Europe (and Britain) unable to supply their own needs. Sites such as Mount Batten (Devon) and Hengistbury Head (Hants) were only two of the many coastal ports through which the metal trade passed on its way to and from the continent.

After about 1450 BC four overlapping stages of metalworking developed, known chronologically as the Acton Park, Taunton, Penard and Wilburton phases. Bronze palstaves or axe-heads with side flanges, short swords called dirks based on European examples, and rapiers – long, thin, two-edged swords with a mid-rib derived from early Bronze Age daggers – all belong to the Acton Park phase, as do socketed spearheads with leaf-shaped blades and side loops, used to tie the heads to the shaft. By the Taunton phase the palstaves had also acquired a lozenge-shaped cross-section. Tools of the early Bronze Age such as chisels and razors continued to be made, and were joined by saw-blades, sickle-blades and socketed hammers. Bronze ornaments include splendid spiral-twisted neckrings or torques, and a smaller version made of bar bronze for bracelets, and tiny coiled finger rings. Pins for woollen clothing and hair were cast, including the curious and massive quoit-headed pins. Most of the metal objects made in Britain during these two phases can be matched in France and Holland, clearly indicating a copying of continental styles

metalworking { Acton Park / Taunton / Penard / Wilburton.

by the British, and perhaps some movement of people backwards and forwards across the Channel.

The Penard and Wilburton phases of metalworking lasted from about 1200 to 900 BC. A variety of new metal types reflecting social changes were introduced. Warriors appeared equipped with long spears tipped with finely pointed heads and swords copying central European styles that had replaced the rapier. Around their arms and legs they displayed elaborate bangles of twisted gold. Flamboyant bronze shields are known, and at least some of them seem to have been reserved for votive offerings since they are most often found in rivers. However, a shield in the Ashmolean Museum from the River Thames has been punctured by sword or rapier thrusts. It is more likely that most shields were made of wood faced with leather, which experiments show was more effective against a sword than a bronze shield. Items of harness equipment found in hoards at Heathery Burn (Durham) and Llyn Fawr (Glamorgan) show that the horse was being used in Britain, though whether for riding by warriors or for pulling waggons is not clear.

The smiths also learnt to work sheet metal to produce large buckets and cauldrons (some more than half a metre (2 ft) in diameter) and luxury items like trumpets. At first they could only beat out small plates of metal using socketed hammers, and these were neatly riveted into larger sheets. The invention of the cauldron created a culinary revolution. It now became much easier to boil food for long periods, something previously impossible due to the lack of a suitable container.

The end of Bronze Age metalworking is marked by the beginning of what is known as the Ewart Park phase. It is often seen as the start of an industrial revolution when a large variety of further specialized weaponry was developed, and carpentry tools evolved into new forms including socketed axes (fig. 50).

By the middle of the eighth century bronze objects equally at home in north-west France were also in use in south-east England. Amongst these were the long carps' tongue swords with narrowed points, bag-shaped chapes to protect the legs of warriors from their sword tips, and curious bugle-shaped objects which were probably part of horse equipment.

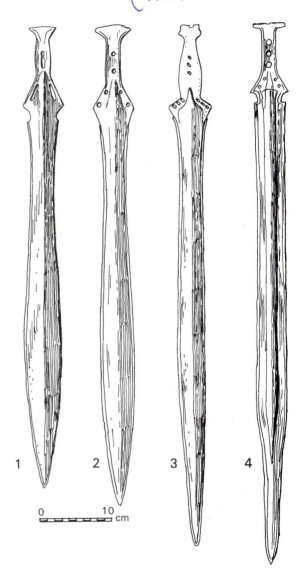

1   2   3   4

0   10
⊏⊏⊏⊏⊏⊏⊏⊏⊏⊐ cm

Fig. 50 *Late Bronze Age swords.*
1 *From the Thames at Battersea;* 2 *Ewart Park (Northumberland);* 3 *Ebberston (Yorks);*
4 *the Thames.* (After C.B. Burgess, 1968)

No sooner did bronze products reach Britain from abroad than they were copied by native craftsmen, who reproduced them on a large scale, presumably more cheaply, and distributed them most effectively around Britain. There is some evidence to show that even by the Penard phase in the coastal and riverine settlements of southern and eastern England an elite had begun to emerge specializing in metal production and trading, not only in Britain but also in north-west France and beyond. In return, food and animal products were provided by communities living inland, perhaps with cattle and sheep as units of exchange.

We have already noticed that many items and metal weapons have been recovered from rivers like the Trent and Thames. Indeed 75 per cent of all the dirks and rapiers known from Britain are from riverine sites. Most of the tools were ostentatious and clearly intended for display rather than utility. Though some facings of sheet metal were mounted on the front of leather shields and used for fighting, others

Plate 41 *The jumble of timbers found on the floor of the Bronze Age hall being excavated at Flag Fen (Cambs). Shaped and jointed timbers can be seen in the photograph. (Francis Pryor)*

could never have been used in battle. Instead it is logical to see them as votive offerings deposited in selected sacred places, in particular the sources of rivers, bogs and pools. There was something magical about the way that water burst out of the earth, particularly in the case of streams such as winterbournes, where the flow is seasonal and can be predicted. Water was essential to life and health, and yet it also had the power to destroy; as such it held a fascination for people which developed particularly towards the end of the second millennium and was to become paramount in the ensuing Iron Age. The water gods needed to be propitiated and this could best be done with costly military weapons in mint condition. It is even possible that human sacrifices were offered to the gods, since human bones and skulls are sometimes found with the weaponry as at Clifton in the River Trent at Nottingham, but this practice is better demonstrated with more assurance in later Celtic Britain.

offered or consecrated in fulfilment of a vow

like a ~~causway~~ enclosure causeway

Flag Fen

On the edge of the Cambridgeshire Fens near Peterborough lies Flag Fen, an artificial island built about 1000 BC and made up of more than a million timbers. It is connected to the mainland by a ritual avenue of posts 820 m. long. It is likely that a number of buildings stood on the island, but at present only one large rectangular hall 6.5 m. (7.1 yd) wide and at least 20 m. (22 yd) long has been uncovered. It was constructed with three aisles, and posts supporting a thatched roof. Many of the timbers used in building it have survived, due to waterlogging, although they now lie in a jumbled confusion (plate 41). Conspicuous, lying just off the shore in a lake of open water into which offerings were

Plate 42 *An aerial view of the complex of enclosures dating from the seventh century BC to the third century AD at Hownam Rings (Roxburgh). The earliest palisaded enclosure is not visible in the photograph. (Denis Harding)*

dropped, the site was one of prestige, perhaps a ceremonial centre, built by people who commanded respect and could control workmen.

There is however an alternative explanation for Flag Fen. Its position on an island might be for reasons of defence; further excavation is required to resolve this issue. We have noticed the great increase in military weapons, particularly swords in the south-east and elaborate spearheads elsewhere. There have also been hints that society was becoming stratified with peasants and farming groups, perhaps to be interpreted as workers and landowners with rich metal distributors somewhere in the picture. Weapons may have existed only as a prestigious deterrent, but it is most probable that they meant conflict between groups possibly disputing land ownership. The appearance of linear dykes to separate territories hints at land division between tribal groups.

can be a ditch or a bank

At the same time, around 1000 BC, the climate

[handwritten: 1000 B.C.]

was changing. As it became cooler and wetter areas of upland like Dartmoor and the North York Moors became impossible to farm due to the growth of blanket bog. The Dartmoor boundary reaves and Deverel Rimbury settlements seem to have been abandoned, so too was the marginal land, and there were new incursions into the chalk lands of the south and east. In northern Britain another natural catastrophe overwhelmed many impoverished settlements. Climatologists have recorded the volcanic activity of Mount Hekla in Iceland about 1159 BC. Prolonged clouds of volcanic dust blocked out the sun and caused low pressure and temperature, resulting in extremely high rainfall and cold weather all over Scotland and northern England. This led to an exodus of highland folk to the south. Settlements at Strath of Kildonan in Caithness were suddenly deserted, as were similar sites on the island of Noth Uist.

In Roxburghshire open settlements on Eildon Hill North were fortified with timber palisades for the first time, and at Broxmouth near Dunbar in East Lothian a large, circular wooden house was enclosed by a strong fence and guarded by dogs. Close by at Dryburn Bridge the same need for defence was observed, and this was repeated many times over in the Cheviot Hills of Northumbria. Hownam Rings in Roxburgh has become the type-site for this sudden enclosure (plate 42). Over many years it was defended by a succession of two palisades, a stone wall and eventually multiple earthen ramparts. Inhabitants of these enclosures seem to have been pastoralists who found their new defences adequate protection for their animals.

Together, the effect of tribal grouping and environmental stress in the uplands due to climatic deterioration, aggravated by the effects of volcanic activity, seems to have been folk migration from the north which caused pressure on land in southern Scotland. Ripples spread out across England leading to an increase in population and heavy demand on resources. This in turn led to the enclosing of many settlements that were formerly open, and the first attempts at fortification and the protection of herds and flocks against human predators.

Major changes were taking place in the countryside. The old familiar rectangular fields of Wessex, sometimes called Celtic fields, were beginning to disappear. Sinuous linear dykes,

with deep V-shaped ditches and often with banks on either side, perhaps planted with hedges, started to straddle the countryside, often running for several kilometres. Some included earlier fields within their bounds but often they cut across them, suggesting that the old arable plots were being replaced by sweeping ranches. The new boundaries usually respected the barrows that dotted the landscape, and often seem to have been aligned on them. Similar dykes were appearing elsewhere. Extensive systems are known on the Yorkshire Wolds, the North York Moors and in the Midlands. Shorter cross-ridge dykes found on the chalk of Wessex, Sussex, Berkshire and the Chilterns probably relate to this same period.

Ann Ellison has suggested that certain major palisaded settlement sites which appear at the beginning of the first millennium fulfilled the function of exchange centres for metalwork and fine pottery. It is not clear how they would have operated but an examination of materials, especially pottery, from the sites suggest that each was situated on a boundary between style zones and acted as a communal meeting-place or market centre. Suggested centres were Rams Hill in Oxfordshire, Norton Fitzwarren in Somerset, Highdown Hill in Sussex and Martin Down in Dorset. With more investigation others may be expected on Dartmoor, in Kent and the Thames Basin.

A group of rather specialized fortified settlements of the late Bronze Age, around 1000 BC are known. One of the best examples has been excavated at Springfield Lyons in Essex, where a circular area 65 m. (71 yd) in diameter was strongly defended by a ditch 1.5 m. (1.6 yd) deep, broken by six causeways, and a bank topped by a timber palisade. Inside were three houses, the main one with an elaborate entrance porch facing the enclosure entrance. Another hut may have been a workshop – the site produced an important find of clay moulds for bronze casting (fig. 51). Similar sites have been excavated nearby at Mucking North and South Rings, and at Thwing in Yorkshire.

At Thwing a chalk bank was piled up inside a massive outer ditch which was more than 100 m. (109 yd) in diameter and 3 m. (3.3 yd) deep. Inside the bank were the paired post holes of a box-type rampart. At the centre of the enclosure was an enormous building 28 m.

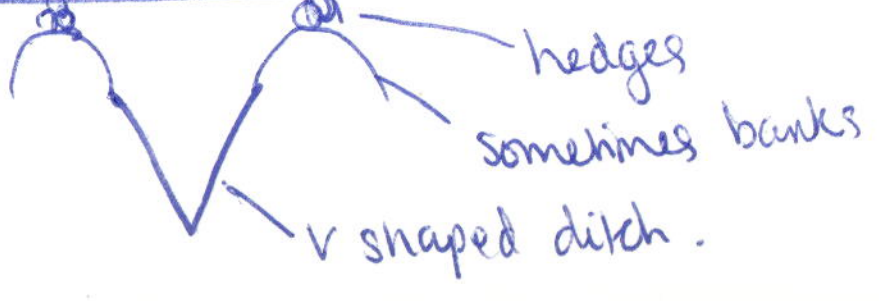

[handwritten annotations at bottom: hedges / sometimes banks / v shaped ditch.]

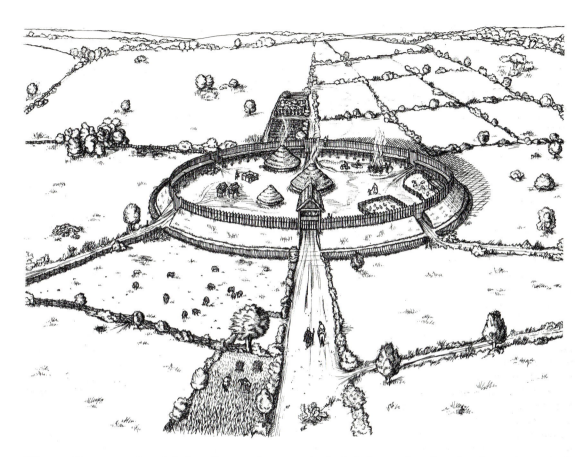

Fig. 51 *Reconstruction of the late Bronze Age settlement at Springfield Lyons, Essex.* (Tracey Croft)

(30.6 yd) in diameter, with an internal ring of posts 19 m. (21 yd) in diameter which would have supported a roof. At the centre a cremation was found in an urn – a dedication perhaps? The building also produced many domestic items including a saddle quern, loom weights and spindle whorls, personal jewellery and weapons, and lots of pottery. Animal bones included those of cattle, pig, sheep, horse and deer.

Hilltop settlements were in existence by 1000 BC that mark the advent of the hillforts and are found initially in the highland zone. Radiocarbon dates show that Dinorben (Clywd) 1032 bc, Mam Tor (Derby) 1274 bc and Grimthorpe (Yorks) 1058 bc were already established, often as open settlements soon to be fortified. Metalwork from Ivinghoe Beacon (Bucks) suggests a late ninth-century BC date for a lowland site.

Chapter Seven

The First Millennium BC

Continental influences

There has long been speculation on the amount of contact that existed between Britain and France at the beginning of the first millennium. A dense concentration of Hallstatt C cavalry swords in the lower Thames valley is especially noticeable. In other places like South Cadbury (Somerset) and Staple Howe (Yorks) continental razors were found. Whilst these objects can be easily explained by way of trade or gift exchange, intermarriage or warfare, we should be aware that there may have been incursions from the continent by small Celtic bands of more warlike adventurers, as well as traders and smiths. Some of the earliest Iron Age pottery in southern central England is very different from the preceding Deverel-Rimbury material, indicating a marked change in tradition; this is difficult to explain without suggesting the arrival of newcomers from the continent, probably also bringing with them the Celtic language. In particular, pottery of the mid-eighth century copies, on a much smaller scale, the metal cauldrons and other vessels produced on the continent. Bi-conical bowls, sometimes with omphalos (indented) bases, are totally new to the British scene, although they are found side by side with bucket and barrel-shaped vessels continuing in the local Bronze Age tradition.

Barry Cunliffe has drawn attention to the intensification of resource exploitation from about 800 BC. Salt, needed for food preservation, was being produced from seawater around the south and east coasts of England. At Walton-on-the-Naze (Essex) workings have been dated as early as 1070 bc, but sites at Kimmeridge and Droitwich were probably exploited rather later. The salt evaporated in large salt pans throughout the summer, and was then reduced by boiling. The raw material may have

been packed into crude clay containers known as briquettage, found on many Iron Age sites in southern England. Shale was quarried in the Isle of Purbeck and worked at sites such as Eldon's Seat (Dorset) into bracelets and pendants. Tin was still extensively mined in Cornwall whilst in north Wales, Cornwall, the Welsh Borders and Scotland copper continued to be exploited. In the Weald of Kent it is probable that iron extraction had not yet begun. Trade in bronze tools flourished, with the importation of axes from Brittany, exemplified by the finding of a wreck in Langdon Bay near Dover (Kent) containing a cargo of bronze implements and scrap metal. We can see the south coast of England and its immediate hinterland acting as a contact zone where intermediaries supervised the transference of goods between Wessex and south-west Britain on the one hand, and between Armorica across the sea to the south on the other. A number of sites in the contact zone achieved a reasonable degree of prosperity.

Hilltop enclosures

On the hilltops of southern England a number of extensive enclosures appeared between 800 and 500 BC. They all tended to be large and defended by one or two rather slight banks and ditches. Where excavated the interiors are reasonably empty suggesting that they were not intended primarily for human settlement. Limited examination of the south-east corner of Harting Beacon, a 12 ha. site in West Sussex produced what are known as four-posters, that is four post holes grouped in a square, believed to be the corner posts of raised buildings, possibly store huts or granaries. In Hampshire, Winkelbury (6.8 ha./18.8 acres) contained 42 four-posters, 3 storage pits and 6 circular wooden houses, whilst Balksbury (18 ha./44.5 acres) in the same county, surrounded by a dumped rampart, also contained four-posters and houses. Further afield at Nottingham Hill (Glos) double banks and ditches cut off a 48 ha. (110 acre) promontory whose sides are protected by steep natural slopes. Its well-ploughed interior is unexcavated. Nadbury Camp in Warwickshire is an oval, 7 ha. (17.3 acre) enclosure surrounded by a single rampart and ditch and bears a superficial resemblance to the group, as does Borough Hill, near Daventry in Northamptonshire.

As has already been said, the linking feature in these sites is their large size and apparent lack of occupation. It is possible that they were built as corrals and were the enclosures for the local community's cattle, or defensive stores for spring-sown grain, thus indicating some centralized authority in early Iron Age society. The four-posters can then be interpreted as granaries or we might consider them as the wooden bases of fodder ricks. Such a use also poses the question of water supply. Cattle drink a great deal. Perhaps there was daily droving backwards and forwards to the nearest stream. Alternatively clay-lined ponds may have existed, the precursors of dew ponds, but none have been identified with certainty. It has been noticed that early arable field systems seem to be missing in the areas of the enclosures, seeming to add weight to the pastoral nature of the sites. This may also be reflected in the nature of the bank and ditch defences which took hundreds of man-hours to construct. Cattle were a valuable commodity and needed careful protection. Wooden fences might have contained them but were of little use against determined cattle rustlers. Earthworks were much more difficult to drive animals across, especially when they were in duplicate, so we must most probably see this group of hilltop enclosures as a response to the pressure of cattle farming.

Plate 43 *The stern end of two log boats of probable Bronze Age date, dredged from the River Trent at Clifton (Notts) in 1938. (City of Nottingham Museums)*

During the first millennium BC the climate was slowly deteriorating, resulting in conditions similar to today in many parts of Britain. In Somerset excessive precipitation led to the growth of peat bog and the local population built new wood trackways across the marshes to facilitate communication as their ancestors had done in the early and middle Bronze Ages. Extensive flooding in the area also led to the use of log boats that could carry five or six people and their belongings (plate 43). Elsewhere in upland Britain blanket bog was already well-developed by this time. The intense occupation of Dartmoor in the Bronze Age came to an end by 800 BC, not to be reinstated until the medieval period. In south and east England pressure for land caused widespread forest clearance to take place, not only on the chalk but also on the lowland clay and less productive soils, where a heavier two-oxen plough made agriculture easier than before. In northern England, eastern Scotland and parts of Wales forest clearance on a smaller scale followed later in the millennium.

Small farmsteads and villages existed widely in most parts of Britain. These can be divided into isolated round houses, usually in enclosures, and nucleated groups of huts often linked by trackways and hedgerows. All differ widely in date, but in rural areas are remarkably consistent in layout and design between 800 and 100 BC. In the lowlands the houses are usually built of wood whilst in highland areas stone foundations are more usual.

Little Woodbury

Normal Iron Age houses were circular and varied in size, with diameters from 15 m. at Little Woodbury (Hut 1) to 10 m. (11 yd) at Shearplace Hill. The Little Woodbury house would have had a conical thatched roof supported on two concentric rings of posts. The outer ring of posts seems also to have supported the walls of the house, the gaps between them being filled with wattle work daubed with clay. On the eastern side of the structure a series of posts formed an entrance porch into the building, probably contrived to house double doors which would alleviate draughts that might prove disastrous in a structure with a central hearth. No obvious provision was made to allow smoke to escape, and it may well have per-

colated through the thatch, incidentally killing insects and helping to 'proof' the thatch, or filtered out through the doorway. Excavation of Little Woodbury in 1938–9 showed that the house timbers had all been replaced twice, and that it may have been occupied for at least 100 years. A second circular house was constructed about 12 m. (13 yd) east of the first. A single ring of posts 10 m. (11 yd) in diameter formed the outer wall, with a porch again on the eastern side. It is not clear if the second hut replaced the first, was contemporary with one of its phases, or merely stood as a stable or store.

With its central fire ablaze and the doors closed life in a round house must have been remarkably comfortable. Each was spacious, with extra room in the rafters for shelves and sleeping platforms for the children. Furs and woollen rugs would have provided warm coverings for wooden benches and beds. Lighting came mainly from the fire, though rush spills or even candles may have been used. A bronze cauldron, perhaps constantly on the boil, hung over the hearth, providing a smell of food that pervaded the whole room and mingled with acrid wood smoke that made the eyes smart and with the stench from the open drain. On shelves around the house jars of various sizes contained food for the household's consumption whilst wooden barrels and tubs held mead and water. Pans contained milk, some of it in the process of being turned to cheese. Salted meat hung from the rafters. On one side stood a quern with freshly ground flour lying beside it; elsewhere a loom was hung with a half-finished blanket. Dogs lazed by the fire, ready to scavenge whenever possible. During the winter cattle probably shared part of the same house, their body heat helping to warm the building (fig. 52).

Outside the Little Woodbury huts a yard was enclosed by a wooden palisade, which was in use long enough to need renewing at least once. Later the palisade was replaced by a ditch 3.4 m. (3.7 yd) wide and 2 m. (2.2 yd) deep, with a bank on its inside, enclosing an oval area of 1.6 ha. (4 acres). Neither the palisade nor the ditch could be seen as defensive and we must assume that they served mainly to keep wild animals out and domestic animals and small children in. Within the palisaded enclosure many post holes were excavated, some of which were either in pairs

Sussex

Fig. 52 *Reconstruction of an Iron Age farmstead of Little Woodbury type. Outside the central hut are various farming activities, as well as hay-drying racks, grain storage pits, raised granaries and beehives. A disused quarrying hollow makes a sheltered workplace.* (Tracey Croft)

or groups of four. The excavator, Gerhard Bersu, suggested most plausibly that the paired post holes, usually between 2.0 m. and 2.5 m. (2.2–2.7 yd) apart, once held drying racks for ears of seed corn or hay. The groups of four post holes, arranged at the corners of approximately 2 m. (2.2 yd) squares, may have supported granaries.

An extensive area on the west of the site was occupied by a shallow hollow measuring some 70 m. by 15 m. (76.5 yd × 16 yd) scooped out of the chalk. Dr Bersu interpreted this as a working place where threshing and parching of the corn may have taken place, but it was more probably just an old quarry. In addition, other domestic chores such as spinning and weaving, basketry and food preparation may have gone on there, or in various smaller hollows, accompanied by the daily chatter of a large family. Traces of corn drying ovens made of cob or clay were found around the enclosure. A number of post holes may relate to unidentified farm structures such as sties, byres, pens and beehives.

At a later date, perhaps contemporary with the digging of the enclosure ditch, more than 190 storage pits gradually appeared at the site. Varying in shape from cylindrical to beehive, they also varied in depth but averaged about 2 m. (2.2 yd). Dug into the solid chalk, they

Wilfshire — Little Woodbury
Dorset — Gussage All Saints

acted as silos for the storage of grain and would each have held about 40 bushels (14.6 cu. m.). The pits were filled with grain in the autumn and the tops were sealed with clay. The seeds which touched the damp sides of the pit began to germinate and as they did so they used up oxygen and gave off carbon dioxide which created a sterile, airtight atmosphere. Such conditions kept the rest of the grain in excellent condition. When the silos were eventually opened the majority of the grain was removed, perhaps leaving only the germinated seeds around the sides and on the bottom to be destroyed by burning in the pit. Discarded pits were filled up with rubbish or used as latrines. Some shallower pits seem to have been lined with clay and were used for water storage, possibly collected from the hut roof.

Animal bones from the excavations show that small oxen (*bos longifrons*), sheep or goats and a few pigs had been kept at the farmstead and were eventually butchered. Small horses and a dog had also been kept for a time. The former would have been used primarily as draught animals, but were also ridden at this time, sometimes by warriors. It is often observed that trousers were introduced during the Iron Age to make riding easier. Worn tight at the ankles, they were decorated with check and stripe patterns which may have been ancestral to the tartan series.

Clearly the growing of corn was a primary occupation at Little Woodbury and outside the enclosure there must have been a whole series of squarish fields from which the corn was harvested with small iron sickles. Traces of these fields can still be seen on aerial photographs. Once it was realized that farmyard manure scattered on the land, or deposited there by grazing animals, increased its fertility, it is probable that a two-field system of rotation was introduced. It has been suggested that in the Iron Age a corn yield of about 10 bushels (36 cu. m.) per acre might be expected. Consequently about 1.5 ha. (4 acres) of corn would be required to fill an average storage pit. Fragments of numerous saddle querns were found inside the enclosure at Little Woodbury, as well as the upper stone of a newer, rotary, beehive quern, which had once revolved upon a lower stone that could not be found.

Little Woodbury has been described at length since it represents a common pattern of farming settlment on the chalk hills of southern England, though others often differ in size and shape. At Ardleigh (Essex) the enclosure was much smaller, only 20 m. by 30 m. (22 yd × 33 yd), but at Hog Cliff Hill in Dorset it covered some 14 ha. (34.6 acres). Similar to Little Woodbury and completely excavated in 1972 was a 1.2 ha. (3 acre) enclosure at Gussage All Saints in Dorset, which has been shown on the evidence of its pottery to have developed in three stages between the fifth century BC and the first AD. The enclosure ditch was very roughly circular in plan with an external bank which may have been capped by a fence or thorn hedge. The main entrance on the east was closed by a strong gate of timber construction. Leading out from the enclosure during stage 2 were two arcs of ditch and bank known to archaeologists as antennae, which formed an impressive, funnel-like feature on either side of the entrance. It may have served as a symbol of the status of the farmstead, as well as being functional and guiding animals towards the gate. A similar feature is known from Little Woodbury but was not investigated in detail.

Owing to deep ploughing most traces of houses at Gussage had been destroyed. During stage 1 it was possible to recognize about a dozen four-post structures, 128 storage pits and half a dozen working hollows. One hut foundation survived from stage 2 together with more storage pits on the north side of the enclosure, whose ditch had by then been enlarged. The final settlement that spanned the last years BC and the first AD was more dispersed, with small internal enclosures as well as 184 storage pits.

The economy of Gussage was clearly arable and there was evidence for a gradual transition from growing barley to wheat during the life of the site. Iron tips from plough ards were found, as well as an ox goad. Livestock included sheep kept for wool and milk rather than meat, cattle and a few goats and pigs, more than 40 horses and about 30 dogs. The remains of red and roe deer show that they were hunted, and domestic geese, ducks and fowls were kept. Considerable debris from bronze and iron working shows that the Gussage folk were metallurgists as well as farmers and specialized at some point in the casting of bronze harness and chariot fittings.

a flesh fork?

Banjo enclosures

In an area roughly defined from Hampshire and Wiltshire north to Oxfordshire are about 50 sites known as 'banjo' enclosures (plate 44). Named from the similarity of their plans to the musical instrument, they consist of circular or semi-circular enclosures, with a long, parallel-sided entrance passage. These passages are from 15 to 85 m. (16.4 × 93 yd) in length, defined by V-shaped ditches some 4 m. (4.4 yd) apart. The external ends of the ditches often extend outwards in a sweeping curve to surround the original enclosure. Excavated examples at Bramdean and Micheldever Wood (both Hants) indicate that they were associated with normal farming practices. At the latter cattle, sheep and pigs were kept and spelt wheat was the dominant cereal. Although no houses were found inside the central enclosure this does not mean that they did not exist. Middle Iron Age houses were almost certainly built of stakes with a light framework whose traces would not have withstood later ploughing. The main function of the long entrance passage seems to have been connected with specialized animal husbandry, possibly being used for shearing, gelding, branding or slaughtering. Linear dykes, often associated with banjo enclosures, again suggest stock raising. A surprising number of infant and child burials were found at Micheldever Wood, either in the ditch of the enclosure, or casually laid in storage pits. This suggests that custom may have allowed young children to be disposed of within the settlement, whilst adult burial took place somewere outside.

—high protein content

Other settlements

At Draughton in Northants a circular enclosure about 30 m. (33 yd) across was surrounded by a bank surmounted by a palisade and an external ditch. Inside were three huts, the largest 10.4 m. (11.4 yd) in diameter, the others both 5.8 m. (6.3 yd) The excavator suggested that the settlement was occupied by a group of iron-workers exploiting the local ironstone.

In East Yorkshire is a small, steep-sided knoll known as Staple Howe (fig. 53). Its oval top was surrounded by a palisade in the seventh-sixth centuries BC. Inside were two circular huts and

Plate 44 *Two banjo enclosures revealed by aerial photography near Popham (Hants). (Cambridge University)*

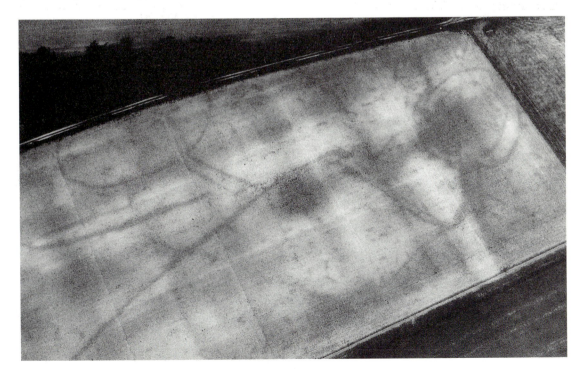

Fig. 53. *A reconstruction of Staple Howe, viewed from the south.* (J. Dyer)

an oval one, together with a massive rectangular setting of five post holes, interpreted as a granary. Other groups of four posts suggest storage sheds and masses of cattle, sheep and pig bones emphasize the agricultural nature of the site, with animals spread between the clay vale and the adjacent chalk downland. Post holes for looms and weights for threads show that weaving was well-established.

In northern England and southern Scotland palisaded enclosures are common, varying in shape from circular to rectangular. Their dates range from the seventh century BC well into the Christian era and can be seen as the first truly permanent settlements in that part of Britain, following the largely impermanent nature of settlements that went before. The palisades were set in bedding trenches rather than individual post holes, thus producing a closely set fence. Two concentric palisades 1.5 m.–3.0 m. (1.6 yd–3.3 yd) apart were common on many sites. At West Brandon (Co. Durham) a double palisade and external ditch enclose a single, large, round house and small pits for iron smelting. At Hownam Rings (Roxburgh) – see

plate 42 – a palisaded enclosure was succeeded by a stone-walled fort, which later increased the number of its walls before finally returning to a non-defensive settlement – a sequence that stretched over six or seven centuries. Throughout the north the same recurring occupational sequence has been observed, consisting of 1) unenclosed settlement, 2) palisaded enclosure, 3) single or multiple ditched defences, and 4) return to undefended settlement (usually by the Romano-British period).

In the south-west of England there were many open settlements of stone-walled round houses amongst extensive small field systems. Later these were enclosed, as at Bodrifty (Cornwall) where eight huts were surrounded by a stone wall which encircled an area of 1.2 ha. (3 acres). The huts varied in internal diameter from 3 to 8 m. (3.3–8.7 yd). The larger examples had hearths and were clearly lived in whilst the smaller ones may have been barns or byres. Some of the huts had small enclosures attached to them, perhaps forming sheltered kitchen gardens or animal pens. Pottery from the site included shouldered jars with finger impressions and open bowls resembling those current in eastern Britain.

Although Dartmoor was showing clear signs

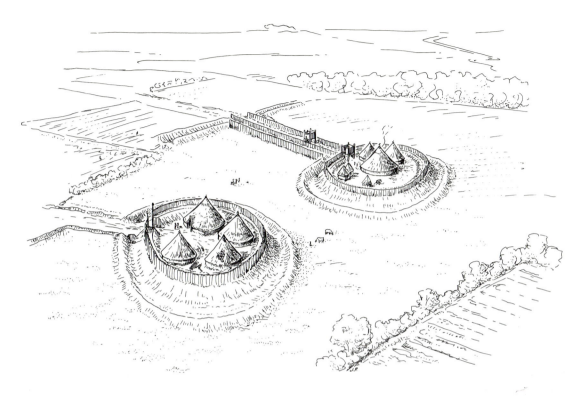

Fig. 54 *A reconstruction of the early phases of the Dan y Coed* (left) *and Woodside enclosures at Llanwhaden, Dyfed. The artist has drawn them slightly closer together than they were in actuality.* (Joshua Pollard)

of depopulation one or two settlements remained, especially on the eastern slopes. Round Pound beside Kestor (Devon) was excavated in 1951–2. It can still be seen as an upstanding walled enclosure 33.5 m. (36.6 yd) in diameter, surrounding a single round house 11.2 m. (12.2 yd) in diameter. The house had stone wall footings and an internal ring of posts to take the main weight of an irregular conical roof. There was evidence of iron smelting, though this may have been medieval.

In south-west Wales there is a profusion of small defended hut groups, but with little evidence of dating save that they are pre-Roman. A group of three banked enclosures, Drim, Woodside and Dan-y-Coed, were excavated near Llawhaden in central Pembrokeshire (fig. 54). Each was roughly circular, 40 m. (44 yd) internally, with massive ditches and internal banks and at Drim and Woodside the entrances were defended by wooden towers. Inside Woodside and Dan-y-Coed circular huts were grouped round the perimeter, with a slightly larger hut at the centre of Woodside, making provision for about 30 people. Four-post granaries were present and together with querns and spindle whorls attest to a mixed agricultural economy with stock raising predominant. Dan-y-Coed was occupied from the second century BC into the first century AD. In the north of the country at Castell Odo (Gwynedd) wooden round houses were surrounded by an unfinished timber palisade during the fourth century BC.

Chapter Eight

The Spread of Hillforts

Defended sites

By far and away the best-known sites of the Iron Age are the hillforts. The name is used to describe a wide variety of earthworks and is somewhat misleading since quite a lot of them were neither on hills nor functioned as forts. At its simplest the term covers any fortified site that is defended by one or more banks and ditches and encloses areas as widely varied as 0.1 ha. (0.2 acres) and 240 ha. (593 acres). In 1979 A. H. A. Hogg defined hillforts when he published an index of 'enclosures with substantial defences, usually on high ground and probably built between about 1000 BC and 700 AD, but showing no significant Roman influence'. The index included some 3,840 sites, the majority in central, southern and western England, Wales and south-east Scotland.

Whilst it is true that many hillforts do lie on high ground – Ingleborough in Yorkshire for example is at 716 m. (783 yd) – others like Holkham in Norfolk are at sea level and Risbury in Herefordshire is overlooked in a valley. Generally speaking a hillfort is a deliberately constructed fortification built of earth, timber or stone, situated in a position which will make it easiest to defend and can offer the best protection for its inhabitants. Whilst taking advantage of such natural features as steep escarpments and cliff-like rock faces for defence whenever they existed, the majority of forts relied on deep external ditches and ramparts faced with timber or stone, topped by wooden stockades. Forts with a single circuit of rampart and ditch are known as univallate; those with additional circuits are called multivallate and are often of more than one period. Whilst some ramparts were constructed in close proximity to one another, others are more widely spaced down a hillslope, giving defence in depth. In other cases there is room between the ramparts,

[handwritten margin note: 1 rampart and ditch = univallate]

possibly for corralling cattle, a feature which was developed in the south-west with a series of annexes outside the main fort.

Entrances

The weakest part of any hillfort was its entrance and consequently few forts have more than two. The builders went to great lengths to strengthen them and protect the wooden gates which were particularly vulnerable to fire and battering. Many early gates were simple straight-through affairs, but more ingenious works were constructed later at either end of long barbican passages, tucked into claw-like outworks, or set obliquely between staggered ramparts (fig. 55). Some were protected by guard chambers; others had a bridge over the top for sentry patrols.

It is worth noticing that sometimes gates were not actually present and entrances may have been blocked by felled tree trunks, as at Bigbury (Kent) according to Caesar, or by thorn bushes. At Crickley Hill (Glos) a wall curved outwards from the main gate forming a hornwork, from the end of which sentries could survey the whole of the entrance area. Similarly at Danebury (Hants) a curving hornwork at the end of a long entrance passage provided what the excavator called a command post, from the top of which a competent slinger could hurl slingstones well over 70 m. (77 yd). In other parts of the country extra lines of rampart in front of the entrance made direct access difficult and in some highland areas carefully placed grids of small upstanding pointed stones or posts called *chevaux de frise* served the same purpose, e.g. Pen-y-Gaer (Gwynedd), Kaimes (Midlothian).

There is a strong possibility that the more elaborate the entrance design, the greater would be considered the social status of the builders and the more impressive it would appear to visitors. Michael Avery has described the

[handwritten note bottom left: 50 cm – 1 m in height. close together outside fort walls. Makes access difficult.]

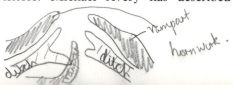

[handwritten labels: ditch, ditch, rampart, hornwork]

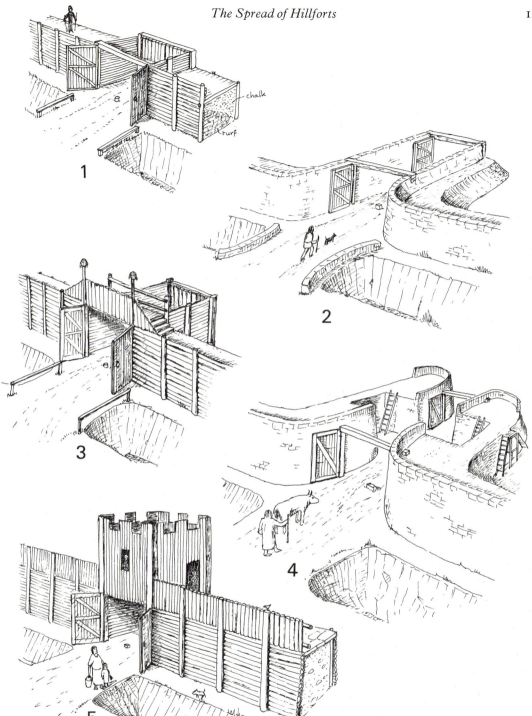

Fig. 55 *Reconstructions of possible gate structures in British hillforts. 1 Simple straight-through example of timber, turf and chalk; 2 An inturned design used in stone territory; 3 Inturned entrance with timber bridge over the gate; 4 Inturned stone entrance with guard chambers or recesses; 5 Timber entrance with defensive tower above the gate (a hypothetical example).* (J. Dyer)

earliest gates being protected by short range weapons such as the sword, axe, spear and stones used in hand-to-hand fighting in a continuation of Bronze Age traditions.

The elaborate entrances of the later Iron Age were designed to place the gate out of easy range of attack. Caesar in the first century BC describes his tactics: first clear the defenders from the ramparts by a barrage of stones and then move under cover of shields to fire the gate. Of course, these were Roman methods; the hillforts were designed for local warfare, but the same principle may have operated, with the defenders also hailing down stones upon the attackers. At Maiden Castle Mortimer Wheeler found pits filled with stones at the eastern gateway, 22,260 in one haul. Wheeler identified them as slingstones, though Avery suggests they were probably hand-thrown.

In southern England the rampart was often of chalk faced with wooden posts, turf, or chalk blocks. Excavation has often shown a sequence beginning with a single palisade, developing into a series of box ramparts in which an outer face of closely set timbers was tied back to a lower inner set by horizontal beams, the gap between them being filled by turf, chalk and earth. The latest ramparts are often nothing more than dumps of loose, slipping rubble known as glacis, although their core consisted of carefully laid layers of soil and they would have been capped with a wooden breastwork. Soil and turf used in the ramparts came either from external ditches or from quarries deliberately dug inside the fort.

In the upland areas of south-west England, Wales, northern England and Scotland, stone walls in a variety of local styles surrounded the forts. Some timber posts were set in a dry-stone wall; in others, vertical or horizontal timbers strengthened the structure. Alternating upright stones and horizontal layers of dry-stones are known as post and panel and occur at Maiden Castle (Dorset) and Moel-y-Gaer (Clwyd). In many Scottish forts transverse timbers ran from back to front of the stone walls, their ends often protruding from the wall face. When these timbers accidentally or deliberately caught fire the burning was often so fierce that the rampart melted and vitrified. An example of this can still be seen at Barry Hill (Perth). Forty-eight such instances are recorded in the Forth-Clyde

isthmus alone (plate 49). Some of the stone used in constructing these forts came from quarries near by; the rest was obtained from surface outcrops and scree slopes.

It is possible to divide hillforts into a number of broad types based on their siting (fig. 56). Those built on hilltops whose ramparts follow the contours are known as contour forts, e.g. Eggardon (Dorset) and Eildon Hill (Roxburgh). Where there is no suitable high land and the fort occurs on more or less flat ground it is identified as a lowland or plateau fort, e.g. Warham (Norfolk). If the sides of a hill spur were steep enough to offer natural defence, the neck of the spur might be cut off by one or two lines of rampart and ditch creating a promontory fort, e.g. Crickley Hill (Glos). If the hillspur jutted into the sea, with steep inaccessible cliffs all round it, the term cliff-castle is used, e.g. The Rumps (Cornwall) and St David's Head (Dyfed). In south-west England and south Wales are a group of forts composed of a number of widely spaced enclosures, usually on the slope of a hill. It is believed that these were for gathering livestock, and they are known as hillslope or multiple enclosure forts. On a much smaller scale a fort like The Ringses (Northumb) in northern England also seems to have provision for enclosing stock.

Hillfort construction

Careful study of two unfinished forts, Ladle Hill (Hants) and Elworthy (Somerset), has enabled us to follow the construction of typical plateau forts (plate 45). At first a shallow marking-out ditch was cut around the perimeter of the fort, some 3 m. (3.3 yd) wide and 0.5 m. (0.55 yd) deep, with a low bank on the inside composed almost entirely of the removed turf. Thus an area of about 3.3 ha. (8 acres) was enclosed. The next stage involved about a dozen groups of people who began to deepen parts of the ditch, piling the excavated chalk into dumps well inside the earthwork. Harder chalk from the bottom of the ditch was used to build the front of the rampart. More people were employed in cutting hundreds of timbers to strengthen the rampart. These were set up in two parallel rows about 3 m. (3.3 yd) apart around the inner edge of the ditch. Cross-timbers laced the two rows together and close-set cladding posts faced the outside of the

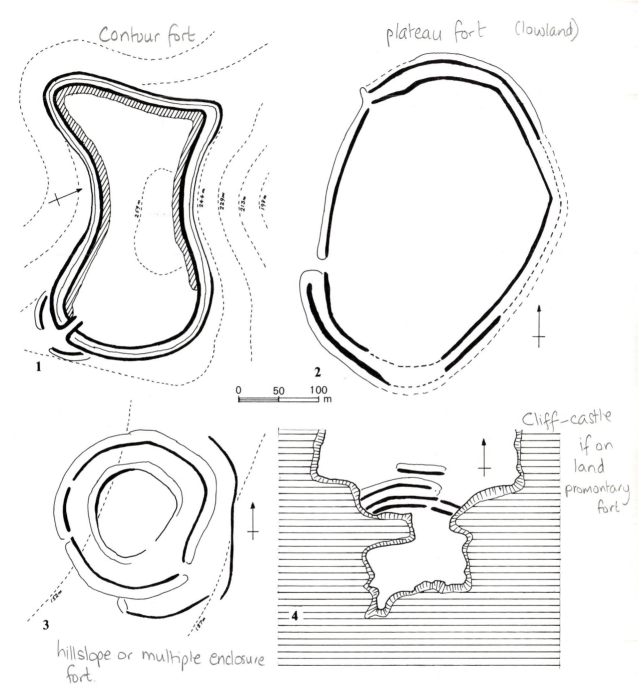

Contour fort

plateau fort (lowland)

Cliff-castle if on land promontary fort

hillslope or multiple enclosure fort.

Fig. 56 *Plans of typical southern hillforts.*
1 Contour fort, Beacon Hill, Hants; 2 Plateau
fort, The Aubreys, Herts; 3 Hillslope or multiple
enclosure fort, Tregeare Rounds, Cornwall;
4 Cliff castle, Penpleidian, Pembroke.
(1,3 after Forde-Johnston, 1976)

Plate 45 *Ladle Hill, Hampshire, an unfinished hillfort. The external ditch is clearly visible with the dumps of soil ready for building the rampart lying in the interior. To the right is a disc-barrow. (Cambridge University)*

structure. The gap between the front and back rows of posts was filled with turf and chalk to form a solid defence and to support a rampart walk. Extra care was needed in the construction of the entrances, especially if they were to incorporate guard chambers and sentry walks over the top.

It has been estimated that a medium-sized hillfort of some 9 ha. (22 acres) (e.g. Ravensburgh Castle, Herts) required at least 1,190 large timber posts and a further 17,850 thinner lacing and cladding posts. Not only does this indicate a vast amount of forest clearance, probably not surpassed until Elizabethan times, but thousands of man-hours employed in carpentry and earth-moving activities.

Interiors
The excavation of hillfort interiors shows that there were considerable variations, which must reflect their function. Careful planning seems to have taken place and distinct areas appear to have been set aside for dwellings and storage, often separated by streets. The majority of forts

contained circular buildings mostly 6–8 m. (6.7–8.7 yd) in diameter, but sometimes as much as 15 m. (16.4 yd). On some sites like Hod Hill (Dorset) huts took up much of the interior. Garn Boduan in Gwynedd still shows the hollows of about 170 huts of Iron Age date. Such sites can probably best be seen as permanently occupied defended villages. At Danebury (Hants) the early period huts were concentrated beside a street on the southern side of the fort, whilst much of the interior was filled with four-post structures, interpreted as granaries, and storage pits. The main road in the centre of the site led to the footings of a rectangular building some 4 m. (4.4 yd) square, which may have been replaced four times. This structure has been interpreted as a shrine, but in view of the concentration of granaries and pits around it with an enormous food storage capacity, it might be more appropriate to see it as the central exchange building from which orders for the distribution of commodities within the fort were controlled.

Conderton Camp (Hereford and Worcs) is very much smaller (1.2 ha./3 acres) and may well have been subservient to the nearby Bredon Hill fort (4.5 ha./11 acres). It contained the stone footings of about a dozen circular huts, each some 6 m. (6.6 yd) in diameter, accompanied by many storage pits, some of them dry-stone lined

Plate 46 *Storage pits at Conderton Camp (Hereford and Worcs). Those which cut into earlier pits have been stone lined, to prevent collapse. (J. Dyer)*

(plate 46). In contrast Arbury Banks (Herts) with an area of 5 ha./12.4 acres seems only to have contained one large round house and a number of small farm buildings.

Many of the circular houses were similar to the example at Little Woodbury described earlier (p. 118). The outer walls might have been of wattle work daubed with clay, or of vertical timbers bedded in a continuous wall slot; 1.5 to 2 m. (1.6 × 2.2 yd) inside the walls a ring of posts often supported the conical thatched roof. It would have been possible for the outer walls to have carried a roof on their own provided that the top of the wall was suitably bound by a ring beam which would prevent the lateral thrust of the roof timbers forcing the walls outwards. In western and northern areas the outer walls were built of dry-stone about 1 m. (1 yd) broad and 1.5 m. (1.6 yd) high, often with interior posts to help support the roof. Houses were thatched with straw, reeds or sometimes turf. Floors were usually of rammed chalk or clay or of bare stone, covered with straw, reeds and possibly herbs. A high standard of carpentry was available and door frames and furnishings were comparable to those produced in medieval times. It is worth comparing the interior area of these round houses with that of twentieth-century homes. A structure 8 m. (8.7 yd) in diameter had a floor space of 50 sq. m. (60 sq. yd), whilst one of 10 m. (11 yd) diameter (78.6 sq. m./94 sq. yd) was comparable to an average modern house with lounge, three bedrooms, kitchen, bathroom and hallway. Certainly such a house would be big enough for quite a large family.

The excavations at Danebury revealed traces of 21 stake-built round houses with walls of wattle-work construction. Their roofs may have been built in the traditional conical fashion and thatched, or the poles may have been bent over to form a beehive-shaped roof, which would then have needed some kind of weather-proofing. Similar stake-built houses may have stood at South Cadbury and Winklebury hillforts. The light construction of these buildings might suggests a temporary or perhaps seasonal function.

We should not assume that all round houses were intended for human habitation. They would have served equally well as storehouses, workshops, or animal and equipment sheds. Thousands of post holes found at places like Danebury cannot be interpreted but must have supported a variety of temporary pens and enclosures for animals and poultry, as well as corn and household drying racks.

Many of the four-post structures, together with six-post examples, seem to have been solidly built and may have supported a platform which stood about a metre off the ground. On this was erected the building proper, avoiding damp and excluding rodents. Whilst the usual interpretation of these as granaries (allowing easy access to quickly needed food) makes good sense, there is no reason why they should not have served an alternative function as storehouses for items such as skins and fleeces. Contemporary storage pits in the forts would have functioned as granaries for seed corn. Whilst most four-posters were too small for houses (about 1.5 m./1.6 yd square), they have been interpreted at Croft Ambrey (Hereford and Worcs) as barracks for soldiers in training and elsewhere as platforms on which the dead were exposed. Four-posters with less robust posts were possibly supports for hay ricks, suggesting the winter foddering of animals inside the hillfort. We should certainly be cautious of assuming that these structures all had the same function.

We have talked at length about circular houses in hillforts. Rectangular buildings are also known, although they are by no means as common in Britain as they are on the continent. Seventh-century examples are best recorded at Crickley Hill (Glos) where half a dozen houses between 10 and 25 m. (11–27 yd) long and well over 3 m. (3.3 yd) broad were ranged along a street leading from the eastern entrance. Structurally they consisted of two rows of aisle posts, with external wattle and daub walls, of which little trace remained. At Moel-y-Gaer (Clwyd) the stone floors of about 20 rectangular structures have been uncovered. Smaller than at Crickley Hill, they average 6 m. (6.7 yd) long by 3.5 m. (3.8 yd) wide and do not seem to have had earth-fast footings. At Credenhill (Hereford and Worcs) rectangular buildings 3.5 m. (3.8 yd) by 2.5 m. (2.7 yd) were found, but the probability that they had raised floors seems to put them in the four-poster class rather than that of dwellings. There is clearly a fine line of differentiation here and it is hard to decide to which group such rectangular structures as those found at Maiden Castle, Rainsborough and Winchester belong. Perhaps the answer is that they were general purpose structures such as workshops and storehouses.

The function of hillforts

It is time to speculate on the function of hillforts. We have already described some as permanently occupied fortified villages, but such a description could only apply to a few where many contemporary huts have been identified. In southern Britain it is likely that most hillforts should best be seen as either administrative or exchange centres, or centralized storage depots, to which people travelled in order to deposit or acquire commodities of which they had excess or need. Whether this was done freely or compulsorily – in the form of tithes for instance – we do not know. There is some evidence to suggest that forts like Danebury and Winklebury were only seasonally occupied during the autumn and winter months when animals and agricultural produce needed storing. In the summer attention may have concentrated on more fertile, low-lying pastures with ample meadowland for grazing and

hay production and a plentiful water supply. It is unlikely that anything more than an administrative staff of maintenance men and security guards lived permanently in the forts.

It is important to question the nature of the Iron Age society that dwelt in the farmsteads, open settlements and hillforts in the mid-first millennium BC. There is little to suggest the emergence of any major hierarchy at this time. Little has been found in forts such as Danebury or South Cadbury to indicate that they were the headquarters of a tribal king or chief. Extra-large houses or sophisticated artefacts have not been recorded and their identification as centres for storage or exchange seems more logical. Whether anything as elaborate as a centre for redistribution of produce was really needed at that time is open to question. It seems reasonable to envisage a fairly egalitarian society in which land was held in common and which elected a local council of leaders or 'magistrates' to administer the affairs of the community. Caesar described such an arrangement operating in Germany in the mid-first century BC. From common ownership of land we can expect common ownership of its products, all of which could be stored and cared for in the communal stronghold. Such a system ensured that wealth was equally divided and in Germany even the land was reallocated annually so that no one was favoured by ownership of particularly rich arable. Cattle, collected as booty after raiding a neighbour, may also have been divided although claims of exceptional prowess might have been rewarded with a larger share.

Consideration of the massive fortifications surrounding many hillforts suggests that the defence of the interior was all-important and we cannot escape the fact that all were capable of serving a belligerent function (plate 47). This would be in the control of the local council or 'magistrates' under the guidance of their elected or hereditary leader. The fortifications were strengthened and remodelled from time to time as necessity dictated and in response to local crises. It seems clear that a powerful driving force would be required to build such enormous earthworks. We have mentioned the rectangular structures, identified by their excavators as shrines, at places like South Cadbury and Danebury, which could perhaps hint at a religious presence. That alone is unlikely to have been

Plate 47 *The ramparts of Eggardon Hill fort (Dorset) were probably faced in timber and stone, making them almost impregnable. (J. Dyer)*

enough to generate the energy needed to dig and build for a half a year. Fear of attack and the loss of valuable commodities including livestock, foodstuff, personal possessions and perhaps personal freedom are great stimuli, and by the middle of the first millennium much of the countryside of southern, central and western Britain was divided up into hundreds of little territories of varying sizes, each with farms and villages and a central hillfort. In the east of the country the farms and villages existed but there were far fewer hillforts.

In peacetime the fort was the commercial and administrative centre for the area but in times of stress it offered protection to both people and their animals. For a brief period folk might crowd inside the defences, sheltering in temporary huts. As soon as the alarm was over they would return to their farms and settlements. Fighting may not have been commonplace but it was a threat and the fort would be kept in good repair, perhaps by a few days' work required from each man during the year. Fighting may have been between one fort and another over ownership of stray cattle, a disputed boundary

or grazing rights. According to later Celtic literature such skirmishes were short and sharp. Sieges were almost unknown, fortunately perhaps, since most forts lacked a permanent water supply and resort to hill-foot springs for drinking and cooking water was frequently necessary.

Although the great strength of many forts suggests that the fear of attack was always present many may never have seen any fighting at all, and the actual evidence from excavation provides few signs of real destruction. The first Iron Age fort at Crickley Hill (Glos) was destroyed by burning, brushwood being piled against its protective wall producing so great a heat when it was fired that the limestone was reduced to quicklime. Not far away a similar state of affairs was revealed at Leckhampton (Glos) where timbers in the eastern wall were ignited. In the Chilterns the skeletons of adults and children thrown into the ditches at Maiden Bower (Beds) and Arbury Banks (Herts) suggest disasters which brought a temporary end to both forts early in the fourth century BC.

Developed hillforts
At about that time, whether as the result of local warfare or of peaceful negotiation, many small forts went out of use, leaving only a few larger hillforts that seem to have gained control over

large areas, some of which correspond roughly with tribal areas known to us from later literature and coin evidence. These big forts were strongly defended, often with a number of banks and ditches and elaborate entrances, and their interiors were carefully planned along existing lines. Massive four-post and six-post granaries and storage pits predominated, but it was still not possible to identify new or extra-large buildings that might suggest that the forts were the headquarters of paramount chiefs. Even so, at this time it is likely that warrior chieftains were beginning to emerge. Expanding population allowed for the growth of a warrior population that could be called upon for military help when necessary. Such soldiers might find a base in the hillforts, though their fighting might often have taken place in the open countryside. It is doubtful if these men should at first be seen as standing armies. They were probably of farming stock, and had undergone a period of military training so that they could be called to arms and pay their dues to the nobility in the form of military service. As time went by more and more became professional warriors and developed the skills of combat and chariotry, so that by the first century BC well-trained tribal armies existed, and in the south-east could be called upon to combine their skills against Caesar in 55 and 54 BC.

The emphasis on forts as centres of storage and distribution seems to have increased as their more normal function from the fourth century BC. At Danebury (Hants) the defences were remodelled, occupation intensified and more roads were constructed. Hod Hill, Maiden Castle and South Cadbury all belong to this class which Cunliffe has called developed forts. In Wessex territories of about 150 sq. km. (58 sq. miles) emerged, each with a fort near its centre, suitably placed to reap the benefits of lush water meadows and fine hill pasture. On the Berkshire-Marlborough Downs, territories with similar facilities were smaller, about 100 sq. km. (39 sq. miles) around Uffington Castle, Liddington and Barbury. In the Chilterns, Ravensburgh and Wilbury may have dominated the same sort of areas. In parts of the Midlands, the Yorkshire Wolds and the Chilterns sets of dykes were constructed as part of a planned landscape.

Open villages

Scattered amongst the developed hillforts, but more often spreading over eastern England where forts are scarce, a series of settlements which we can best call open villages (some known since about 800 BC) now began to proliferate. An expanding population may have led to overcrowding in single farmsteads and the growth of nucleated clusters of houses in which the occupants could diversify their talents, for instance as metalsmiths, weavers, potters and carpenters, as well as farm and general labourers. Unenclosed round houses with streets and paddocks formed extensive groups which were usually located on the lower lying ground, and seemed to favour the river gravels.

Francis Pryor's excavations of the Cat's Water site on the extreme edge of the Fens at Fengate near Peterborough (Cambs) show that it dates from between 400 and 100 BC, and revealed more than 50 circular buildings. Clearly they were not all contemporary, nor were they all used for habitation. It was suggested that not more than a dozen would have been in use at any one time, perhaps occupied by a total of 25 to 30 people together with their animals. In general the houses were placed around the outside of the settlements, whilst the animals were penned in fenced and ditched enclosures in the centre. The site was divided up by numerous drainage ditches, made necessary by the high water-table so close to the Fens. Wild animals, fish and waterfowl supplemented the meat from cattle and sheep which the village produced. There was much evidence for pasture and meadow land around Fengate but cereal cultivation was poorly rep-represented. Four-post granaries were absent and the subsoil was too waterlogged for storage pits. A crucible with tin traces in it suggests that some metallurgy was practised at Cat's Water.

The construction of a bypass at Little Waltham (Essex) revealed part of an open village settlement (fig. 57). Fifteen circular houses were uncovered dating from about 250 BC. Assuming that the unexcavated area was equally densely occupied, we can estimate a total of 30 to 35 houses. They stood on slightly raised ground above the river Chelmer, and each averaged 12.5 m. (13.7 yd) in diameter. The hut walls were made of wattle and daub panels supported by substantial timbers 0.20 to

melting pot for metals

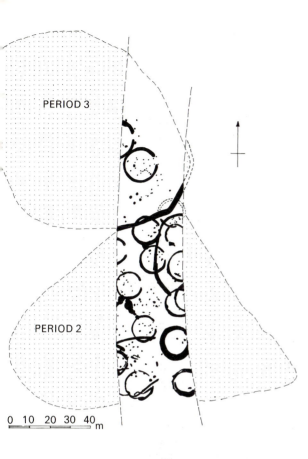

PERIOD 3

PERIOD 2

0 10 20 30 40 m

Fig. 57 *Plan of huts excavated at*
Little Waltham, Essex. The Period 2 settlement
about 250 BC was unenclosed, whilst a ditch
surrounded the Period 3 huts about 50 BC.
(After P.J. Drury, 1978)

0.35 m. (0.22–0.38 yd) thick which stood in
deep wall trenches. An inner ring of posts to
support the roofs was inferred from the great
span of the rafters which would have needed
internal support. There were no storage pits at
Little Waltham, probably due to the poor soil
conditions. Instead 8 four-post granaries were
traced and more than 30 two-post drying racks.
Bones of cattle, horses, pigs and sheep suggest
that a mixed agricultural economy was practised. Pottery bowls of local manufacture were
found in large quantities, together with everted-
rim and footring bowls transported from the
Mucking-Chadwell area of the Thames estuary.

At Mucking, also in Essex, the sites of more
than 100 round houses have been uncovered in
rescue excavations which are still largely un-
published. Little remained of the actual houses,
but the circular drainage gullies that caught the
water as it fell from the roofs were clearly
visible. Some of the houses were in small
garden-like compounds, but most were free-
standing. Pits and post holes were common on
the site, but were difficult to interpret as they
ranged in date from the Bronze Age through to
the Anglo-Saxon period.

On the south side of Bredon Hill beneath the
hillforts of Bredon and Conderton Camp lies
Beckford (Hereford and Worcs), an extensive
village of houses and enclosures dating from
250–50 BC and covering several hectares. The
enclosures seem to have been non-defensive,
their ditches most probably for drainage. Each
may have been individually owned. Inside were
houses marked by rings of stakes and doorposts,
cobbled yards, four-poster granaries and grain
storage pits 0.5–1.0 m. (0.55–1.1 yd) deep and
1.0–2.0 m. (1–1–2.2 yd) in diameter. Examination of bones from the site shows that cattle
and sheep were the main animals kept, but pigs,
dogs and horses were also present. Under one of
the cobbled yards a bundle of ten spit-shaped
iron 'currency bars' was found. (See pp. 136 and
166.)

On the north-eastern side of Winchester
aerial photography revealed an enclosure on
Winnall Down. Excavation has shown that it
had a long history beginning in the neolithic
period and continuing until medieval times. In
the late Bronze Age four possible post-built
round houses with west-facing porches were
constructed. Later a D-shaped enclosure ditch
surrounding half a dozen round houses, 24
storage pits and 19 four-post structures was
dated by radiocarbon to the sixth century BC. By
the second century BC the ditch had silted up
and an open village of 10 round houses had been
built over it, together with a large rectangular
structure that may have been a sheep-fold, and a
group of 80 storage pits to the east, along with
some 16 four-posters. Eighteen burials were
associated with the village, 12 of them children
or infants. They had mostly been buried in
crouched positions in quarry hollows and
storage pits. The only adult male burial was also
the only one with grave goods – a shale bracelet
and a bronze thumb ring. The economy of the

village seems to have been based like the others on mixed farming, which consisted of rearing sheep, cattle, pigs and horses, and growing six-row hulled barley and wheat (sown in the autumn) together with beans and peas. The pottery used on the site consisted mainly of saucepan pots common throughout central southern England by the third century BC. Pieces of briquettage vessels, probably used for transporting salt, were also found.

As with the hillforts of the mid-first century BC there is little in the layout of the villages to suggest that they housed a hierarchy; every one seems to have been more or less equal. Currency bars and salt containers are seen by some as symbols of exchange. Perhaps villages could also be exchange centres? In Somerset the marsh villages of Glastonbury and Meare produced a range of semi-exotic goods. Meare

Fig. 58 *A reconstruction of the Glastonbury lake village.* (Tracey Croft)

Village West stood on the edge of a raised bog. Its houses had clay floors but very flimsy superstructures suggesting that they might only have been tents. The village was occupied only in the summer when its residents concentrated on the production of a wide range of specialist crafts, including glass beads, loom weights and antler combs. Among the many other materials used in the village were iron, tin and lead, shale, bone, wood and wool. Bryony Coles, one of the excavators of Meare, finds the situation of such a prosperous village in such a wet marginal location puzzling – but perhaps it was deliberate. She suggests that Meare may have been a market centre, a meeting-place, or seasonal fair on the periphery of a number of adjoining communities, sited in a neutral 'no-man's-land' position, rather than a private hillfort: a clever expedient for keeping the peace. For a flourishing rural economy such exchange centres would be essential, and if she is right many more must remain to be identified.

Glastonbury lake village

The nearby village of Glastonbury was very different, partly because of the waterlogged nature of the site; it was excavated by Arthur Bulleid and Harold St George Gray more than 80 years ago and many otherwise perishable items have been preserved. It was built on an artificial island or crannog composed of tree trunks and brushwood and was completely surrounded by water, making it accessible only by boat (fig. 58). Alder logs, together with some of oak, ash and birch, had been felled on the shores of the lake and brought to the island, where they were laid in layers at right angles. The surface had then been levelled with bracken and peat, rubble and clay. A close-set wooden palisade around the edge of the site enclosed 1.4 ha. (3.5 acres). The posts, sharply pointed with axes, had been driven down into the peaty bed of the lake.

Within the enclosure were about 80 buildings, which were certainly not all contempor-ary, and only a few were major dwelling houses. A number of attempts have been made to reinterpret the old excavation report, and the writer is inclined to accept some of the views of the late Professor E. K. Tratman (1970), who considered that the village had passed through two distinct periods of occupation. At first square or rectangular houses were built, supported above the ground on oak piles. The builders were fine carpenters and all the wood was carefully jointed and the houses were skilfully constructed with walls of daubed hurdle work. After a period of abandonment, the artificial island was constructed around the ruins of the old houses, which were replaced by new circular buildings between 5.5 and 8.5 m. (6–9.3 yd) in diameter. They had walls of wattle and daub, floors of clay, some with central hearths and ovens, and reed-thatched roofs. The excavators observed the huts as low mounds, created by the build-up of as many as ten successive clay floors. Eight houses had wooden floorboards.

The most recent study of Glastonbury, by Bryony and John Coles, speculates that the village may have been occupied for 300 to 400 years into the first century AD. They suggest

Fig. 59 *Examples of coarse and fine decorated pottery from Glastonbury and Meare villages. The largest pot is approximately 24 cm. (9.4 in.) high.*

Iron age pottery usually black.

that as well as a series of dwelling houses, the village contained specialized areas for working wood and bone, bronze and iron objects and pottery manufacture. Most weaving and basketry probably took place in individual houses. Because the site was waterlogged numerous wooden objects have survived, including bowls and tubs turned on a pole lathe, containers and baskets, a ladder and a stout door a metre high. Turned axle boxes and wheel spokes belonged to chariots or carts pulled by pony-sized horses which wore iron snaffle bits and bronze terret rings, as well as old-fashioned bone and antler cheek pieces in a late Bronze Age style. The wooden handles of many iron tools such as sickles and saws, knives and billhooks can still be seen in Taunton Museum, together with weaving equipment and loom weights, local glass beads and fine pottery with beautiful flowing linear patterns (fig. 59).

Glastonbury also produced two iron currency bars; these were long iron bars resembling swords with rounded tips. Caesar referred to them in the mid-first century BC as one of three types of currency in use in Britain at that time, the others being coins of bronze and gold. Rotary handmills or querns were replacing the earlier saddle querns and were used to grind mixtures of wheat, barley and oats, some of which were combined with honey to make bread and small cakes or buns. Wild berries, acorns, parsnips, peas and dwarf broad beans were gathered. Meat in the form of mutton and lamb was most common, followed by beef and pork and perhaps horse flesh. This was supplemented with wild birds, including the pelican, and freshwater and sea fish. Perhaps indicating the inhabitants' relaxations were finds of bone and antler dice and dice-boxes.

Courtyard houses

200BC

As one moves from central southern England to the west and north, areas begin to display their own regional peculiarities. In western Cornwall and Scilly are about 60 courtyard houses, usually sited on fairly high ground. The best known examples have been excavated at Chysauster and Carn Euny where they occur in groups, but they are more frequently found as isolated farmsteads set amongst fields. A typical house was oval in plan and consisted of a central courtyard, sometimes paved, and almost certainly open to the sky (plate 48). Around it were ranged four to seven rooms with thatched roofs, the largest opposite the courtyard entrance. This big circular room was often raised above the level of the yard and was most probably the living room. As well as a central hearth it often contained benches and drains. Other rooms may have been used for sleeping, working, storage and perhaps housing animals. The houses were very strongly built with carefully designed granite walls often 2–3 m. (2.2–3.3 yd) thick. A number of the houses had small paddocks or gardens attached, whilst beyond were extensive field systems. Most courtyard houses seem to date from around 200 BC and continue into the Roman period.

Another feature of western Cornwall are underground structures known locally as fogous. Most are found attached to settlements like Chysauster, Halligye and Carn Euny. They vary considerably in size but consist basically of a stone-lined and roofed underground passage. At Chysauster it is very short, but at Carn Euny the passage is 20 m. (22 yd) long with a corbelled stone chamber 4.5 m. (5 yd) in diameter on one side. It is almost certain that these structures were cellars or storage places, where food could be kept at a fairly even temperature. As hiding places they would have been death traps. A radiocarbon date from Carn Euny suggests that some may be as early as the fifth century BC thus pre-dating the courtyard houses, but they continued in use throughout the later Iron Age.

Banked and ditched enclosures known as rounds are another feature of the Cornish and Devon countryside in the late first millennium BC. Essentially agricultural in economy they are difficult to define since they come in many shapes and sizes. Suffice to describe them both as farmsteads and hamlets, surrounded by a non-defensive bank and shallow ditch, and seldom more than a hectare in extent. Each contains a number of huts, usually sited against the inner face of the bank. They fit without difficulty into the pattern of enclosed farmsteads found in the rest of Britain.

Many similar sites also existed in south-west Wales where banks and ditches sometimes make it difficult to decide whether the site is not in fact a very small hillfort, since 50 per cent of Welsh forts enclose less than 0.5 ha. (1.2 acres). One such site, extensively excavated in 1967–8

Plate 48 *The interior of a courtyard house at Chysauster (Cornwall) with small rooms leading off from the central open area. (J. Dyer)*

was Walesland Rath in central Dyfed (fig. 60). Earliest occupation began in the third century BC with a settlement enclosed by a low clay bank and shallow external ditch. The western entrance had limestone walls leading up to a timber gateway. Over the south-east gate was a bridge or tower supported by six massive posts. The inner edge of the bank was lined with a continuous run of roughly rectangular wooden huts, with hard earth floors, occasional paving and indications that some had been used for animal housing. Evidence of grinding grain and metallurgy suggest that most of the buildings were occupied by people. Other circular houses with conical roofs stood inside the enclosures, together with at least one of rectangular shape.

The peripheral buildings at Walesland Rath have been compared with similar structures at Clickhimin broch in Shetland and various Scottish duns, and it is possible that they were a feature of contemporary sites along the Irish Sea coast. One word of caution; some of these buildings at Walesland may be interpreted as four-post granaries.

The northern Iron Age

So far our attention has been concentrated on the Iron Age in southern Britain. In most parts of Scotland after the climatic deterioration at the beginning of the first millennium BC, there was a gradual expansion of the population. Bronze Age traditions survived and there was cultural continuity through into the Iron Age. Regionally the country is very diverse, with sparse settlement along the edges of the Atlantic coast and in the north-east, and greater density between the Tyne and the Forth, and along the Solway and Clyde estuaries.

The most intensive research has taken place in the Tyne and Forth area and this might slightly distort the overall view. Tiny hillforts, often less than a hectare in extent, are thick on the ground there. Hownham Rings (Roxburgh), developing from palisaded enclosure to defended hillfort, has already been quoted, and this sequential pattern seems to have been common, though many palisaded homesteads existed side by side with hillforts. The excavation of Broxmouth, on a low hill near Dunbar

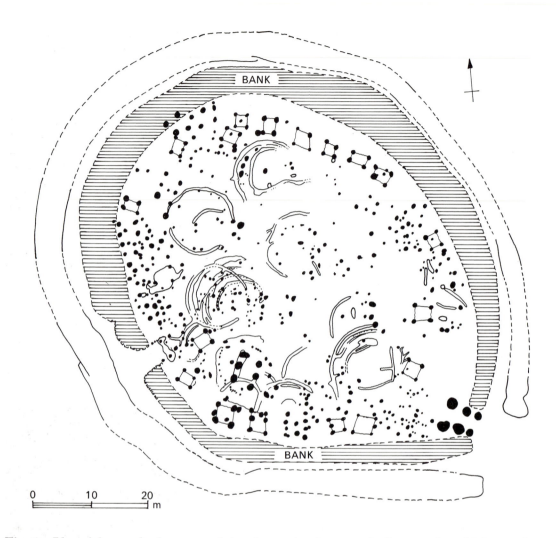

Fig. 60 *Plan of the completely excavated site of Walesland Rath, Pembroke, showing circular huts and rectangular structures, not all of which were contemporary. The excavator interpreted some of the buildings close to the bank as a continuous run of huts, but some of these could be interpreted as four-post structures as indicated.* (After Wainwright, 1969)

(East Lothian) revealed a very complex hillfort. An unenclosed homestead containing a single round house was succeeded by a fort with a single rampart and ditch. This defence was later doubled, and then reduced to a univallate form with a variety of entrances throughout. Five wooden round houses each about 11 m. (12 yd) in diameter, were detected in the fort, as well as

circular stone-built examples which were later than the defences. The latter had timber posts to support the roof and beaten earth floors. Later the floors were paved and the roof posts must have stood on stone supports. A deposit of ox skulls beneath a house wall may have been a dedication burial.

Most hillforts in central and eastern Scotland were timber-laced. This means that horizontal timbers were laid within the core of both stone walls and earthen ramparts, rather than being set vertically as in southern Britain. Sometimes when the fort accidentally caught fire (or was deliberately fired) the timbers burnt at temperatures over 900°C, causing the stones to fuse together producing vitrification. This is seen clearly at Carradale (Argyll) and Dunagoil

[handwritten annotation] 1 rampart and ditch

[handwritten annotation] Converted into glass or glass like substance.

(Bute). There has been much debate as to whether vitrified forts were the result of a deliberate attempt to strengthen the defences, but the general consensus seems to be against the suggestion. Although some very early radio-carbon dates have been obtained for timber-laced forts, a beginning perhaps in the eighth century BC seems most acceptable. Finavon (Angus) is the best known of the timber-laced forts which suffered extensive vitrification. Although only enclosing 0.4 ha. it is defended by a massive stone wall some 6 m. thick, surviving to a height of 4.9 m. externally. Excavation by Gordon Childe in 1933–4 showed that only the top of the wall had vitrified, perhaps because the upper section had contained more timber to strengthen it. The excavator found traces of timber houses against the fort wall, and hearths, a possible oven, domestic refuse and crucibles for metalworking. Childe also uncovered a

Plate 49 *Castle Law fort, Abernethy (Perth), showing the slots for timber lacing on the outer face of the inner wall. (R.C.H.M. Scotland)*

rock-cut cistern or well to a depth of 6.3 m. Such cisterns occur in other north-eastern forts, such as Castle Law (Abernethy, Midlothian) (plate 49).

This latter site, also excavated by Childe, passed through at least three phases consisting of palisade, single timber-laced rampart and multivallate fort. In the fort ditch an under-ground storage place or souterrain had been constructed, similar to the Cornish fogous. About 200 examples of souterrains are known from northern Scotland, though most are dated between the last century BC and the third AD. Those in Orkney and Shetland tend to be entirely underground, but in eastern Scotland they are only partially subterranean. As in Cornwall their function is uncertain though storage seems to be most probable.

The duns
Characteristic of western Scotland from Gallo-way to Lewis is a dense concentration of small stone-walled forts called duns. Circular or oval in plan, they have exceptionally thick walls

enclosing an area of up to 375 sq. m. (448 sq. yd) which contains timber buildings. The layout of the dun was often determined by its location on a rocky knoll or promontory, an island in a loch or occasionally on flat ground (plate 50). The walls were usually solid and stood about 3 m. (3.3 yd) high, often with an inward sloping batter on the outside. Sometimes they had timber lacing to give them extra stability. The only break was an entrance passage, often with door-checks and bar-holes. There might be a cell built into the thickness of the wall which acted as a guard chamber.

On top of a long ridge on the island of Luing (Argyll), near Leccamore farm, stands a well-preserved dun measuring some 20 m. by 13 m. (22 yd × 14.2 yd), enclosed by a wall 5 m. (5.5 yd) thick and still standing 3 m. (3.3 yd) high. It is slightly unusual in having two opposing entrances, that on the south-west with well-preserved door jambs and a bar-hole and slot for securing a heavy wooden door. On

Plate 50 *The dun of Castell-an-Sticir (North Uist) is situated on an island in a tidal loch. It is linked to the shore by a narrow causeway. (J. Dyer)*

either side of the north-east entrance are guard cells. The western one is carefully corbelled and contains a stair that allows access to the wall-head. To give the dun extra strength it is protected by an outer wall and two rock-cut ditches.

Dun excavations have not been particularly helpful in revealing details of interior structures but there is some evidence for timber buildings placed against the inner stone walls. A ledge or scarcement 1.5 m. (1.6 yd) above the floor of a dun at Ardifuar (Argyll) is seen as evidence for the anchoring of such constructions. Although we know next to nothing of their economy it seems almost certain that duns were fortified homesteads eking a fragile living from a difficult environment, and each jealously guarding its own immediate territory. The earliest duns may have originated in the seventh or sixth centuries BC but their type persisted until at least the third century AD. It should be pointed out that this part of Scotland was not occupied by the Romans and so an Iron Age way of life persisted into the first millennium AD.

The brochs
To the north of the dun territory, in Orkney and

Shetland, Caithness and Skye, appeared a series of tall, tapering, stone towers, clearly designed as fortifications and known as brochs. As Euan MacKie has observed, these were the only advanced architectural buildings ever to be created entirely within prehistoric Britain, apart from Stonehenge. About 500 of them are known in northern Scotland where some of them once stood 9 m. (10 yd) or more in height and over 20 m. (22 yd) in diameter (plate 51). Each circular tower consists of an inner and outer layer of dry-stone walling tied together with a series of horizontal lintels which bridge the gap between them. In this space, which is about 1 m. (1 yd) wide, are a series of galleries superimposed one above the other and a slab-built staircase which climbs clock-wise to the top of the tower. The galleries were probably intended only to lighten the weight of the tower wall, thus allowing it to be built higher. The total thickness of the wall at its base was about 4.5 m. (5 yd).

Plate 51 *Dun Carloway broch (Lewis) still stands almost 9 m. (9.8 yd) high. The galleries between the walls are easily seen, and the smooth outer profile can be appreciated. (Colin Ramsay)*

The outer wall of the broch has no windows and is unbroken, except for an entrance, and rises upwards for two storeys or more, with a gentle, inward batter, like an electricity cooling-tower. The inner wall face is sometimes broken by vertical openings called voids which allowed light and air into the staircase and relieved some of the weight of the walls, especially above the entrance. The long entrance passages needed to be strongly built to withstand attack. They averaged 1.5 m. (1.6 yd) high and 0.75 m. (0.8 yd) wide. About half-way along the passage were stone door jambs and a slot into which a bar could be placed to secure a heavy wooden door, to which was attached a strong iron ring handle, like the one found at Dun Ardtreck (Skye). (Confusingly duns and brochs are both called duns or duins in Gaelic.) Behind the door was a corbelled guard chamber in the thickness of the wall.

Around the inside of the broch ran a ledge or scarcement, varying between 1.5 m. and 3.5 m. (1.6 yd–3.8 yd) above the floor, which seems to have supported a wooden gallery which jutted forward on to a ring of posts. Higher up, a second scarcement probably carried a roof over the gallery. It seems likely that the central part

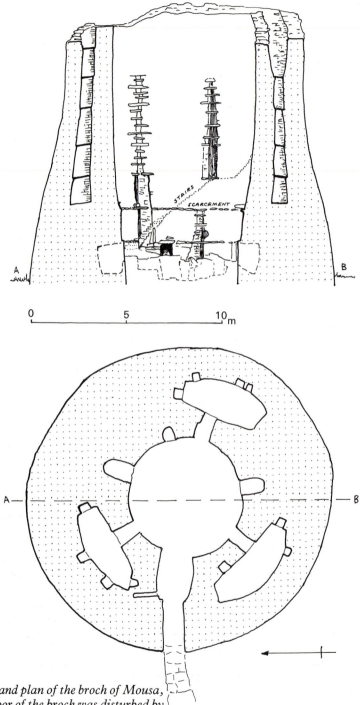

Fig. 61 *Section and plan of the broch of Mousa,
Shetland. The floor of the broch was disturbed by
later use of the building. It is unlikely that all
brochs were as high as Mousa; the majority
probably did not exceed 9 m. (10 yd).*

of the tower was open to the sky which must have provided problems in bad weather for the central cooking hearths that were often present, though storage tanks in the same area could have been filled with rain water from the gallery roof. Drinking water was often provided by a well.

Some brochs have outer defensive walls or ditches added, like the bailey of a Norman castle, which contain small villages of domestic buildings. At the Broch of Gurness (Orkney) there were sufficient houses for 30 to 40 families enclosed within three stone-faced ramparts and ditches. Enclosed buildings at the broch of Howe (Orkney) would have accommodated about 250 people.

Although there is considerable uniformity in broch design, on one point there is a major variation between those in the Hebrides and those in north Scotland and the Northern Isles. This shows in the ground plans which are usually ground-galleried in the Western Isles and normally solid-based in the rest of Scotland. As the names imply the ground-galleried brochs have cells and galleries starting at ground level, whilst the solid-based examples have an almost continuous solid wall of masonry at ground level, broken only by the entrance passage and two or three corbelled cells.

The classic broch is Mousa on Shetland, standing on a rocky headland guarding Mousa Sound (fig. 61). The tower is almost complete, standing to a height of 13 m. (14.2 yd). Although its external diameter is 15 m. (16.4 yd) at the base, the thick walls leave room for an interior only 5.5 m. (6 yd) across. The entrance passage leads directly into the interior with no guard chambers. Inside are three large cells with tiny wall-cupboards all set in the thickness of the wall. The continuous staircase passes up through five floor levels or galleries in the wall before reaching the walk-way at the top of the tower. The galleries were lit by three voids. Two ledges or scarcements projecting from the inner wall face at heights of 2.1 m. (2.3 yd) and 3.7 m. (4 yd) above the floor of the broch probably represent the floor and roof height of a wooden gallery, which could be reached from an entrance on the stairway. The interior of Mousa is now partially blocked by a wheelhouse-type structure of perhaps the third or fourth centuries AD, though recent work in

Orkney may suggest that this is contemporary with the main broch occupation.

Many brochs, though not all, stand on the seashore, and this has led to speculation that they were erected against seaborne attack by people united by maritime interests. It is likely that over many centuries they guarded the small tracts of good farming land that were dispersed in an inhospitable terrain, hemmed in by mountains and moorland. It is clear that in the closing centuries BC life in northern Britain was ever more turbulent and attack was always a possibility. The loss of livestock or personal belongings or capture for a southern slave market must have been a constant fear. The brochs probably acted as temporary refuges into which the local community could retreat to withstand a short attack or siege. It would be difficult for an enemy to overcome the great height of the broch tower which would prove impregnable to spear or slingstone. Scaling would be incredibly dangerous and battering of the door difficult due to the narrowness of the passage and the presence of guard chambers and armed guards. The excavation of Dun Mor Vaul (Tiree) showed that although the broch was in use for about 250 years, occupation was only sporadic and for short periods.

There have been years of debate regarding the origin of the brochs. It now seems likely that they developed in the Orkneys as prestigious fortified towers. Recent study has begun to show various round houses that could be claimed as ancestral to them there. That they can have originated in the mid-first millennium BC is shown by a radiocarbon date around 600 BC that has been obtained for the demolished broch site at Bu, near Stromness (Orkney). To the south-west, in the Hebrides, Dun Ardtreck on Skye has given a radiocarbon date of 115 BC. As has already been suggested, the great similarity between the brochs reflects a certain unity amongst the people of north-western Scotland, which may have led to a specialist group of local architects responsible for their design, who travelled from one community to another and passed on their knowledge from one generation to another. It is clear, however, that not all of them were built with the same degree of sophistication.

Crannogs

All over Scotland, but particularly in the west, are small, artificially constructed islands in lochs, marshes, rivers and estuaries known as crannogs. They were built of timber, brush-wood or stones and often utilized natural features on the lake bed to give them greater stability. Many began as wooden platforms which were later reinforced with boulders and it is these which now appear as stone mounds protruding above the surface of a loch, or in reclaimed fields close to the water's edge.

On the islands stood wooden buildings, usually circular huts, although rectangular ones are known. It is assumed that these were permanent dwellings which would also have served as refuges in times of emergency, providing safe store huts for food and livestock away from predators and vermin and also acting as fishing and fowling bases. Some were connected to the shore by stone or wooden causeways and it is likely that good farming land existed close by. From time to time log boats have been found offering an alternative means of access. Although excavated sites such as Milton Loch (Kirkcudbright) give dates in the fifth century BC, and Lochmaben (Dumfries) in the first century BC, it is very clear that crannogs were built over an excessively long period from early in the first millennium BC until at least the sixteenth century AD.

Mrs C. M. Piggot's excavation of one of the crannogs in Milton Loch in 1953 is one of the

Fig. 62 *Reconstruction of the crannog on Milton Loch excavated in 1953.* (Tracey Croft)

best documented (fig. 62). An island constructed of timbers over clay lay some 35 m. (38 yd) from the present shoreline, to which it was connected by a wooden causeway. It had its own small wooden jetty and harbour leading out into deep water, which was partially supported by a rock outcrop. The island was mainly occupied by a round house with a conical reed-thatched roof. It was 12.8 m. (14 yd) in diameter, and had been partitioned into a series of rooms, one with a central hearth. Around the edge was a gangway 1.5 m. (1.6 yd) wide supported on a framework of stout wooden piles.

The plough head and stilt of a wooden ard was uncovered beneath the foundations and was dated to 460–500 BC; an enamelled bronze dress-fastener from within the house dated from the second century AD. These divergent dates suggest an intermittent use of the crannog over some seven centuries, and any attempt to interpret the excavation should bear in mind that all the features uncovered were not necessarily contemporary. Fragments of a quern and a spindle-whorl, together with the plough ard, suggest a simple economy of mixed farming on the loch shore, supplemented by fishing and fowling, during the late Iron Age.

Wheelhouses

One final group of buildings remains to be described, found mainly in the Outer Hebrides and, to a lesser extent, in the Northern Isles. Known as wheelhouses, these structures are usually circular and are divided up into compartments by internal stone walls arranged like the spokes of a wheel, with an open central area, often occupied by a stone hearth. In some examples, known as aisled wheelhouses the radial walls are separated from the house wall by a narrow gap. Wheelhouses can be free-standing structures but more often they are sunk into a sand dune, the inner wall acting as a revetment against unstable sand. The radial walls must have helped support the roof which may well have been strengthened with rafters of whale bone, there being no local wood.

At Middlequarter, Sollas on North Uist the refuse from the house was piled in a midden over its roof, creating a virtually subterranean structure, entered from a long, funnel-shaped passage (plate 52; fig. 63). The central room, about 9 m. (9.8 yd) in diameter, was divided into 12 bays, each wide enough to sleep two or three persons, or to act as store rooms. On one side a door led into an extramural oval chamber. Beside the central hearth, a stone-lined pit was used for storing water or shellfish. A stone quern indicated that grain had been grown and ground. The most bizarre feature of the Sollas wheelhouse was the discovery of some 200 sheep buried beneath the floor, mostly head downwards in small, conical pits. On the island of South Uist at the wheelhouse of A Cheardach Bheag some 20 deer jawbones had been set in an arc around the central hearth, and at the neighbouring site of A Cheardach Mhor 32 ox teeth were found beside one of the piers.

Wheelhouses usually occur close to fertile machair land and are not defended in any way. They seem to have been the Iron Age equivalent of the modern island croft. There is no clear dating for the beginning of wheelhouses although there are good reasons for thinking that they follow the demise of the brochs, their open, unprotected sites perhaps indicating less troublesome times. They seem to have flourished in the later Scottish Iron Age of the second to fifth centuries AD.

Plate 52 *The wheelhouse at Middlequarter (North Uist) during excavation in 1957. The entrance is on the left. The floor has been disturbed by pits containing the remains of sheep. (J. Dyer)*

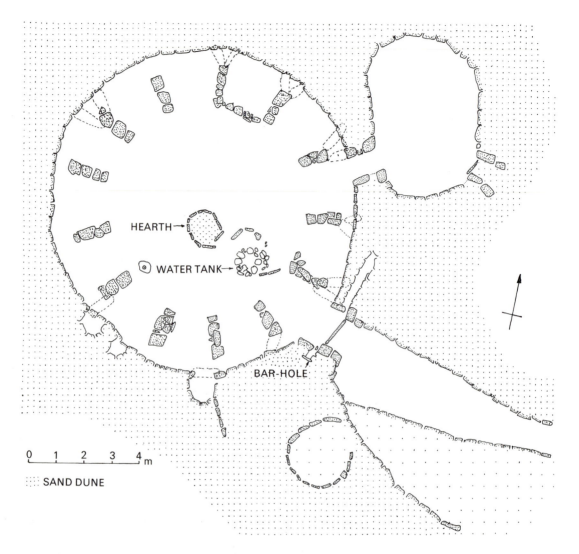

HEARTH→

WATER TANK→

BAR-HOLE

0 1 2 3 4
m

SAND DUNE

Fig. 63 *The aisled wheelhouse at Middlequarter, Sollas, North Uist was inserted into a sand dune. It may have been partially roofed over, with an opening above the hearth. The door could be sealed by a draw-bar. There were cupboards in the house walls. The structure is unusual in having an additional side chamber on the north-east.* (R.J.C. Atkinson)

Metalwork

Iron was manufactured in Britain by the seventh century BC and was used for making a variety of tools and weapons. By the first century BC it was being extensively worked in many places, including the Weald of Kent, the Forest of Dean and the ironstone regions of Northamptonshire and Oxfordshire. Bronze still remained the favourite material for the more prestigious items, especially personal ornaments such as brooches and pins, many of which were based on styles which were popular on the continent. These styles are named after two successive Iron Age cultures, called Hallstatt and La Tène, after sites in Austria and Switzerland where this material was first found. The transition between the two took place around 500 BC. It was at that time that the first brooches in early La Tène forms reached Britain and they were soon copied. Essentially they were of safety-pin design but they became

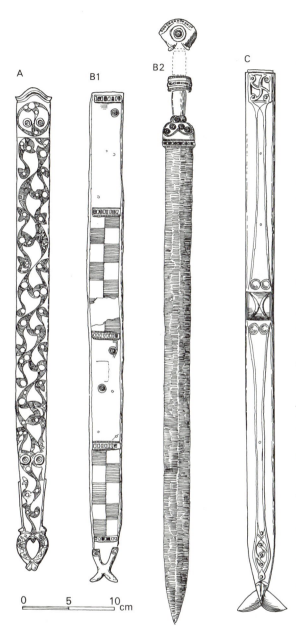

more elaborate as fashions changed and the Iron Age progressed.

Bronze swords of Gundlingen type (Hallstatt C about 700 BC) have been found in large numbers in the middle Thames valley and up the eastern coast of Scotland. Some may be British-made copies of continental originals but how the originals reached Britain is unknown (fig. 64). Some archaeologists favour the theory of infiltration by a small group of warriors: the exchange of gifts or the employment of foreign mercenaries seems equally plausible. The swords were protected by sheaths made of wood or leather, terminating in a winged chape. This device is believed to have been devised to allow a mounted rider to steady his sheath with his feet whilst he drew his sword.

A century later swords passed briefly out of fashion in favour of iron daggers, again based on European originals, which continued in use until the end of the third century BC. Some of the dagger sheaths were decorated in a simple La Tène art style (see below). Around 300 BC iron swords, some influenced by the European La Tène types and others being local derivations, made a reappearance, their scabbards often elaborately decorated. Careful study of the swords had made it possible for at least six regional groups to be recognized in Britain; these remained in use up to the time of the Roman conquest.

Shields were normally made of wood covered in leather, with iron bosses to protect the hand, but prestige items were fashioned in bronze (backed with wood) and were highly ornamented. Examples like those found in the River Witham (Lincoln) and the Thames at Battersea (London) (plate 53) would have been created for rich patrons. The splendid horned helmet from Waterloo Bridge adds to our knowledge of military equipment and was richly decorated with tendril patterns highlighted with red glass roundels.

Fig. 64 *Iron Age sheaths and sword: A Bugthorpe, North Humberside; B1 and B2 sheath and sword from Embleton, Cumbria; C Morton Hall, Edinburgh. The Bugthorpe scabbard is a particularly fine example of the type of Celtic art known as the 'mirror style', made up of many segments of finely hatched design.* (After Piggott, 1950)

La Tène art

La Tène art originated in Europe during the fifth century BC and very soon after its influence reached Britain where it was copied and developed along new lines until it surpassed much that was appearing on the continent. The original elements consisted of geometric abstract designs, archaic oriental symbols and

of an earlier period

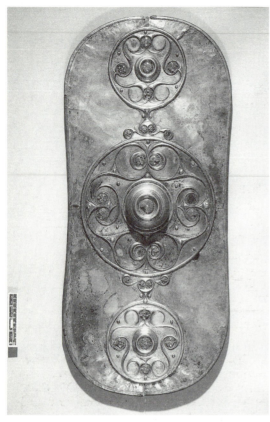

Plate 53 *Dredged from the River Thames at Battersea, this shield is one of the finest examples of Celtic art to be found in Britain. It was probably a ritual piece flung into the river to placate a Celtic god. (British Museum)*

classical plant decoration. Combinations of these were used to decorate a great variety of objects of bronze, iron and gold, which were sometimes also enhanced with red glass (often called enamel) or coral. These varied from simple pieces of personal jewellery such as pins, brooches, bracelets and finger rings, to the magnificent gold neck rings or torques, like those found by a ploughman at Snettisham in Norfolk in 1948 and 1950, and a builder at Ipswich in 1968. A number of bronze mirrors have been found, their faces of polished metal and their backs elaborately engraved with intricate patterns. Being heavy, they were probably suspended from their looped handles.

Even households items like iron firedogs,

bronze buckets and tankards were ornamented. Mention has already been made of the decoration on prestigious swords and daggers, and this was also extended to harness and chariot fittings. Known on the continent some centuries previously, where it had become obsolete as a war vehicle, the chariot continued in use in Britain during the first century BC.

Iron Age pottery

For most of the Iron Age pottery continued to be hand-made in the late Bronze Age tradition although this does not mean that it did not include extremely fine biscuit-like wares. The material (800–600 BC) from sites such as Ram's Hill (Berks) and Ivinghoe Beacon (Bucks) consists of large, tall jars, often with an angular profile and fingertip decoration. After this, between 600 and 300 BC, in lowland Britain three types of pottery dominate; angular tripartite bowls with incised patterns, rounded jars with pedestal bases, and bowls with flaring rims, rounded body and pedestal or omphalos (a navel-like depression) bases (fig. 65). Sometimes in Wessex these latter bowls are decorated with horizontal grooves at the shoulders and are coated with a red haematite slip.

By 300 BC the pottery became less angular, and although there is a general similarity in shapes a wide variety of decoration denotes regional groups which include small barrel-shaped saucepan pots appearing in central southern England, the beginning of the so-called Glastonbury ware in the south-west, and globular bowls in the south Midlands with simple curvilinear decoration. It is clear that many of the finer Iron Age wares were made by potters in regional workshops. Petrological studies of the fabric of vessels by David Peacock have identified the various clay sources, showing for example that the skilfully decorated vessels from Glastonbury and Meare, originated in the Quantock Hills and that workshops using gabbroic clays from the Lizard peninsula (Cornwall) supplied pottery that reached at least as far east as Hampshire.

By the first century BC wheel-made pottery appeared in the form of globular pedestal urns, and necked bowls and jars. Regional styles are clearly defined in their decorative motifs, and can sometimes be linked to known emerging tribes, such as the Durotriges of Dorset and the

[handwritten: wheel turned. amphalos base]

[handwritten: angular]

[handwritten: tiny layers of clay put on]

Fig. 65 *Early and Middle Iron Age pots.*
1 Coarse urn from Puddlehill, Beds; 2 Haematite-coated cordoned bowl from All Cannings Cross, Wilts; 3 Urn from Swallowcliffe, Wilts;
4 Saucepan pot from Blewburton Hill, Berks (12 cm. (4.7 in.) high); 5 Angular bowl from Ravensburgh Castle, Herts.

Atrebates of Hampshire and Wiltshire. In south-east England two cremation cemeteries at Aylesford and Swarling in Kent contained the finely made pedestal urns which characterize late Iron Age pottery. Related vessels are known from Colchester in Essex and Prae Wood in Hertfordshire. In Wales and north Yorkshire stretching into Scotland the story is very different with pottery either non-existent or in short supply with impoverished designs. Plain open jars tend to persist there throughout most of the

Iron Age. Only in northern Scotland are well-made globular and shouldered jars found quite extensively, some in the Western and Northern Isles heavily decorated with concentric arcs and hatched zigzag designs.

In the final years of the first century from about 15 BC until the Roman occupation large quantities of Gallo-Belgic wares were imported into Britain from north-east France and the Rhinelands. Although this high-quality wheel-made pottery was developed initially to supply the Roman army, it was soon traded across the whole of southern England in the form of cups, platters, flagons and butt-beakers which were quickly copied by local craftsmen. Roman wine amphorae and Arretine wares from the Mediterranean and early south Gaulish samian ware were received as prestigious imports, especially in south-east England.

[handwritten: samian made in Italy (1st BC rarely found in Brit.]

[handwritten: Butt Beaker]

Chapter Nine

Burials, Society and the End of Prehistoric Britain

Reappearance of burial

Throughout the earlier periods of prehistory we were able to deduce a certain amount about the population from the various methods of burial. After 1000 BC in the late Bronze Age, for the next 700 years or more throughout much of the Iron Age, burial as a rite practically disappeared and did not recur until after 300 BC. As a result we are left with a tantalizing blank. A method for the disposal of the dead was introduced which left no obvious trace that we can detect. Inhumations were not buried in the ground and cremations were not placed in urnfields or cemeteries. Until the late Bronze Age cremation had been practised, with the ashes buried in urns. Then something occurred which caused this to cease. It is possible that the act of cremation continued, but the method of disposal changed. The simplest explanation would be the scattering of the ashes in the countryside, either on land or into water. Wind and rain and perhaps ploughing would soon disperse them.

Alternatively, the corpse might have been exposed, much as in the neolithic periods, until it fell to pieces, at which point the bones were scattered and some of them eaten by scavenging animals. In view of the many centuries involved, this would almost certainly have resulted in thousands of larger bones littering the landscape. Excavation does often reveal scattered human bones in settlement and hillfort sites, but no clearly ritual structures have been found that might have been mortuary houses. It is conceivable that some of the post holes on Iron Age sites might have supported exposure platforms. Corpses might even have been placed on the roofs of houses, on convenient rocks or in nearby trees – the possibilities are endless.

Burial rites

It is only at the end of the Iron Age that several regional inhumation traditions can be observed, which represent local minority rites. In many areas, particularly central and north-west England, Wales and Scotland, burial customs remain unknown. In central southern England about 200 skeletons have been found in storage and similar pits in hillforts and settlements. These seem to have been deliberate burials which follow a predetermined pattern. Many bodies lie on their left sides (occasionally right) in a flexed or crouched position, often with their heads to the north or east and with no accompanying grave goods. At Danebury (Hants) about 100 pits (10 per cent of the total) contained human bones, though not all were complete individuals. Barry Cunliffe has suggested that they were placed in the freshly emptied storage pits as a thank offering to the gods. If so, who were these people? Why were they singled out for this particular method of burial? Had they died naturally, or were they sacrificial victims, executions, prisoners of war or expendable slaves? More burials have been found beneath the ramparts of hillforts which have been interpreted as foundation burials. At Maiden Castle (Dorset) Mortimer Wheeler found the crouched skeleton of a young man carefully placed in a pit at the junction of two rampart phases, and another male burial was found crouched within the rampart of Sutton Walls (Hereford and Worcs). Although the first pit burials may be dated as early as the fourth century BC the majority belong to the first century BC.

[handwritten annotation: legs drawn up under the chin / limbs close to the chest]

Cist burials

In western Devon, Cornwall and the Isles of Scilly a number of inhumation burials have been found in small stone cists, which can be dated between the second century BC and the early second century AD. They occurred in cemeteries at Trelan Bahow, St Keverne; Porth Cressa, St Mary's and Stamford Hill overlooking Plymouth Sound, but the best recorded discovery is the Harlyn Bay cemetery above a delightful sandy bay near Padstow. Harlyn Bay was crudely excavated between 1900 and 1905 when 130 inhumation burials were dug up. Most of them were crouched with their heads to the north, in stone-lined graves which were covered with slabs of stone. The cemetery seems to have been in use for a long time since up to four levels of graves were found in places.

Plate 54 *Arras burials in square ditches excavated at Burton Flemming, North Humberside. (British Museum)*

A date beginning in the third century BC is suggested, perhaps lasting until Roman times. Many objects found at the site have been lost, but a few survive in Truro Museum, including two similar disc-footed brooches made locally, but whose style originated in northern Spain or south-west France.

Arras culture burials

Only in south-east Yorkshire (Humberside) in an area centred on the chalk Wolds does an almost unique state of affairs prevail. In practically every dry valley there is evidence of a large scale funeral rite with hundreds of graves but little information about settlement or domestic goods. This is likely to change as more new sites are discovered by aerial photography: clusters of round houses are already known from excavations at Wetwang, but cannot be seen from the air. Extensive cemeteries like those at Arras, Burton Flemming and Wetwang Slack are made up of rock or gravel-cut graves often once

[handwritten: ? thought under chin ???]

covered by low barrows and enclosed by square or, less often, circular ditches (plate 54). The earliest burials were placed in fairly shallow graves in the large barrows. As land became scarce the barrows seem to get smaller and the graves deeper. Since so many graves are known it is probable that most of the adult population was buried in this way, although children under the age of about 16 are very rare.

[handwritten left margin: like Roman idea of didn't get a memorial tablet if you die before maturity]

Most of the skeletons are found in a crouched or flexed position lying on their side, with heads to the north. Only at Burton Flemming were the bodies extended and lying east-west. Traces of coffins and shrouds have sometimes been observed. Locally made pots, jewellery and a joint of meat often accompanied the burials. All the graves can be seen as part of a unified group which is known as the Arras culture. Particularly interesting are more than a dozen burials reflecting a higher social status. In these the body had been placed in a large irregular grave with a dismantled cart or chariot and harness fittings. Such burials were for both sexes.

Plate 55 *The skeleton of an Iron Age chieftain, buried with his cart and excavated in 1971 at Garton Slack, Yorkshire. (English Heritage)*

At Garton Slack traces of a two-wheeled cart were found beneath a square barrow (plate 55). It had been dismantled and the 12-spoked wheels with iron tyres laid side by side. An adult male lay flexed on his left side between them, accompanied by the carcass of a pig. The pole-shaft of the cart had been broken in two to fit into the grave. Two iron bridle bits lay over the body whilst five terrets (rings fitted to the yoke through which the reins passed), two harness buckles and a possible whip were close by. A similar grave found at Wetwang Slack in 1984 contained a woman's skeleton with the remains of a cart, bronze horse bits and terrets. She was buried in a crouched position with a joint of pork, a swan's neck bronze dress pin, an iron mirror and a curious sealed bronze canister a few centimetres in diameter decorated with a flowing scroll pattern. Its function is unknown. An earlier female burial had been found with a cart and bronze mirror at Arras in 1870.

Also at Wetwang Slack two cart burials have been excavated containing male warriors with weapons. In one a sword with scabbard, seven spears and traces of a shield were found; in the other was a similar sword and shield. During 1988 a cart burial at Garton Station was un-

HIGH STATUS

Fig. 66 *A warrior, wearing a suit of chain mail, similar to one found in a grave at Garton Station, Kirkburn, Humberside.* (Tracey Croft)

covered in a very large grave pit measuring some 5.2 m. by 3.6 m. (5.7 yd × 4 yd) and 1.2 m. (1.3 yd) deep. The body of the vehicle lay upside down over its male driver, whilst the wheels lay beneath him. Although it contained no weapons the burial was unique in that it was covered by a suit of chain mail, badly corroded but sufficiently preserved to reveal its shape and fastening device (fig. 66).

There seems little doubt that the people afforded cart burials were rather special, a local elite perhaps who were borne to their funerals on their carts, which were then intended to speed them on their way to the next world. Their graves have been dated to between the fourth and second centuries BC. There are a number of similarities between the Arras culture burials and those found in the Champagne region of France in the La Tène period, but there are also a lot of differences. As a result many archaeologists believe that there may have been an actual movement of people to Yorkshire from that area. As Ian Stead has written, 'they need not have been numerically strong: perhaps they were adventurers, mercenaries, evangelists, or a few farmers'.

Durotrigian burials

In the first century BC a number of distinctive burials were made in a relatively small area close to the coast of southern Dorset. These were in flat graves often grouped in cemeteries such as Jordan Hill, Weymouth and at Maiden Castle. The burials were usually crouched or flexed on their right side and were accompanied by locally made pottery, some copying Gallo-Belgic wares and imported samian vessels. The local pots belong to types being made by the Durotriges, a native tribe which was emerging in Dorset. Also in the graves were joints of meat, usually sheep or pig, but occasionally horse, ox or chicken.

One common theme links all the Iron Age burials so far described: their preference for interment in a crouched or flexed position with the head to the north. This can hardly be seen as an ancient tradition harking back to the Bronze Age when a gap of 700 years separates them.

Rather less obvious as a regional group are some two dozen graves containing warriors buried with swords and dated to the second half of the first century BC, which are widely scattered in southern England and Anglesey, and

Plate 56 *The decorated back of a bronze mirror found in a woman's grave at Birdlip (Glos) in 1879. (Gloucester Museum)*

concentrated around Arras in Yorkshire. Each corpse lay extended on its back and was accompanied by a La Tène sword, scabbard fittings and sometimes spears and a shield. These isolated burials seem to be a purely British phenomenon found only in England, Wales and the Channel Islands. Half a dozen women's graves, mostly spread along the south coast, may possibly be the female counterparts to the warriors. They were buried with bronze mirrors, bowls and jewellery. The best known, at Birdlip (Glos), was discovered in 1879 when an extended female skeleton was found in a stone cist covered with a slab of limestone. She was accompanied by a magnificent bronze mirror, bowls, a silver-gilt late La Tène brooch, four bronze rings, a bronze bracelet and bead necklace – everything to suggest a lady of considerable social standing (plate 56).

Aylesford graves

In the second half of the first century BC an extensive group of cremation burials appeared, loosely spread across north-east Kent, Essex and the eastern Chilterns. They belong to the Aylesford culture, named after a cemetery in Kent. Most of the cemeteries are very small, containing less than a dozen burials, but larger ones are known at Colchester and St Albans. Sometimes the graves were laid out in rows as at Stone in Kent, at others they were in rings as at Aylesford (Kent). The ashes were usually placed in a variety of wheel-turned urns (fig. 67), although some, possibly poorer, individuals had no containers at all, as at Puddlehill (Beds). Often the burials were accompanied by additional pots, some locally made, others imported samian or Gallo-Belgic wares. It seems reasonable to assume that they once contained offerings of food and drink. Gallo-Roman brooches have been found in large numbers, for example 222 from a total of 454 graves at King Harry Lane, St Albans (Herts) (plate 57). Burials at that site lay close together and may possibly have each been marked with a wooden headboard or very small, low mound. Groups of burials were separated by shallow trenches, perhaps demarcating family plots. The cemetery dates from between 15 BC and AD 43 (fig. 68).

At Aylesford a grave contained a bronze pan and wine jugs from Italy and a great wooden bucket, bound in bronze and decorated with stylized horse-like creatures and two grotesque face-masks.

Aylesford cremations in wheel-made urns arranged in cemeteries can be seen as an intrusive La Tène burial custom derived from the Belgae of northern France. This almost certainly means that groups of Belgic immigrants moved into parts of Kent and the Chilterns during the second half of the first century BC, perhaps as refugees from Roman oppression. Less plausibly, only the ideas and technology may have reached Britain as a result of trade.

Amongst the Aylesford cremations were about a dozen very rich graves similar to contemporary examples found in France and known in Britain as Welwyn type burials. Concentrated mainly in the Hertfordshire, Bedfordshire and Cambridgeshire area, they might even be termed princely graves. They tend to contain exotic imported items and may be best exemplified by one excavated at Welwyn Garden City in 1965 (plate 58). The rectangular grave pit measured 3.1 m. by 2.0 m. (3.4 yd × 2.2 yd). At its northern end were the cremated remains of a man. Amongst the goods buried with him were

Fig. 67 *Wheel-turned Aylesford style pottery consisting of: 1 Undecorated pedestal urn; 2 Taza; 3 Pedestal urn with horizontal cordons.*

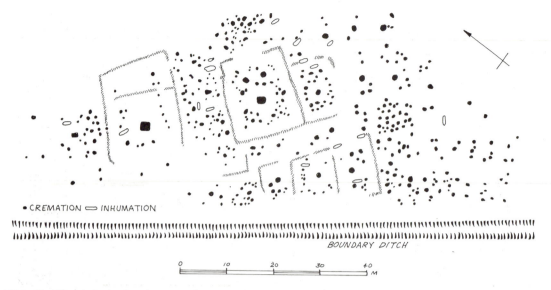

• CREMATION ⟺ INHUMATION

BOUNDARY DITCH

0   10   20   30   40
                                         M

Fig. 68 *The Aylesford style cremation cemetery at King Harry Lane, St Albans, Herts. Family plots may have been separated by the rectangular ditches. (After Stead, 1969)*

Plate 57 *A La Tène III grave found at King Harry Lane, St Albans (Herts). (British Museum)*

Plate 58 *Objects found at Welwyn Garden City (Herts) in 1965. At the back stand Italian wine amphorae and in the foreground imported pottery vessels and a silver cup. (British Museum)*

36 pottery vessels, mostly imported, 5 Italian wine amphorae, a silver Roman drinking cup and bronze wine strainer and 24 coloured glass gaming pieces. The burial probably took place between 40 and 15 BC.

One outstanding Welwyn-type burial occurred under a round barrow 30 m. (33 yd) in diameter at Lexden, within the *oppidum* of Colchester. In a grave pit measuring 9 m. by 5.5 m (9.8 yd × 6 yd) were cremated human bones, together with many rich grave goods all damaged by fire. These included high quality bronzes, a shirt embroidered with gold threads, some silver ears of wheat, iron box or chest fittings, chain mail, wine amphorae and a silver portrait medallion of the Roman Emperor Augustus, which must date after 17 BC. It has been suggested that this might be the grave of Addedomarus, king of the native Trinovantes.

Two later Welwyn-style burial pits were found at Stanfordbury in Bedfordshire as long ago as 1832 and 1834. Each, measuring about 4.5 m. by 3.5 m. (4.9 yd × 3.8 yd) and 1.5 m. (1.6 yd) deep, was paved with clay tiles. Apart from cremated human bone, one contained a bronze shield boss, six wine amphorae, samian cups, a bronze jug, two pairs of iron fire dogs, two iron roasting spits, a large iron tripod with hooks for a cauldron, bone gaming pieces and a bone flute. All were objects that might be associated with a prolonged funeral banquet in the next world, with gently roasting meat, games of chance, mellow music and wine in each amphora equivalent to about 34 standard bottles. The Stanfordbury vaults are dated to about the time of the Roman conquest.

The after life

The grave goods found with the late Iron Age burials indicate a strong preoccupation with the after life. Great care was taken to propitiate the gods in order to secure a safe entry to the next world, and this was made easier by the intercession of a priestly class known as druids.

The druids have been figures of romantic antiquarianism since the eighteenth century but were known historically in Europe from at least the third century BC. In Britain they were a group of high-ranking holy men with considerable political power, whose duties included teaching and arbitration in judicial matters. There was also a barbarian side to their duties which included overseeing human sacrifice and divining the future from the movements of their expiring victims, and also from the flights of birds. A 12-year-old boy found in South Uist in the Outer Hebrides may have been a divination sacrifice. He had been killed by stabbing in the back. After his flesh had disintegrated his bones were buried in four separate pits, together with the bodies of two cows and two sheep. Diodoris Siculus writing about 8 BC records that the

Plate 59 *The upper part of the body of an Iron Age man found in the peat at Lindow Moss (Cheshire). (British Museum)*

druids 'stab a man in the region of the mid-riff and foretell the future by the convulsions of his limbs and the pouring of his blood'.

The Iron Age people found the deities in natural places like forests and groves, marshes, lakes, rivers and springs. The poet Lucan, writing about AD 60, says of the druids, 'the innermost groves of far-off forests are your abodes' and Tacitus, describing the woods of Anglesey in AD 60, refers to 'groves devoted to inhuman superstitions'. There are suggestions that some of the tree trunks were carved and painted with grotesque Celtic designs.

Watery locations were often chosen for the deposition of votive offerings from the late Bronze Age onwards. Many rapiers and swords have been found while dredging rivers, and the Thames is particularly notable for the large numbers of fine Iron Age swords and highly decorated bronze shields that were deliberately deposited there. The peat bog at Llyn Cerrig Bach (Anglesey) contained a large hoard of La Tène metalwork, almost certainly votive, which included iron swords and scabbards, spears,

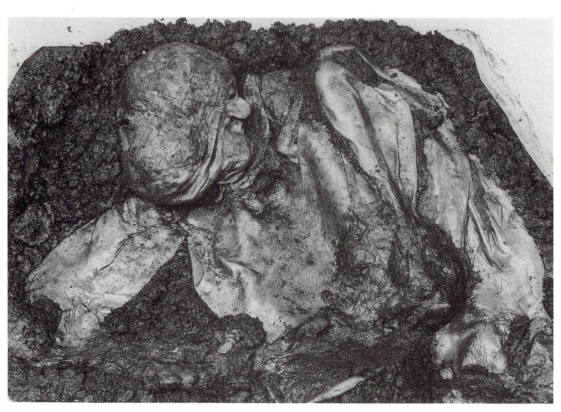

shields, chariot and harness fittings, gang chains for prisoners, a bronze trumpet and iron currency bars.

Many human corpses have been found in waterlogged sites in Britain over the centuries, although few are documented, and only one has been studied in detail. A human body, excellently preserved by the peat, was found at Lindow Moss (Cheshire) in 1984 (plate 59). It was the corpse of a well-built young man, a little

over 25 years of age, who had been killed by blows to the head followed by garroting. He probably died in the latter years of the Iron Age and may have been the victim of murder, execution or sacrifice. Describing Celtic punishments in Iron Age Germany Tacitus wrote, 'traitors and deserters are hanged from trees; cowards, shirkers and sodomites are plunged in the mud of marshes with a hurdle on their heads'. He also talked of 'barbarous rites' culminating in 'human sacrifice for the good of the community'.

Shrines

No formal temples were required by the druids but a small number of possible purpose-built shrines have been recognized in Britain, prob-

Fig. 69 *Examples of possible Celtic temples and shrines.* 1 *Heathrow, Middx* (Grimes, 1961); 2 *Danebury, Hants* (Cunliffe, 1978); 3 *Harlow, Essex* (Bartlett, 1988); 4 *Frilford, Berks* (Bradford and Goodchild, 1939)

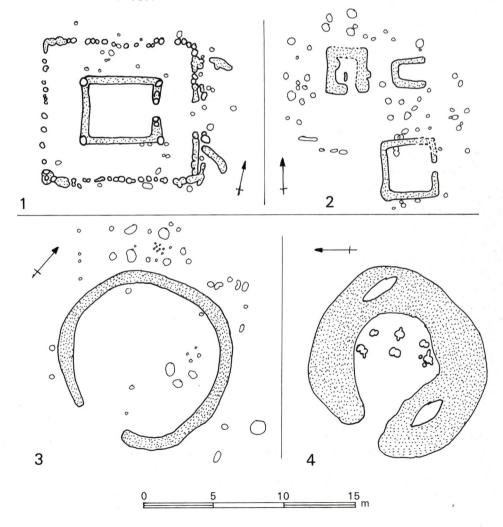

0   5   10   15 m

ably dedicated to a local deity and presided over by a priest who would make the necessary sacrifices and offerings. Some of these buildings were circular in shape, but the majority identified were square or rectangular (fig. 69). Clearly, many circular structures may not have been recognized as they could easily be mistaken for round houses. The shrines vary considerably in size but most are very small. They are usually taken to consist of a central square room surrounded on all sides by a verandah or portico as in the example excavated at Heathrow airport (Middx). Such a plan resembles the later Romano-Celtic temples found in Gaul and Britain. Beneath some of these later temples the foundations of circular timber buildings have been found, as at Harlow (Essex), Frilford (Berks) and Thistleton Dyer (Leics). More than 800 Celtic coins were found at the Harlow site, clearly votive offerings. Often shrines are set in a *temenos* enclosure like those at Gosbecks (Essex) and Lancing Down and Hayling Island (both Sussex). Where no *temenos* existed the shrine was usually set apart from any domestic sites, thus emphasizing its special religious nature.

Shrines were also used for the display of human heads which were collected as trophies of war. According to Didorus Siculus heads of their most distinguished enemies were embalmed in cedar oil and stored in a chest where they were proudly displayed to strangers. Other heads were placed on poles above the entrances to hillforts as at Bredon Hill (Hereford and Worcs). The head and neck of an adult woman was found buried behind the lining of a well at Odell (Beds). This may signify a linking of the cult of the head and a votive offering.

Continental contacts

It is clear from the description of Iron Age burials given earlier that Britain had resumed its contacts with continental Europe, particularly north-west France. Much of France between the lower Rhine and the lower Seine was occupied by people called the Belgae who had their own late La Tène civilization. Not only were imported wares like Gallo-Roman and samian vessels reaching southern England, but trade was also developing with the import of Italian wine in what are known as Dressel I amphorae. In return, Strabo tells us, Britain

was exporting corn, cattle and hides, gold and silver, iron, slaves and hunting dogs. This was certainly taking place through trading ports like Poole Harbour (Cleavel Point) and the old-established Hengistbury Head (Dorset), which also served as a manufacturing and distribution centre. It seems quite certain that British mercenaries were fighting in Gaul, and that refugees from France were also crossing back to southern England. Caesar claimed that one of the reasons for his expeditions to Britain in 55 and 54 BC was as punishment for the help that had been given to the Gauls. In 52 BC Commius, the leader of the Atrebates, fled from defeat in France to set up a capital at Silchester (Hants).

Oppida

In a number of places in eastern and southern Britain large new open settlements were appearing, loosely called *oppida*. The hillforts in these areas were for the most part abandoned, although a few larger ones were adapted. There is little precise agreement on what constituted an *oppidum*. For some they were settlements of large size, often on low-lying ground and protected by linear dykes. Suetonius, writing of Vespasian's campaign in AD 43, refers to the capture of 20 *oppida* in the Dorset area. Such a comment can only refer to large hillforts. It would seem that they were semi-urban sites, minting their own coinage, producing a variety of commodities and trading in imported goods of many kinds. They are often referred to as administrative and royal capitals. Some two dozen large *oppida* recognized in southern Britain include Verulamium (St Albans, Herts), Colchester (Essex) (fig. 70), Chichester (Sussex), Bagendon (Glos) and perhaps hillforts like Maiden Castle (Dorset). In the north it seems reasonable to see Stanwick (Yorks), Traprain Law (East Lothian), and possibly Eildon Hill North (Roxburgh), as related sites. Some smaller, low-lying sites, which seem to have replaced local hillforts, might also be considered. Dyke Hills (Oxon) seem to have replaced Wittenham Clumps (Oxon) for example.

In a number of cases British *oppida* are characterized by large scale linear dykes though these were unknown on the continent. At Colchester, Silchester, Chichester and Verulamium these dykes cover a number of kilometres, not always in a pattern comprehensible

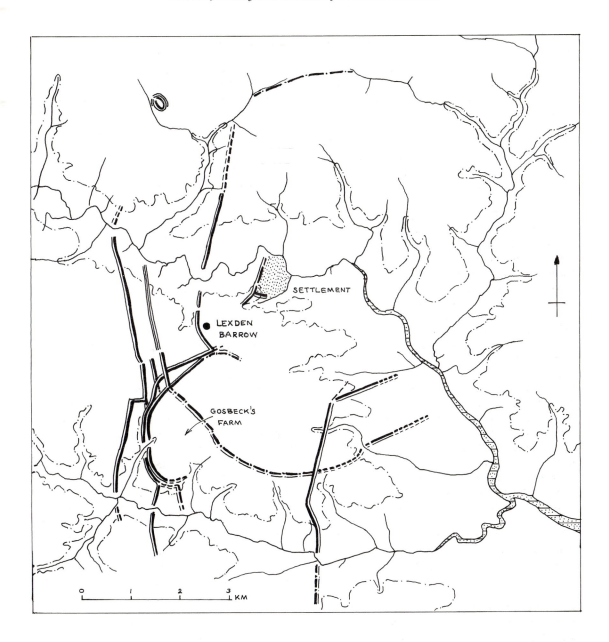

Fig. 70 *The* oppidum *of Camulodunum (Colchester, Essex) protected by a series of massive dykes, constructed at different periods during the late Iron Age. In the north-west corner of the map is the earlier oval hillfort of Pitchbury.*

to modern eyes. They may indicate phases of expansion. The area within them was not totally occupied with settlement. Many different activities were taking place, with fields and enclosures separating them. Evidence so far available does not really suggest a close-knit urban community, and yet the presence of many imported goods, rich burials and the minting of coins, Iron Age shrines and rectangular buildings all point to something bigger than just a local market centre.

A complex of dykes marks the landward side of Colchester (Camulodunum), Essex, where development probably began around the Gosbeck's farm site and then expanded north-east to take in Sheepen. Excavations have revealed circular and rectangular buildings and a ritual site, surrounded by pits and drainage ditches. Much imported pottery and amphorae were found, together with clay moulds indicating the remains of a mint. The imports may well have reached Colchester by way of a port on the River Colne. Metalworking and pottery making were amongst the local industries represented.

Occupation at Verulamium (St Albans, Herts) began at the end of the first century BC on a plateau west of the later Roman town, known as Prae Wood. Here Mortimer Wheeler found traces of a rather primitive settlement with many circular huts, pits and gullies enclosed by strong boundary earthworks and larger linear dykes, one of which still runs between the Ver and Lea valleys. Outside the settlement were at least two Aylesford-type cemeteries and the site of a mint in the vicinity of the later Roman forum.

At Braughing (Skeleton Green, Herts) initial settlement, perhaps as early as the third century BC, might have centred on a small earthwork known as Gatesbury Wood. By about 20 BC occupation had expanded rapidly to the south and west of Gatesbury, on both sides of the River Rib, until it covered about 100 ha. (247 acres). Analysis of fragments of coin moulds shows that silver coins were minted at Braughing. Linear dykes are missing; only small-scale enclosure ditches are known. Natural features may have taken their place. The scattered nature of the excavations has revealed isolated areas of settlement, which include rectangular buildings, roads, storage pits and the inevitable gullies. A very wide range of imported pottery, including Gallo-Belgic wares, was found, together with metalwork and Celtic coins.

Whether some of the large hillforts should be considered as *oppida* is open to question. Although the majority of forts were abandoned by the first century BC some were increased in strength and, as Wheeler describes at Maiden Castle (Dorset), 'the whole enclosure was packed as closely as might be with dwellings and storage pits; the place was wholly urban in the density of its population and had nothing of the straggling character of village settlement'. At

South Cadbury (Somerset) Leslie Alcock has similarly written, 'within the defences, storage pits and timber round-houses proliferated. The settlement can no longer be considered as a village, still less as a hamlet, it is reasonable to describe it as a town.' Clearly both these forts had become industrial and commercial centres, as well as providing permanent residential facilities. Caesar describes defeating Cassivellaunus at an *oppidum* somewhere in Hertfordshire. From his account he is clearly describing a hillfort such as Ravensburgh near Hexton (Herts) (plate 60). In northern England, Stanwick (Yorks) is by far the largest of the *oppida* to have been identified. Though small in comparison to Colchester, it is 300 ha. (741 acres) in extent. Its size and the nature of the terrain would have made it ideal for cattle production. Like the sites in the south it was also most

Plate 60 *An aerial view of Ravensburgh Castle (Herts), 'a place of great natural strength and well fortified'. It is one of the possible sites of Cassivellaunus's oppidum. (Cambridge University)*

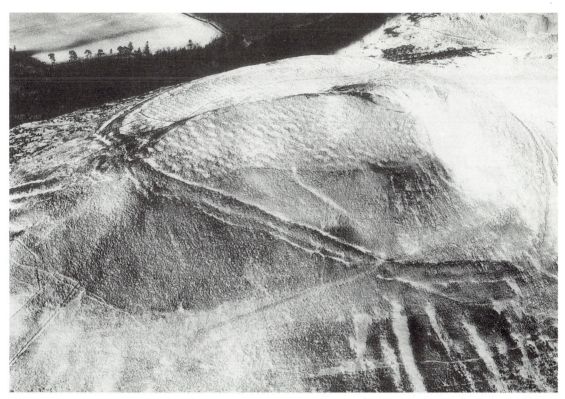

Plate 61 *An aerial view of Eildon Hill North (Roxburgh). The native settlement covers about 16 ha. (39.5 acres). Hut platforms are clearly visible. (R.C.H.N. Scotland)*

probably a centre for the import and distribution of fine, continental pottery, amphorae and glassware.

In Scotland two hillforts have been singled out as being of *oppida* potential, though their minute size shows that they are not in the same class as those in the south. Traprain Law (East Lothian) increased its size during the late Iron Age, eventually reaching 16 ha. (39.5 acres) by the Roman conquest. It seems to have been the capital of the local tribe, the Votadini, and continued to be used during Roman times. The identification of Eildon Hill North (Roxburgh) is even more doubtful (plate 61). It is a complex site also covering 16 ha. (39.5 acres) on the top of a great dome-shaped hill. It was enlarged at least three times and eventually enclosed over 500 hut platforms that may have housed up to 3,000 people. This was the head-

quarters of the Selgovae, and appears to have been abandoned after the arrival of the Romans in AD 79. No particular hillforts in Wales have been singled out as *oppida*, but a dramatically sited hilltop fortress such as Tre'r Ceiri (Gwynedd) might be a serious contender. Probably dating from the end of the first century BC until the fourth century AD, it is packed with 120 stone-built huts, most of which belong to the later years of occupation.

Late Iron Age settlements

Alongside the great *oppida* of the south and east were the open villages and farmsteads of late Iron Age Britain. Many of these have been destroyed by gravel working in the fertile valleys of rivers such as the Thames, Nene and Great Ouse. Typical of such sites is Claydon Pike, Lechlade (Glos) where the Oxford Archaeological Unit uncovered an extensive late Iron Age complex of irregular tracks and enclosures, with circular houses, barns and storage pits which continued in use into the first century AD. About AD 70 the whole area was

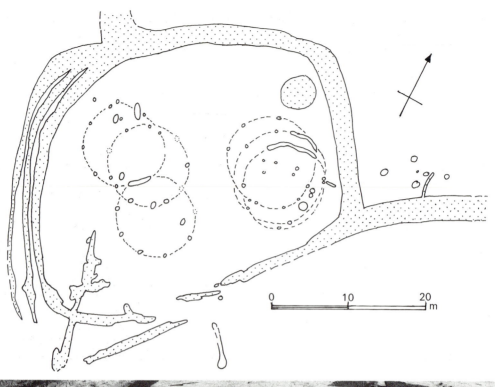

Fig. 71 *The late Iron Age farmstead at Odell, Beds. The two circular huts were each rebuilt at least three times.* (After B. Dix, 1979)

reorganized along more formal, Romano-British lines with rectangular enclosures and straight roads, in the midst of which a shrine was set up.

At Odell in Bedfordshire a farmstead was found consisting of two circular wooden houses in an enclosure, approached by a broad droveway and set amongst rectangular fields (plate 62; fig. 71). Water was obtained from ponds and wells. Evidence for mixed farming was provided by the bones of cattle, sheep, goats, pigs and domestic fowls, and the presence of drying pits, silos and querns, together with the discovery of a wooden crook-ard type of plough. Wooden ards (ploughs without mould boards) were in use throughout the Iron Age. Many continued to have stone shares as they had done in the Bronze Age, but iron foreshares became fashionable, were more efficient and lasted much longer.

Iron Age society

We may question who lived in the *oppida*, and who in the scattered farmsteads and villages that proliferated in Britain by the end of the Iron Age. The classical writers of Greece and Rome give us some idea of how society was divided in Celtic Europe at that time. In Britain by the first century BC a relatively egalitarian society had given way to one in which the upper classes were represented by a class of nobles. At their head was a chieftain or king. At times women could assume this role, as in the case of Boudica of the Iceni and Cartimandua of the Brigantes. The nobles were powerful aristocrats probably bound to the king as military leaders, who might have been rewarded with wealth in the form of land and cattle. In a similar class were the priests or druids already mentioned (p. 158) and the bards who were singers and poets who learnt by heart the history and folklore of the tribe and transmitted it orally at

Plate 62 *A view along the north-west corner of the ditches of the earliest farmstead enclosure at Odell (Beds) looking west. (Beds C.C.)*

Druids

times of feasting and ceremonial. They were given free licence to travel between tribes, thus disseminating the news.

Amongst the non-noble freemen were the highly skilled craftsmen like the potters and carpenters, and especially the metalsmiths who were held in the greatest esteem. The peasant farmers were tied to the land which they owned by the need to produce crops and meat for the nobles, to whom all the non-noble freemen were bound by bonds of clientship. In exchange for protection and patronage they would be expected to produce goods as their lord required and sometimes fight for him if the need arose. The freemen might also expect their children to be fostered by the nobles. Boys in particular were trained in the martial arts, sports and manners of a nobleman, whilst girls learnt needle and home crafts. A slave class also existed, probably made up of captives acquired after raiding. Slave chains worn round the neck have been found at Park Street (St Albans, Herts) and Llyn Cerrig Bach (Anglesey) (plate 63).

What sort of physical picture can we form of

Plate 63 *An iron slave chain with six collars from Lords Bridge (Cambs). (Museum of Archaeology and Anthropology, Cambridge University)*

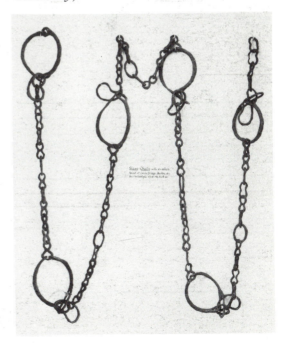

these various people? Again we turn to contemporary writers from the Mediterranean whose travel books and military histories described the various Celtic people who were living on the edge of classical civilization. We know that they were quite distinctive in appearance from the Greeks and Romans, being tall and fair-skinned, with blue eyes and fair or red hair. Men were expected to be slim of figure; corpulence was considered a disgrace. Most of them wore long hair and some grew beards. The nobles were notable for full moustaches that covered the mouth. Diodorus Siculus tells us that they wore 'tunics dyed and stained in various colours, and trousers. They wear striped cloaks, fastened with buckles, thick in winter and light in summer, picked out with small check patterns.' In battle they are reputed to have fought naked, though they decorated their bodies with blue woad dye. Women were considered equal to men, and often stronger. According to Dio Cassius, Queen Boudica of the Iceni (Norfolk) was 'huge of frame and terrifying of aspect and with a harsh voice. A mass of bright red hair fell to her knees. She wore a great twisted golden necklace (torque) and a tunic of many colours, over which was a thick mantle, fastened with a brooch.' Both men and women wore leather shoes or sandals.

Coinage

The idea of coinage was introduced to Britain from the continent. Initially so-called iron currency bars were produced which Caesar tells us were iron ingots of fixed standard weights. Shaped like swords they would have been clumsy and heavy to handle and any village blacksmith worth his salt could have made his own copies. The bars could have been only worth as much as the iron of which they were made. They are best seen as a way of trading iron in fixed quantities.

Caesar adds that coins of bronze and gold were also used, and we know that later, silver and potin (tin-rich bronze) were also common. The earliest coins originated in northern France and appear as imports in Britain. They first occur in six recognizable groups which are known as Gallo-Belgic A to F. These were then copied in southern and eastern England and a number of native types were produced called British A to Q. They were followed by coins of

Plate 64 *Celtic gold coins. The front and back of a Catuvellaunian coin with an ear of barley and the inscription CUNO (Cunobelin); also a coin of the Dobunni of Gloucestershire inscribed EISU. The ears of barley are a reinterpretation of the head wreath of the god Apollo. (British Museum)*

the native tribes inscribed with the names of their leaders. These coins were based on the fourth century BC gold staters of King Philip of Macedonia which had the wreathed head of the god Apollo on one side and a chariot and horses on the other. Successive Celtic craftsmen copied these designs which gradually devolved into a series of meaningless dots, although on some a stylized horse is still recognizable and resembles the chalk hill-figure, the white horse of Uffington, carved into the Berkshire Downs.

The best-known coins are perhaps those of the Catuvellauni who were based in Hertfordshire. The first to be inscribed were those of Tasciovanus who ruled between 20 BC and AD 10, and minted coins at Verulamium (Herts). His kingdom expanded rapidly into the territories to north and south. Cunobelinus, who claimed to be Tasciovanus's son, minted in Camulodunum (Colchester, Essex), showing that he had overrun the land of the Trinovantes to the east. In west Sussex, Hampshire and

Fig. 72 *A map of Britain showing the approximate position of the main tribes at the end of the Iron Age.*

Surrey a tribe called the Atrebates were producing coins by 15 BC, modelled on Roman originals under their king Commius and his son Tincommius. His brother Eppillus minted coins at Silchester inscribed in good Roman letters styling himself REX, 'king' (plate 64).

Tribal origins

The origins of the various tribes in Britain is a somewhat contentious subject. Many clearly evolved from small local communities, amalgamating to form larger groups. This may have been what happened in the southern Chilterns where Keith Branigan suggests that small tribes mentioned by Caesar as the Cenimagni, Segontiaci, Ancalites, Bibroci and Cassi united under a common leader, Tasciovanus, to form the Catuvellauni of Hertfordshire, south Bedfordshire, south Buckinghamshire and eastern Oxfordshire. In the same way the extensive Brigantes that stretched from coast to coast across northern England, were made up of smaller tribes including the Carvetii, Setantii, Gabrantovices and many others.

On the other hand the Trinovantes of Essex seem to have been long-established, as were their northern neighbours the Iceni, and further afield the Cornovii of Shropshire. Along the south coast of England Caesar tells us that the inhabitants had crossed from Belgic Gaul for war and plunder, but had remained to settle and till the soil. In this area the Cantiaci and Atrebates flourished, but the latter tribe lost much of its territory under Verica at the beginning of the first century AD. It later emerged under Roman domination as the territory of the pro-Roman king Cogidubnus of the Regni (fig. 72).

The Roman Conquest

When the army of the Emperor Claudius invaded in AD 43, Britain was still largely a forested agricultural country, with centres of industrial activity in the south and west. Large areas belonged to tribal confederacies, some of whom were prepared to ally themselves with Rome, whilst others fiercely opposed any form of contact. The south had long been trading with the Roman world and could appreciate its luxuries. Diplomatic contact existed between some of the tribes and Italy and some Britons could probably speak Latin. Camulodunum (Colchester) had become the main port, though maritime trade still came to the south coast. But in AD 43 there was considerable unrest in Britain, partly brought about by the death of the powerful king Cunobelinus of the Catuvellauni, whose impetuous sons Caractacus and Togodumnus drove out King Verica of the Atrebates and annexed the last surviving part of his kingdom. Verica fled to Rome to seek the help of the Emperor, which was the catalyst for the invasion of Britain, led by Aulus Plautius, in AD 43. Britain was disunited and a policy of annexation by the Romans, which had long been planned, could now be put into practice. This intertribal strife probably made the conquest easier, Plautius playing off one tribe against another. Tradesmen and travellers had been visiting southern Britain for years and Roman army intelligence had gained a fairly clear idea of the country's layout. The south-east was fairly quickly subdued, though the Legate Vespasian met some opposition along the south coast. There he attacked surviving hillforts of the Durotriges in Dorset such as Maiden Castle, where the excavation of the war cemetery revealed skeletons with sword cuts and iron arrow wounds, and Hod Hill with its evidence for a barrage of ballista bolts. By AD 47 the Romans had reached the line of the Fosse Way from Devon to the Humber. The conquest of the rest of Britain was slow and painful. Rough terrain in Wales and Scotland made progress difficult. By AD 84, under Agricola, Rome advanced to the edge of the Scottish highlands, but in spite of inroads from time to time, northern Scotland was never conquered and remained an Iron Age backwater for the next five centuries.

—————— Bibliography ——————

General surveys

Bradley, R., *The Prehistoric Settlement of Britain* (1978) Routledge and
  Kegan Paul
Darvil, T.C., *Prehistoric Britain* (1987) Batsford
Longworth, I.H., *Prehistoric Britain* (1985) British Museum
  Publications
Longworth, I.H., and Cherry, J., *Archaeology in Britain since 1945*
  (1986) British Museum Publications
Megaw, J.V.S., and Simpson, D.D.A., *Introduction to British
  Prehistory* (1979) Leicester University Press
Renfrew, C., (ed.), *British Prehistory – a new outline* (1974) Duckworth

Aspects of prehistory

Ashbee, P., *The Bronze Age Round Barrow in Britain* (1960) Dent
Ashbee, P., *The Earthen Long Barrow in Britain* (1984) Geo Books
Burgess, C.B., *The Age of Stonehenge* (1980) Dent
Burl, A., *Stone Circles of the British Isles* (1976) Yale
Cunliffe, B.W., *Iron Age Britain* (1995) English Heritage/Batsford
Cunliffe, B.W., *Iron Age Communities in Britain* (3rd edn 1991)
  Routledge and Kegan Paul
Elsdon, S.M., *Later Prehistoric Pottery in England and Wales* (1989)
  Shire
Fowler, P.J., *The Farming of Prehistoric Britain* (1983) Cambridge
  University Press
Gibson, A., *Neolithic and Early Bronze Age Pottery* (1986) Shire
Harding, D.W., *The Iron Age in Lowland Britain* (1974) Routledge and
  Kegan Paul
Harrison, R.J., *The Beaker Folk* (1980) Thames and Hudson
James, S., and Rigby, V., *Britain and the Celtic Iron Age* (1997)
  British Museum Press
Lynch, F., *Megalithic Tombs and Long Barrows* (1997) Shire
Morrison, A., *Early Man in Britain and Ireland* (1980) Croom Helm
Pollard, J., *Neolithic Britain* (1997) Shire
Reynolds, P.J., *Ancient Farming* (1988) Shire
Roe, D.A., *The Lower and Middle Palaeolithic Periods in Britain* (1981)
  Routledge and Kegan Paul
Ross, A., *The Pagan Celts* (1986) Batsford
Stead, I.M., *Celtic Art* (1985) British Museum Publications
Wickham-Jones, C.R., *Scotland's First Settlers* (1994)
  Batsford/Historic Scotland

Wymer, J.J., *Mesolithic Britain* (1991) Shire
Wymer, J.J., *The Palaeolithic Age* (1982) Croom Helm

Sites and regions
Atkinson, R.J.C., *Stonehenge: archaeology and interpretation* (1979) Penguin
Bewley, R., *Prehistoric Settlements* (1994) English Heritage/Batsford
Burl, A., *Prehistoric Avebury* (1979) Yale
Burl, A., *Prehistoric Henges* (1991) Shire
Burl, A., *The Stonehenge People* (1987) Dent
Clarke, J.G.D., *Excavations at Star Carr* (1954) Cambridge University Press
Coles, B., and J., *Sweet Track to Glastonbury* (1986) Thames and Hudson
Crawford, H., (ed.), *Subterranean Britain* (1979) John Baker
Cunliffe, B.W., *Danebury, the anatomy of a hillfort* (1983) Batsford
Drewett, P., *et al*, *The South-East to AD 1000* (1988) Longman
Dyer, J., *Discovering Prehistoric England* (1993) Shire
Dyer, J., *The Penguin Guide to Prehistoric England and Wales* (1982) Penguin
Fleming, A., *The Dartmoor Reaves* (1988) Batsford
Higham, N., *The Northern Counties to AD 1000* (1986) Longman
Hogg, A.H.A., *Hill-forts of Britain* (1975) Hart-Davis
Holgate, R., *Prehistoric Flint Mines* (1991) Shire
Houlder, C., *Wales: an archaeological guide* (1974) Faber and Faber
Lynch, F., *Prehistoric Anglesey* (1970) Anglesey Antiquarian Society
Mercer, R., *Hambledon Hill, a neolithic landscape* (1980) Edinburgh University Press
Pryor, F., *Fengate* (1982) Shire
Renfrew, C., (ed.), *The Prehistory of Orkney* (1985) Edinburgh University Press
Ritchie, A., *Scotland BC* (1988) Scottish Development Department
Ritchie, A., and G., *Ancient Monuments of Orkney* (1989) Scottish Development Department
Ritchie, J.N.G., *The Brochs of Scotland* (1988) Shire
Ritchie, G., and A., *Scotland: Archaeology and Early History* (1981) Thames and Hudson
Smith, B., (ed.), *Shetland Archaeology* (1985) Shetland Times
Todd, M., *The South-West to AD 1000* (1987) Longman

More information
Dyer, J., (ed.), *British Archaeology, an introductory booklist* (1987) Council for British Archaeology

Glossary

Adze Axe-like wood-working tool, but with blade at right-angles to the handle, used with pick-like motion.

Awl A pointed tool of flint, bone or bronze, used for making holes in skins, etc.

Barrow An earthen burial mound, either circular or rectangular in plan.

Burin Engraving or piercing tool, used with rotary action.

Berm Flat platform separating a mound or bank from a quarry ditch.

Cairn A heap of stones, varying in size, usually covering a burial.

Carinated A shoulder or sharp change in direction in the profile of a pot.

Chape Decorative terminal of a sword scabbard.

Cist Small rectangular pit lined with stone slabs and covered with a capstone; often a grave.

Corbelling Roofing method in which successive layers of stone rise one above the other and overlap inwards until they meet.

Cursus Long, narrow parallel-sided enclosure of the neolithic period. (See page 50f)

Dolerite Basaltic type rock used for making axes, also in the construction of Stonehenge.

Dysse Long megalithic burial mound found in Denmark.

Gabbroic clay Clay containing crystals of the igneous rock gabbro from the Lizard peninsula.

Graver Engraving tool made from pointed, longitudinal flake, used with a straight action.

Hafted axe Axe with a wooden handle.

Halberd Bronze Age dagger at right angles to a wooden handle with metal rivets.

Henge Later neolithic circular enclosure surrounded by a bank and internal ditch, broken by one or more entrances. (See page 64ff)

Hunebeden Long megalithic burial mound found in the Netherlands.

Inhumation An unburnt human burial.

Machair Gaelic word describing lush meadowland.

Mattock Heads Pick-like tool with chisel shaped blade.

Megalithic Constructed of large stones, e.g. Stonehenge.

Midden Rubbish dump, often composed of discarded shells, bones or charcoal.

Quern Two stones used for grinding corn, either by rubbing backwards and forwards, or revolving one upon another.

Revetment A facing of timber, stone or turf intended to stop the sides of a bank or mound collapsing.

Scalene triangle Unequal sided microlith, probably used as an arrow tip.

Sherds Fragments of broken pottery.

Skeuomorph An imitation.

Spelt A species of wheat: *triticum spelta*.

Tanged Projection at base of dagger or arrowhead used to fasten it to a handle.

Temenos Spacious enclosure of 'consecrated' land, attached to a temple.

Trepanation A form of brain surgery practised in the Bronze Age.

Index